STABILIZATION AND STRUCTURAL ADJUSTMENT

The past decade has been disastrous for Africa. Different solutions have been proposed for this crisis, but the stabilization and structural adjustment packages of the World Bank and the IMF have had much the greatest influence. Characteristically these packages are designed to diminish the role of the state and enhance that of the market, but a whole range of strategies have been pursued to achieve these ends.

Given that much of the literature in this area is descriptive, and orientated around case studies, it is difficult to disentangle the key features of the debate. *Stabilization and Structural Adjustment* offers clarification by looking beyond individual programmes to assess the relevance of the macroeconomic theory and models that underlie them. It begins by examining the peculiar weaknesses of the African economies and the issues of macroeconomic management they create, before proceeding to outline the different frameworks within which stabilization and structural adjustment packages can be analysed. Whilst particular attention is paid to IMF and World Bank models, because of their unique influence, alternative perspectives are also considered.

The result is the clearest overview to date of the economic theory underlying this key area of development economics.

Finn Tarp is Associate Professor of Development Economics at the Institute of Economics of the University of Copenhagen. Formerly with the Food and Agricultural Organization of the United Nations, he worked as an economist for a decade in southern Africa from 1978 to 1988. He has previously published on agricultural price policy, agrarian transformation and income distribution and growth.

D1502793

STABILIZATION AND STRUCTURAL ADJUSTMENT

Macroeconomic frameworks for analysing
the crisis in sub-Saharan Africa

Finn Tarp

London and New York

First published 1993
by Routledge
11 New Fetter Lane, London EC4P 4EE

Simultaneously published in the USA and Canada
by Routledge
29 West 35th Street, New York, NY 10001

New in paperback 1994

Reprinted in 1997

© 1993 Finn Tarp

Printed and bound in Great Britain by
Biddles Ltd, Guildford and King's Lynn

British Library Cataloguing in Publication Data
A catalogue reference for this book is available from the British Library
ISBN 0–415–08179–3
0–415–08180–7 (Pbk)

Library of Congress Cataloging in Publication Data
Tarp, Finn, 1951–
Stabilization and structural adjustment: macroeconomic frameworks for
analysing the crisis in sub-Saharan Africa / by Finn Tarp.
p. cm.
Includes bibliographical references and index.
ISBN 0–415–08179–3
0–415–08180–7 (Pbk)
1. Economic stabilization—Africa, Sub-Saharan. 2. Structural
adjustment (Economic policy)—Africa, Sub-Saharan. I. Title.
HC800.T37 1993 399.5'0967—dc20 92–7431 CIP

CONTENTS

TABLES

PREFACE

I was introduced to the field of development economics during the Second United Nations Development Decade, and was immediately intrigued by the coexistence of a variety of competing theoretical and practical approaches to development problems in the Third World. I took note of the fact that the orthodox, neo-classically-inspired school of thought was largely on the defensive. Planned development with a focus on distributional goals became, in my understanding, a realistic goal to strive at for an economically-active, interventionistic state, committed to development.

From 1978 I spent a decade as an employee of the Food and Agriculture Organization of the United Nations (FAO) in various field assignments in southern Africa. In this way, I was effectively exposed to the extremely difficult socio-economic and political conditions of sub-Saharan Africa. I was introduced to widely-different political and economic systems with dissimilar approaches to development, and became gradually more realistic about 'the possibilities of development planning', and the fact that governments may not be representative of the aspirations of their people.[1]

Deficiencies in the formulation of plans and their implementation, insufficient and unreliable data, unanticipated external and internal economic disturbances, institutional and managerial weaknesses, and so on, are obstacles which by now have a very real meaning to me. I came, in other words, to perceive the crisis in planning in sub-Saharan Africa (SSA) and accepted that there is a need to rethink and reformulate government strategies and policies and that market relations have a role to play even in the development of planned Third World countries.[2]

From 1981 onwards I devoted a substantial part of my efforts towards participating in the process of redirecting the Mozambican agricultural policies and planning systems. I was, however, taken by surprise by the strength of what has since been termed the 'neo-classical counter-revolution of the early 1980s'.[3] This approach even offered a new political economy with a theory of the nature of government and public choice, which did not correspond with the rational actor concept of the earlier decades of development economics.[4] The profession had started to yield what Ranis and Fei (1988: 100) have characterized as 'an extraordinary outpouring of agonizing reappraisals and laments about the state of development economics, remarkable for even this difficult branch of our dismal science'.

I agreed to, and had − as just noted − in fact tried to address the need for reform in economic policies and planning systems as well as in the economic role of the government. Yet I was left speculating about the orthodox stabilization and structural adjustment package of free-market, outward-oriented policy advice, developed in conjunction with the 'counter-revolution', and offered *inter alia* by the International Monetary Fund (IMF) and the World Bank to the Mozambican government after 1984 as somewhat of a panacea to the complex economic problems which it was facing.[5] After all, the contradictions between the standard neo-classically-inspired adjustment approach and economic reality can hardly be greater than in sub-Saharan Africa in general and in Mozambique in particular.

I did not then have the possibility of studying in-depth, and at theoretical and pan-African level, the rationale and empirical basis of the 'counter-revolution', the adjacent and evolving views of the nature and economic role of the state, including the issue of the 'proper' demarcation of boundaries for the functions of the government and market forces, and finally, the elaboration of adequate policy advice for stabilization, rehabilitation, recovery and development; but my desire to do so had been awakened.

Upon taking up my present position at the Institute of Economics at the University of Copenhagen, I was therefore highly motivated to devote research efforts to the above issues. However, analysing the African economic crisis involves disentangling a bewildering set of topics of economic as well as political, historical, social and cultural character. It therefore took me a while to develop more clearly the particular theme for this book.

While the role of the state is subject to intense debate, it is, nevertheless, generally accepted that governments must assume responsibility for macroeconomic management and stability. This implies that governments, in addition to striking a proper balance between market and administrative resource allocations, confront a series of routine and strategic planning issues.[6]

The routine issues involve the continuing need for systematic fiscal planning, the use of budgets as policy instruments and the necessary improvements of expenditure planning and budgeting (including basic accounting, co-ordinating decision-making, choosing among investments, and so on). The strategic economic issues which a government must face, and the choices it has to make to fulfil its political mandate, may be grouped under three headings: (a) short-term macroeconomic management, (b) medium-term production and (c) trade policies and distributional issues.

I shall not engage myself here in the routine questions, although they are admittedly of significant importance in developing practical solutions to the problems faced by African governments.[7] Similarly, I do not intend to review the extensive array of operational aspects of the design and implementation of actual adjustment programmes in selected African countries and their financing.[8] It follows – more specifically – that I shall not discuss the diplomatic and other problems which have arisen as a corollary of the more active IMF/World Bank involvement in macroeconomic policy-making in sub-Saharan Africa. The same accounts for the particular style and method of work of the Bretton Woods institutions and the relationships between macroeconomic and sectoral policies and variables.[9]

What I shall do is to focus on the basic macroeconomic aspects of the African crisis and a number of key issues of an overall conceptual nature, related to the stabilization and structural adjustment programmes undertaken by many African countries during the 1980s. Alternative theoretical frameworks (including in particular those of the IMF and the World Bank) to solving the African crisis will therefore be described and critically examined. I shall point out what the policy implications and limitations of existing models and concepts are, explore whether their main elements are appropriate and discuss the linkages between the analytical models and the policy packages as they are typically designed in adjustment programmes.[10]

In addition, I shall assess to what extent the various approaches are indeed alternatives or rather supplementary in nature. As a starting point, I will have to set out what I perceive as the fundamental characteristics of the economies of sub-Saharan Africa and the nature of the economic constraints they face, involving both internal structural and policy variables as well as the external economic setting.

Following the above account of my motivation for writing this book

and the description of its background and overall scope, I would like
to conclude these preliminaries by setting out my purpose. Following
the intensification of the African crisis, the 1980s witnessed an
outpouring of literature on this subject.[11] Yet many of the existing
contributions are of a descriptive nature, and the theoretical core of
the debate has remained somehow submerged and difficult to disentangle. Relevant analytical material is widely scattered, often in unpublished sources, and of very uneven quality. Thus, it is no easy task to
join the existing information and establish a basis for further work.
This book will hopefully be useful to the reader in this regard.

A word of caution is required at the outset. In this volume,
sub-Saharan Africa will be treated as a homogenous whole. This is in
no way meant to underestimate individual country characteristics.
Nevertheless, most of the more than forty countries in sub-Saharan
Africa are small (excluding Nigeria), open economies which were,
during the 1970s and 1980s, subject to major internal and external
shocks. They also share important historical and structural characteristics, and a prominent dependence on imported inputs and ma-
terials is widespread. This is the justification for treating the economies
of sub-Saharan Africa as being basically alike here. However, all the
statements and conclusions made in what follows should be seen as
tentative suggestions rather than as definite affirmations.

Many more country studies and additional empirical work is required. But there is also a need to search for more up-to-date
generalizing principles and assess whether ongoing attempts in this
regard are 'on the right track'. New generalizations once developed
will not, of course, be true at all times. Circumstances change and
general theoretical models and assumptions must constantly be tested.
In other words, generalizations are exactly what the very term implies
– generalizations. On the other hand, my hypothesis is that previously
proposed models neither capture essential features of the sub-Saharan
economies, nor cover the actual scope of the adjustment process that
is pursued.

I hope with this book to provide a comprehensive analytic review
of a crucial topic within the discipline of development economics that
can serve both as a general reference and as an inspiration to further
research on sub-Saharan Africa and macroeconomic management.

ACKNOWLEDGEMENTS

My intention of writing this book developed decisively during the month of August 1989, when I participated in study seminar 125 on Economic Management for Structural Adjustment in sub-Saharan Africa. The seminar was organized jointly by the Institute of Development Studies at the University of Sussex (IDS) and the Economic Development Institute of the World Bank (EDI). I am grateful to these two institutions for inviting me to the seminar. Particular thanks go to Professors John Toye and Reginald H. Green of the IDS. They have also on a number of other occasions stimulated my interest in the issues taken up in the present volume.

My participation in the above seminar was made possible with financial assistance from the Council for Development Research of the Danish Ministry of Foreign Affairs (Danida), the Carlsberg Foundation and the Institute of Economics at the University of Copenhagen. I owe gratitude for the generous and expeditious approval of my applications for support.

Special mention must be made of my former directors in the Ministry of Agriculture in Mozambique, Messrs A. Maleiane and Ragendra de Sousa. It was through my daily working relationship with them and other Mozambican colleagues during four hectic years after Mozambique joined the IMF and the World Bank in 1984, that I gained much of the inspiration and insights necessary to carry out this research. Thanks also to the former director of FAO's Economic and Social Policy Analysis Division (ESP), Jan VanAs, who supported me during my assignment in Mozambique.

A number of unpublished IMF and World Bank documents were kindly provided by Dr Robert G. Liebenthal, Chief of the Review and Analysis Division of the World Bank's Policy and Review Department. I am also grateful to him for the inspiring discussions we had on structural adjustment and the role of the World Bank and IMF during his visit to Denmark in early 1989.

A word of thanks is due as well to the director of the Centre for Development Research (CDR), Professor Knud Erik Svendsen. His patient and fine counsel has contributed to my getting settled in the Danish development research environment after my return to Denmark in August 1988, after almost a decade of field work in southern Africa. Senior adviser in Danida, Anders Serup Rasmussen contributed valid comments and suggestions on my drafts. The same accounts for Professor Lance Taylor of Massachusetts Institute of Technology (MIT) and Associate Professor Alan Matthews of the University of Dublin.

I would furthermore like to express my sincere appreciation to present and former colleagues at the Institute of Economics at the University of Copenhagen for welcoming me as a member of a highly dedicated and hard-working group of economists. I am in particular indebted to Associate Professor Jørgen Peter Christensen, who has aided me from the very beginning of this book as well as in my other duties at the Institute. Associate Professor Søren Bo Nielsen and Professor Peter Birk Sørensen made useful observations on my work and contributed together with Associate Professor Jørgen Birk Mortensen to making me feel at home in my new working environment.

Feedback from students in seminar discussions helped in identifying blurry points in the presentation, and Peter Hjertholm assisted in updating the statistics and in the final proof-reading. I hope they benefited as much as I did.

Without the never failing attention of the above-mentioned friends and colleagues, as well as many others not mentioned, I would never have completed this volume. I personally bear full responsibility for any remaining errors of fact or judgement.

Finn Tarp
Copenhagen

ABBREVIATIONS

AAF–SAP	African Alternative Framework–Structural Adjustment Programme
CDR	Centre for Development Research (Copenhagen)
CEPAL	*see* ECLA
CGE	Computable General Equilibrium
DUP	Directly Unproductive
ECA	UN Economic Commission for Africa
ECLA	UN Economic Commission for Latin America
EDI	Economic Development Institute (of the World Bank)
ESAF	Enhanced Structural Adjustment Facility
ESP	Economic and Social Policy Division (of the FAO)
FAO	Food and Agriculture Organization of the United Nations
FOF	Flow of Funds
GDP	Gross Domestic Product
GLS	Generalized Least Squares
GNP	Gross National Product
IBRD	International Bank for Reconstruction and Development
ICOR	Incremental Capital–Output Ratio
ICSID	International Centre for the Settlement of Investment Disputes
IDA	International Development Association
IDS	Institute of Development Studies (Sussex)
IFC	International Finance Co-operation
ILO	International Labour Organization
ISS	Institute of Social Studies (The Hague)
ITO	International Trade Organization
MADIA	Managing Agricultural Development in Africa
MIGA	Multilateral Investment Guarantee Agency
NIC	Newly Industrializing Country

NIEO	New International Economic Order
OAU	Organization of African Unity
ODI	Overseas Development Institute (London)
OECD	Organization for Economic Co-operation and Development
OLS	Ordinary Least Squares
PFP	Policy Framework Paper
PPR	Policy Planning and Research Division (of the World Bank)
RMSM	Revised Minimum Standard Modelling
SAF	Structural Adjustment Facility
SAL	Structural Adjustment Loan
SAM	Social Accounting Matrix
SSA	Sub-Saharan Africa
UNDP	United Nations Development Programme
UNECA	*see* ECA
UNICEF	United Nations Children Fund
WIDER	World Institute for Development Economics Research of the United Nations University

INTRODUCTION

Since 1979 a majority of the countries of sub-Saharan Africa (SSA) have experienced sharply-worsening economic difficulties. The past decade has in fact been disastrous. The overall global external context of SSA could hardly have been worse with a strenuous constellation of circumstances contributing to macroeconomic problems. However, it is now generally accepted that deficiencies in national policy-making and weaknesses in economic structure also contributed. Whatever the causes, the generality of the African crisis since 1979 implies that previous development policies have not been sustainable.[1]

It is against this background – and in view of the probable future trends, which do not appear encouraging – that African countries initiated during the 1980s a reorientation of economic policies, in particular in the form of stabilization and structural adjustment programmes in whose formulation and implementation the IMF and the World Bank have played a key role.[2] The Bretton Woods institutions have in fact by now gained an unprecedented and pervasive influence over policy-making in African countries, which has obviously stimulated a lively and at times very heated debate in academic and policy-making circles.[3]

Agreement on an IMF supported set of stabilization measures has normally been a pre-condition to entering into structural adjustment programmes supported by the World Bank. Similarly, bilateral donors and commercial banks (in the London and Paris Club fora) insist that agreements be reached with the Bretton Woods institutions before they support initiatives concerning balance of payments and development financing. The main elements in adjustment programmes as they have been formulated since the beginning of the 1980s have centred around the following immediate objectives:[4]

1

(a) strengthening the balance of payments position;
(b) reduction in domestic financial imbalances, including less government deficit financing;
(c) elimination of price distortions in various sectors of the economy;
(d) promotion of domestic savings in public and private sectors;
(e) increasing trade liberalization;
(f) revival of orderly relationships with trading partners and creditors;
(g) mobilization of additional external resources.

In recent years, higher level development objectives have gained more prominence. It is therefore now common to encounter the following overall objectives: (i) restoring positive per capita growth, (ii) averting pauperization of the poor and vulnerable groups and (iii) avoiding such drastic compression of personal consumption and basic services as to erode the fabric of society.

The specific policy instruments have generally included:

(a) credit ceilings and control of money supply;
(b) exchange rate adjustment, mainly devaluation;
(c) interest rate policy;
(d) deregulation of prices of goods, services and factor inputs;
(e) fiscal policy, including measures for resource mobilization as well as the reduction of public expenditure;
(f) trade and payments liberalization entailing, for example, the removal of import quotas;
(g) institutional reforms with emphasis on increased capacity to implement public investments and privatization;
(h) debt reschedulings.

These instruments combined in complex policy packages have served as the basis for the definition of criteria (conditionalities) against which a given government's performance has been assessed. Conditionality is, as Helleiner (1986b:66) aptly puts it, 'in', and automaticity and low-conditionality are 'out'. It is indeed very much through this kind of policy conditionality that adjustment programmes are implemented. For the IMF there is nothing new in this, as conditionalities have been standard in cases where countries had to borrow more than 25 per cent of their quotas. But for the World Bank the imposition of conditionality in this form marks a reversal of earlier practices.[5]

The IMF/World Bank packages obviously have implicit implications for income distribution, and explicit prescriptions for wage and price policy measures are often part of adjustment programmes. More recently, attention to the alleviation of the social costs of adjustment and the protection of the environment has appeared, but these considerations have not yet taken the form of conditionalities put forward by the IMF/World Bank.[6]

Three basic perspectives can be identified in the debate on stabilization and adjustment in sub-Saharan Africa:

(a) a transitory phase in which a series of economic balances (such as balance of payments and domestic fiscal balances) are restored in an orderly manner;
(b) a transitory process of policy reform intended to address policy changes to raise the efficiency of resource use, strengthen basic institutions and revive the balance of payments;
(c) a part of a continuous process of structural change and economic transformation, reflecting induced or planned adaption and adjustment policies as instruments chosen to respond to long-run development objectives and trends.

These different adjustment approaches have often been mixed, and terms are used in a very loose way, making it rather difficult, at times, to trace the origins and implications of a particular objective and policy proposal (or conditionality). Furthermore, it has on many occasions been difficult to establish whether demands put forward to African countries reflect the implications of a particular theoretical economic model, which should in principle be tested empirically, or whether broader, more ideologically-based, motives were the driving force. In practice, a combination of the two will be at work, but clarity about the conceptual framework (that is, the underlying model) and objectives is a first and indispensable condition for effective negotiation and implementation of adjustment programmes.

The first 'restoration of balance' (short-term) perspective has been identified as the IMF approach (also named 'the stabilization approach'). Policy advice is derived from a focus on monetary aggregates and puts considerable emphasis on demand restraint. Supply-side issues have not generally been directly addressed, but 'restoring the conditions for renewed growth' is a stated objective. Such adjustment does not therefore by itself provide a growth dynamic.

The second 'policy reform' (medium-term) approach has been identified with the World Bank. Economic policy is seen as part of the problem as clearly expressed in the 'Berg Report' (World Bank 1981). A range of issues, including, more recently, distributional and

3

environmental questions, are therefore covered. Ultimate concerns are real as opposed to narrowly monetary. This approach is therefore 'supply-side focused' and is preoccupied with the establishment of a growth dynamic. Focus is put on macro prices such as the exchange, interest and wage rates, and the need for removing price controls and distortions is stressed. The 'policy reform' approach remains somewhat transitory in nature, a characteristic it shares with the IMF approach. Furthermore, this perspective of adjustment may easily become identified with the views of the international donor community giving it a rather arbitrary character, and it must at all times be kept in mind that adjustment will not be successful if externally driven. 'Ownership' must be that of the sub-Saharan countries.

The third 'transformation' (longer-term) approach is much broader in its inspiration, and reflects contributions from structuralist and more radical approaches to economic development.[7] This perspective is not narrowly identified with an institution, but corresponds broadly with the views of, for example, the Organization for African Unity/Economic Commission for Africa (OAU/ECA) and a number of critics of the orthodox approaches.[8] This approach is concerned with the continuous, long-run needs of growth, transformation and development. As such, it is as much concerned with the establishment of a growth dynamic as the World Bank concept, but in a wider context, and 'policy is part of the solution'. All economies have to be continuously adapting to changing circumstances and both the first and second concept of adjustment are therefore in this view nothing more than subsets of the wider and longer-term process of development.

The above classification does not, however, fit all situations, and the overall picture has become much more blurred than at the beginning of the 1980s. Most policies cannot be classified as either demand or supply measures, and neither the World Bank/IMF, nor proponents of so-called 'alternative' approaches have been 'static' in their views during the past decade. The World Bank has gradually put increasing emphasis on the transformation approach, and the IMF is giving signs of concern with the overall growth and poverty impact of its programmes.[9] Finally, African policy-makers are now openly recognizing that mistakes have been made in the past, and accept more fully the need for addressing problems created by macroeconomic imbalances.

In other words, perspectives on structural adjustment are evolving in a dynamic manner. The need for adjustment is no longer part of controversy, and more emphasis is put by all involved on distributional as well as growth and supply-side issues.[10] Furthermore, while it was originally thought by the IMF and World Bank that adjustment programmes would only be required for a duration of up to five years from the start of their implementation, there is now recognition of the need for a long-term perspective.[11]

Nevertheless, tensions between demand and supply management remain. Demand management cannot be neglected due to the need of closing resource gaps. There are, however, various ways of doing this with differing implications for macroeconomic balance, growth and development. World Bank and IMF approaches and views differ in subtle ways, which are not always fully perceived. This raises topics like what the IMF and World Bank macroeconomic models are, how they relate to real and monetary variables, and whether they are compatible (in theory and in actual practice).

Furthermore, while much of this kind of analysis refers to technical models, matters of general development theory and practice loom in the background. A series of unsettled questions on the overall World Bank/IMF strategy, emphasizing *inter alia* the role of market prices and a high degree of openness of the economy, remain. It is by no means settled that the IMF/World Bank approaches will actually work in the SSA environment, and that the overall strategy is consistent with the requirements of long-run development. Reformist approaches could be pursued, but it has also been suggested by the ECA (1989) and Loxley (in Helleiner 1986a) that viable alternatives exist.

The search for a 'right' approach is still relatively new. The analytical models of the IMF and the World Bank, and the way in which they are used, continue largely unaltered, and an integrated framework for analysing stabilization and structural adjustment measures and programmes is still lacking. It remains a fact, that structural adjustment is not revealed truth, and on some elements reasonable people and professional economists can disagree. However, a search for alternatives – or more moderately – modified designs of appropriate adjustment programmes has begun, and the same accounts for the integrated analytic framework.

It is within the above context, and to explore the kinds of issues raised above, that this book was written. Chapter 1 sets out in somewhat greater detail the particular features of the economies of sub-Saharan Africa, the sources of their stagnation and the set of macroeconomic management issues their governments face. The aim of Chapter 1, which serves as a common reference point in the remainder of the volume, is not to be all inclusive, but to focus on key macroeconomic aspects. In Chapter 2 a macroeconomic accounting framework is developed. Fundamental concepts are outlined and the possible impact of specific adjustment policies is discussed. Consistency is basic to all macroeconomic analysis, but issue-oriented, partial-equilibrium policy analysis remains, for the time being, indispensable in applied policy-work. Consequently, Chapter 2 provides a link between the review in Chapter 1 of the crisis in sub-Saharan Africa and Chapters 3–6. In these four analytical chapters, policy-oriented, economy-wide frameworks for analysing stabilization and structural adjustment are in focus. Particular attention and space is devoted to the IMF and World Bank models due to their importance in shaping the character of adjustment programmes as they are presently being negotiated and implemented. Chapter 7 concludes and ties together the various threads.

1

MACROECONOMICS OF
AFRICA

The main body of macroeconomic theory and policy analysis is concerned with developed market economies. An attempt will therefore be made here to provide a brief sketch of the particular characteristics of the economies of sub-Saharan Africa (excluding the Republic of South Africa) and the dimensions and causes of the present crisis. An initial disclaimer is necessary. African economies are diverse; economic contexts, structures and policies differ, and available statistics are notoriously unreliable and vary widely from one source to the other. Methodological problems with exchange rates and deflators as well as the unknown size of the unrecorded economy are just a few important reasons for this.

Furthermore, average data are heavily affected by the performance of the Nigerian economy, which accounts for close to 25 per cent of population as well as gross national product (GNP). Also the significant differences between oil-exporting and oil-importing countries are concealed, and the same accounts for a range of other inter- and intra-regional variations. These differences are not in focus here. The generality of the economic crisis is widely confirmed by country studies across sub-Saharan Africa, and while the overall picture to be drawn up does not necessarily fit particular countries, the overall trend seems, nevertheless, to reflect quite well the situation of a majority of African countries. In addition, a frame of reference is required as background to the analytical approaches reviewed in subsequent chapters.

NATURE OF THE AFRICAN ECONOMY

The countries of sub-Saharan Africa are small, poor and open economies. With a rapidly growing population of some 480 million, SSA had a total GNP of only US $163 billion in 1989. This is not even

7

Table 1.1 Comparative structural data on sub-Saharan Africa, other developing regions and OECD economies

Indicator[a]	Sub-Saharan Africa	Latin America[b]	East Asia[c]	South Asia[d]	OECD
GNP per capita (US$)	340	1,950	540	320	19,090
GDP per capita (US$)	337	1,922	588	280	18,489
Share of agriculture in gross domestic product (GDP)	32	—	24	32	3[e]
Share of industry in GDP	27	—	44	26	31[e]
Share of rural population in total population	72	29	53	74	23
Share of government consumption in GDP	15	9	8	12	17
Share of private consumption in GDP	72	67	57	69	61
Share of gross domestic investment in GDP	15	20	34	22	22
Share of gross domestic savings in GDP	13	24	35	7	22
Share of exports of goods and non-factor services in GDP	25	14	25	—	21
Share of imports of goods and non-factor services in GDP	28	11	29	—	21
Resource balance in per cent of GDP	-3	3	-4	-2	0
Share of primary commodities in merchandise exports	89	66	31	30	19
Share of manufactures in merchandise imports	77	73	74	62	73
Life expectancy at birth (years)	51	67	68	58	76
Annual 1980–89 annual population growth	3.2	2.1	1.6	2.3	0.6
Daily calorie supply per capita[f]	2,011	2,724	2,596	2,116	3,417
Primary school enrolment as share of age group[g]	67	107	128	90	103
Secondary school enrolment as share of age group[g]	18	48	46	37	95
Tertiary school enrolment as share of age group[g]	2	17	5	—	41

Source: World Bank (1991b).

Notes:

a Data refer to 1989 and are stated in per cent unless otherwise indicated.

b Includes the Caribbean.

c Comprises all the low- and middle-income economies of East and Southeast Asia and the Pacific, east of and including China and Thailand.

d Comprises Bangladesh, Bhutan, India, Myanmar (formerly Burma), Nepal, Pakistan and Sri Lanka.

e 1987 data.

f 1988 data. See the text for further comments on calorie needs.

g 1988 data. Students do not necessarily belong to the age group in reference.

double the GNP of Denmark with only five million people. A major share of the African population live and work in the rural sector. Production, which is severely affected by an array of human, physical, infrastructural and technological constraints, including the vagaries of weather conditions,[1] is therefore largely in the primary sector.

Commercial activities are crucially dependent on imported factor inputs, and exports are based on only a few, mainly primary, export commodities. Savings are limited, and a continuous inflow of external financial resources is required to maintain domestic absorption, including a low rate of capital formation. Poverty in all its dimensions is widespread, and living conditions are extremely difficult. This is clearly demonstrated in Table 1.1, which shows a number of indicators of economic development from sub-Saharan Africa, other developing regions and the Organization for Economic Co-operation and Development (OECD) area. The data reveal, in a self-explanatory manner, the predicament of the economies of sub-Saharan Africa. Only in South Asia can similar conditions be observed at national and regional levels.

It can be added to the above characteristics that the African economies are seriously fragmented as well as inflexible and dualistic in nature. The production base is narrow both in terms of size and the range of goods produced.[2] A modernized sector of monetized enclaves has been super-imposed over a large low-productivity subsistence sector, which has seen little technological development, and which continues to use traditional tools and techniques of production. Linkages with the modern sector are few and may have weakened during the 1980s. Furthermore, intra-regional trade remains insignificant.

Despite considerable progress since independence, human resources are critically underdeveloped. The acute scarcity of trained manpower at many levels has constrained efficiency and the capacity to govern effectively, and the consequent reliance on expatriate advisers, willingly supplied through a rapidly-growing international system of technical assistance, has had at best mixed results.[3] The lack of institutional capability is also rampant in SSA. The apparatus of modern states including the provision of public services are either not in place or work very inefficiently,[4] and the size of the private entrepreneurial sector is limited.

Social organization and the political system, as well as the cultural milieu, interact with the institutional set-up and the management of the economy to determine the dynamism and relative viability of the development process.[5] In perceiving the basic characteristics of the

10

economies of sub-Saharan Africa reference to the socio-political structure is therefore important, and it is beyond doubt that political
instability and civil strife have had an important negative impact on
the economic performance of SSA during the 1980s. These aspects
of the development process of sub-Saharan Africa will not, however,
be discussed further here, and the same accounts for the physical
development potentials which do, of course, influence and constrain
the feasibility of alternative courses of action in the field of economic
management.

ECONOMIC PERFORMANCE

The 1980s have been disastrous for most of sub-Saharan Africa.
Nevertheless, the economic performance, since political independence
was achieved, is not consistently bleak. A few countries have managed
well, and for the continent as a whole, the 1960s witnessed, in fact,
considerable progress in most economic indicators. The 1970s show
an uneven record and there were uncomfortable signs of future
problems on the horizon, but it can be argued that by and large
sub-Saharan countries 'rode through' the 1974–6 external shocks
successfully, and that from 1976 to 1979 Africa performed as well as
anyone.[6]

There is reason, as noted above, to be very cautious in the use of
data and averages in the African context,[7] but some overall trends
make sense, as they are confirmed by observation of a more qualitative
character, and by common sense. Tables 1.2 and 1.3 are an attempt
to capture some of the more important quantitative aspects of the
macroeconomic developments from 1965 to 1989 on which there are
relevant data available.

The average annual rate of growth in GDP, which reached a
respectable 5 per cent from 1965 to 1973, decreased during the latter
part of the 1970s to only 3.2 per cent, and from 1980 dropped further
to 2.1 per cent. Taking account of a rapidly-increasing population,
real GDP per capita actually fell by 1.1 per cent during the 1980s. It
can, furthermore, be noted that real GNP per capita in 1980 prices,
which grew at 1.7 per cent from 1965 to 1973, dropped by 1.2 per
cent annually from 1980. The overall average annual rate of growth
of GNP per capita almost stagnated at 0.3 per cent from 1965 to
1989.

Production in the industrial sector, which had shown much progress
in the earlier two decades, grew little from 1980, and agricultural

Table 1.2 Gross domestic product, aggregate demand and other economic indicators, 1965–89 (average annual change in per cent)

Indicator[a]	1965–73	1973–80	1980–89
GDP	4.8	3.2	2.1
GDP per capita	3.3	− 0.3	− 1.1
Agricultural production	2.4	1.1	2.0
Industrial production	10.4	4.3	0.7
Service production	3.4	4.2	2.3
Government consumption	9.0	7.0	1.1
Private consumption	3.9	2.6	0.7
Gross domestic investment	9.8	4.0	− 3.9
Merchandise exports[b]	15.1	0.2	− 0.6
Merchandise imports[b]	3.7	7.6	− 5.9
GNP per capita	1.7	0.6	− 1.2
Inflation	7.5	6.8	19.0
Terms of trade	− 6.7	5.4	− 4.9
Long-term debt outstanding and disbursed[c]	20.1[d]	23.9	14.5
Population growth	2.6	2.8	3.2

Sources: World Bank (1989a, 1989b, 1989c and 1991b).
Notes:
a Data refer to real changes unless otherwise indicated. For information on how the data have been compiled see the sources indicated. Prudence is, as already pointed out, necessary in interpreting average data, and a variety of technical issues regarding, for example, appropriate weights remain unresolved. The data reported here do seem, however, to be the best available.
b Do not include services.
c Average annual percentage change of nominal amounts.
d Data refer to 1970–73.

output could not keep pace with population growth. Food production per capita had by 1987–9 fallen to 95 per cent of the level in 1980. The daily per capita calorie supply in 1988 was at around 2,000 calories, equivalent to the level of 1965, which is far below minimum nutritional requirements.[8] Consequently, hunger and malnutrition became widespread. The combined share of agriculture and industry remained constant at around 60 per cent of GDP from 1965 to 1989, but agriculture increased its share from 28 to 32 per cent, while industry fell from 32 to 27 per cent from 1980 to 1989. A process of de-industrialization therefore took place in SSA during the 1980s.

However, manufactured exports, which accounted for only 5 per cent of merchandise exports in 1980, increased to 11 per cent in 1989. This illustrates the importance of relatively better export prices, but also that total merchandise exports contracted considerably in volume terms. Data on trade vary in coverage and are not directly comparable,[9]

Table 1.3 Aggregate demand, external resource balance and external debt, 1965–89

Indicator[a]	1965	1980	1989
General government consumption	10	13	14
Private consumption[b]	73	66	73
Total consumption	83	78	87
Gross domestic investment	14	20	15
Absorption	97	98	102
Gross domestic savings	14	21	13
– excluding Nigeria	18	13	11
Exports of goods and non-factor services	23	26	25
Resource balance[c]	1.0	1.0	– 3.0
– excluding Nigeria	1.4[d]	– 6.1	– 5.4
Total external debt (percentage of GNP)	13.4[d]	27.4	98.3[g]
Debt service (percentage of GNP)[e]	1.4[d]	3.1	5.9[g]
Debt service as share of total exports[e]	7.1[d]	10.9	22.2[g]
Debt service as share of scheduled obligations[f]	—	96.6	38.9
Share of long-term debt with variable interest	6.3[d]	23.7	23.8

Sources: World Bank (1989b, 1990c, 1991a and 1991b).
Notes:
a Stated in per cent of GDP unless otherwise indicated.
b Includes some statistical discrepancies (World Bank 1989b:285).
c The resource balance indicates the difference between exports (f.o.b.) and imports (c.i.f.) of goods and non-factor services (or the difference between gross domestic savings and gross domestic investment) (see also Chapter 2). Estimates of GDP by expenditure are, according to World Bank (1989a:33), generally considered less reliable than those of GDP by industrial origin. Figures shown here are therefore only as accurate as the underlying national estimates, which implies that the sum of the shares of total consumption, gross domestic investment and the resource balance does not in all cases add up to 100 per cent, and savings minus investment is not in all cases equal to the resource balance.
d Data refer to 1970.
e Data on debt service in 1970 excludes interest payments on short-term debt.
f Calculated by adding outstanding arrears as well as principal and interests forgiven or rescheduled to actual payments.
g 1990 figures for the debt/GNP ratio, the debt ratio and the debt service ratio are 111.9, 7.8 and 24.2, respectively, as projected by the World Bank (1990c).

but taking account of the rate of population growth of 3.2 per cent per annum, per capita merchandise exports dropped by 29 per cent between 1980 and 1989. Per capita merchandise imports began falling at an average rate of 9.1 per cent per year from 1980, and by 1989 had dropped by 57.6 per cent in volume terms. The overall terms of trade also developed very unfavourably after the positive trend during the 1970s, although it should be noted that terms of trade also fell during the 1970s for the poorer oil-importing African countries. Finally, net inflows of foreign resources started to dwindle rather than increase.

13

External long-term debt continued to increase in nominal terms during the 1980s, but at a reduced pace as compared to the 1960s and 1970s. In fact, real increases in external debt were modest from 1980, and commercial bank lending collapsed.[10] However, from 1973 an increasing share of total long-term debt was contracted at variable interest rates, and debt service payments actually reached 5.9 and 22.2 per cent of, respectively, GNP and total exports in 1989.

As a consequence of the above developments, significant resource gaps developed, inflation reached unprecedented levels averaging over 19 per cent annually from 1980, and past investment and consumption levels became unsustainable.[11] Government and private consumption and gross domestic investment fell in real terms by 17, 20 and 48 per cent respectively per capita, from 1980 to 1989. However, the share of total absorption (that is, consumption and investment) as a share of GDP showed an upward trend during the 1965–89 period. Gross domestic savings therefore fell from a level of 21 per cent of GDP in 1980 to only 13 per cent in 1989, which is lower than the savings rate in 1965. It should be noted though, that if Nigeria is excluded, gross domestic savings fell by only two percentage points from 13 per cent of GDP in 1980 to 11 per cent in 1989.[12]

In other words, it is obvious that much of the economic and social progress realized during the 1960s was lost during the 1980s. Important economic and social infrastructure has deteriorated, human suffering has increased and utilization rates as low as 30 per cent of industrial capacity have been reported in some countries.[13] The quality of health care and education is declining almost everywhere, the supply of expendables (drugs for health services, books for pupils, and so on) is grossly insufficient and maintenance budgets are inadequate. Progress in reducing child death-rates has slowed down and in some cases even reversed, and at the same time population growth continues to soar.

SOURCES OF THE CRISIS

Many of the structural and other features of the economies of sub-Saharan Africa reflect closely the historical legacy of hundreds of years of colonialism. This sets the background against which the development failure of sub-Saharan Africa during the 1980s must be seen. Viewed in this broader perspective, the three decades of post-independence history do indeed appear as a very brief span of time. Nevertheless, there are many mutually-reinforcing sources of the crisis, and while legacies may be historical facts of overwhelming importance, they must be taken as given in economic policy-making. The topic to be reviewed here is, therefore, the more immediate sources of the crisis.

Most of the countries in sub-Saharan Africa became independent in the 1960s, at a time when the state was assigned a leading role in economic development. It appeared self-evident that an active state, pursuing interventionistic economic policies in accordance with a central development plan, and adequately supported by an inflow of foreign aid, could master the art of breaking the vicious circle of poverty and underdevelopment within a relatively short period. With hindsight, this was over-optimistic, and in the early 1980s it became, in addition, politically opportune to perceive state interventionism and ill-conceived domestic economic policies as the primary source of the impending crisis in sub-Saharan Africa.[14]

The 'Berg Report' was a major contribution along this line of thought, and it is, as Ravenhill (1988:179) points out, difficult to overemphasize the extent to which this publication changed the nature of the debate on Africa's development problems.[15] It is now widely accepted that domestic policy matters, and that includes overall development strategies as well as the investment, price, trade and exchange rate policies pursued by many African countries – often at the advice of foreign advisers and institutions – have not yielded the desired results.

As suggested by the World Bank (1989b), there is little dispute that the origins of the problems in the industrial sector in SSA can be traced to high levels of protection and to the erroneous perception that development is equivalent to industrial growth. Governments have consequently relied too much on import-substituting policies, allowing vested interests, including many foreign investors, to exploit their position to the detriment of the overall economic performance.[16]

Even ECA (1989), which is highly critical of the orthodox approach to adjustment put forward by the IMF and the World Bank, refers to the neglected informal sector, to 'lopsided development' (that is, urban-biased) and to policies that have been biased against traditional agriculture. These were, indeed, some of the major points made in the 'Berg Report'. In addition, recent OAU statements make reference to the inadequacy and/or misdirection of human and financial resources, inappropriate economic strategies and policies, and poor economic management.[17] These concerns also appeared in the 'Berg Report'. Domestic policy failure is, therefore, well documented. The same

Table 1.4 Domestic macroeconomic variables and policies, 1980–9

Variable	1980	1981	1982	1983	1984	1985	1986	1987	1988	1989
Private sector balance (per cent of GDP)[a]	7.7	2.6	1.7	3.3	6.5	7.7	4.7	3.9	3.1	3.9
Government balance (per cent of GDP)	-6.3	-8.1	-8.4	-7.3	-6.4	-7.3	-7.9	-7.2	-7.1	-6.9
Overall balance (per cent of GDP)	1.4	-5.5	-6.7	-4.0	0.1	0.4	-3.2	-3.3	-4.0	-3.0
Consumer prices – weighted average (per cent annual change)	24.6	29.3	19.2	25.6	21.6	19.8	20.5	23.1	21.7	19.6
Consumer prices – median estimate (per cent annual change)	12.5	12.7	12.7	11.5	12.0	10.3	6.8	7.2	8.3	8.8
Growth of money supply (per cent annual change)	16.1	19.2	12.5	10.0	17.2	18.4	15.5	—	—	—
Domestic credit (per cent annual change)	21.2	22.8	21.1	17.4	12.0	15.8	15.5	—	—	—
Real effective exchange rate index[b]	100.0	92.6	90.7	85.4	73.6	79.1	113.5	168.6	—	—
Export crop price index/urban wage rate index[c]	100.0	124.0	140.0	144.0	158.0	163.0	174.0	—	—	—
Food crop price index/urban wage rate index[c]	100.0	127.0	127.0	153.0	177.0	143.0	145.0	—	—	—

Sources: World Bank (1989a, 1990a and 1991b), IMF (1988, 1989a and 1990) and Development Committee (1988:36).

Notes:

a Calculated as a residual on the basis of the overall external resource balance and the government balance (deficit). The figures for 1988 and 1989 should be interpreted with caution as the overall balances are from World Bank sources while the government balances are from IMF sources.

b Defined on the basis of the number of local currency unit per unit of foreign currency in thirty-five sub-Saharan African countries (see Development Committee 1988: 36).

c Debt-distressed countries only (see Development Committee 1988:40). Caution is required in interpreting these data, but it does seem apparent that incentives of agricultural producers were improved during the first half of the 1980s in debt-distressed countries.

accounts for the much too liberal domestic credit expansion, insolvent state companies, mounting fiscal deficits and inflation, which have been just a few of the unwanted corollaries.

The particular features of the role of the state in SSA does not, however, arise so much because of its mere size relative to GDP. In fact, although central government is relatively large in sub-Saharan Africa as compared to other developing country regions, general government consumption in SSA in 1989 amounted to 14 per cent of GDP as compared to 17 per cent in OECD countries and 12 per cent in South Asia. Furthermore, indirect government intervention in the allocation of resources through macroeconomic policy and the direct provision of public services is obviously not a special feature of SSA governments.

None the less, public participation in directly-productive activities in the form of state-owned enterprises, and direct control of the allocation of resources, have been very prevalent features in sub-Saharan Africa. Furthermore, the expansion in government activity in general, and of state-owned enterprises in particular, has been very rapid. This has increased financing needs during the 1970s accordingly, as revenues could not keep up with spending pressures.[18]

Table 1.4 summarizes background data on some key domestic macroeconomic indicators for which data for SSA as a whole are available. Domestic monetary and fiscal policy remained largely passive in the early years of the 1980s despite mounting imbalances in the overall resource balance. Government deficits were partly monetized through an expansion in domestic credit, and even when inflation reached very high levels in 1980–1, no action was taken on the real interest rate, and the real effective exchange rate was allowed to appreciate.

Early action was initiated on agricultural incentives and wages, and by 1983 stabilization and adjustment programmes had gained momentum. Such programmes have since then become an important feature of economic policy in the sub-Saharan African region. SSA government consumption and investment were cut back, contributing to import compression. The only component of the government budget, which increased its share of total expenditure between 1980–2 and 1986–7 was that of interest,[19] and interest payments have in this way become a substantial burden on fiscal outlays.

In real terms, cuts in government consumption and capital investment were particularly severe if account is taken of the population increase. Although consolidated data on the parastatal sector are

17

difficult to obtain, it is clear that an important contributor to the cut-back in government spending is a decrease in the losses by public enterprises. Another important contributor is the effort of governments to contain their expenditure on civil service wages and salaries.[20] Expenditure in the social sectors was also curtailed.

Efforts were made to improve domestic policy formulation and implementation in general, and government budget deficits were increasingly financed through domestic and foreign financing. Domestic credit expansion was curbed and increased less than the money supply from 1985. In 1980, 1983 and 1987 respectively, 67.7, 87.1 and 93.6 per cent of the fiscal deficit was financed through an improved private sector balance and increased foreign borrowing rather than being monetized. Parallel with this, real interest rates were increased substantially.[21]

Measures were also taken to liberalize trade, and one of the more striking areas of reform has been action on the exchange rate since 1985–6, which led to an increase in the index of the real effective exchange rate to 168.6 in 1987. This was more than double the level in 1983–5. However, in comparison with the evolution of exchange rates in other low-income countries, especially in Asia, exchange rates remain relatively high in Africa.[22] Action on agricultural prices was, as already noted, initiated relatively early. As a result of the movements of agricultural prices and government urban wage policy, internal terms of trade have, during at least the first half of the 1980s, moved in favour of the rural sector. A dip was, however, experienced in 1985–6 due to successive years of good harvests.

The overall resource balance turned positive (representing a net real resource outflow from SSA) in 1984–5. This situation changed again from 1986 following the initiation of stabilization and adjustment programmes. The overall public sector deficit remained around 6–8 per cent of GDP for the whole of the 1980s, but the decrease in the private sector balance in the early 1980s was reversed, with relatively large private balances occurring in 1984–5. Rather than being associated with substantial changes in the savings rate, this development was due to the occurrence of capital flight and a sharp fall in domestic investment.[23] After 1985, external financial assistance increased, and private sector balances fell to a lower level of 3 to 4 per cent in 1987–9.[24]

Based on the information in Tables 1.1 to 1.4 and the above comments, it is apparent that the post-colonial governments of sub-Saharan Africa have, with due account for wide differences from country to country, been 'weak', in the sense that the goals of economic development set at independence have not been accomplished. It also appears that government policies and strategies, which were generally successful in the 1960s and part of the 1970s, have had a negative impact on economic performance during the 1980s, and the deceleration in growth certainly set in long before the crisis in the 1980s. The 'Berg Report' (World Bank 1981) was therefore indisputably pointing to what were to become very real problems.

Estimating the impact of the various internal and external sources of the crisis and assigning 'blame' is fraught with difficulties of both a practical and theoretical nature. It is therefore not surprising that

some blame the region's economic decline on factors beyond Africa's control – bad weather, weak world economic prices, fluctuating international interest rates, and too little aid. Others blame policies, especially poor management of public resources and inappropriate incentives. Most recognize the importance of structural factors, especially high population growth.

(World Bank 1989b:23)

It remains, however, that the 'Berg approach' of singling out deficiencies in domestic policy-making as the primary and dominant source of the African crisis in the 1970s and 1980s is vulnerable to justified criticism. First of all, external factors over which the sub-Saharan countries have no, or at best, limited control, have always had a significant impact on the economies of SSA. And the international economic environment worsened considerably during the 1980s. Second, it must be recalled that significant economic reforms were in fact undertaken after 1983. What stands out clearly from the experience of the 1980s is that whatever positive effects the economic reforms might have had, they were completely overwhelmed by the negative international environment. Tables 1.5 to 1.7 illustrate the magnitude of these external factors and summarize relevant aspects of trade and financial relations between sub-Saharan Africa and the rest of the world from 1980 to 1989.

Many African countries had easy access to foreign resources and borrowed heavily during the 1970s and early 1980s. They therefore managed to 'ride through' the crisis of the mid-1970s, and until 1979 they did as well, in terms of growth, as many other developing countries. However, the situation quickly deteriorated. The balance of trade and services broke down and the current account deficit almost quintupled between 1980 and 1982. Private transfers remained in the

Table 1.5 Balance of payments – current account, 1980–9
(current US$ billions)

	Trade balance (f.o.b)	Services net	Net private transfers	Net official transfers	Current account balance
1980	5.6[a]	− 14.0	− 1.3	2.9	− 3.5
1981	− 8.2	− 13.6	− 0.8	3.1	− 16.1
1982	− 8.5	− 13.3	− 0.6	2.9	− 17.1
1983	− 3.9	− 12.1	− 0.3	3.4	− 10.5
1984	2.8	− 11.3	0.0	3.4	− 3.0
1985	3.4	− 12.1	0.3	3.6	− 0.4
1986	− 3.5	− 10.3	0.3	4.4	− 5.3
1987	− 3.8	− 10.0[b]	0.8	4.8	− 6.5[b]
1988	− 4.0	− 10.8[b]	—	—	− 8.2[b]
1989	− 0.9	− 10.5[b]	—	—	− 7.4[b]

Sources: World Bank (1989a, 1991a and 1991b) and IMF (1990).
Notes:
a This positive trade balance is due to Nigeria. If Nigeria is excluded the trade balance was negative.
b Not strictly comparable with the other data as the source is IMF (1990).

Table 1.6 Balance of payments – current account, 1980–9
(current US$ billions)

	Net foreign investment	Net long-term borrowing (net flows on debt)	Other capital flows	Use of foreign reserves
1980	0.0	7.8	− 0.3	− 3.9[b]
1981	1.0	8.1	1.6[a]	6.9
1982	1.2	9.3	− 0.5	3.6
1983	0.9	6.8	0.0	1.1
1984	0.5	4.9	− 1.2	− 0.3
1985	1.1	2.6	− 1.3	− 0.8
1986	0.5	4.9	− 1.7	− 0.4
1987	1.2	5.9	− 1.3	− 0.5
1988	0.7	5.3	− 1.0	—
1989	2.3	5.6	− 1.2	—

Sources: World Bank (1988d, 1989a, 1989d and 1990c).
Notes:
a Excludes IMF charges and interest payments on short-term debt.
b If Nigeria is excluded reserves decreased by US$ 0.5 billion this year.

negative until the mid-1980s, while net official transfers (in current prices) stagnated.

There were significant increases in the international rate of interest, and debt service obligations began skyrocketing. Long-term borrowing

Table 1.7 Terms of trade, net financial transfers and external debt, 1980–9

	Terms of trade (index 1980 = 100)	Aggregate net financial transfers[a] (current US$ billion)	Total external debt (current US$ billion)	Total external debt service[b] (current US$ billions)	Debt service ratio[b] (per cent of total)
1980	100.0	11[c]	56.2	6.3	10.9
1981	100.5	11[c]	64.0	5.9	12.5
1982	94.8	11[c]	70.3	7.4	19.3
1983	95.0	8	79.8	8.1	22.8
1984	96.5	6	83.4	10.1	25.9
1985	91.2	8	96.5	11.2	28.2
1986	69.8	14	113.8	10.0	29.4
1987	70.2	16	138.8	8.6	22.6
1988	92.0	14	141.5	9.7	26.1
1989	73.0	14	147.0	8.8	22.2

Sources: World Bank (1989a, 1989d, 1990c and 1991b) and OECD (1990).

Notes:

a Net financial transfers are a mixture of items from the current and capital accounts. They are defined as total resource flows minus investment payments (interest and dividends) (see OECD 1989:219). Total net flows include official and private grants (including technical co-operation), direct investment and total long- and short-term loans minus loan repayments. As such it is a very useful overall indicator of financial flows.

b Debt service actually paid, which in 1989 had declined to only about 39 per cent of scheduled obligations (see Table 1.3).

c Average for 1980–2.

fell from a level of US$ 7.8 billion in 1980 to only 2.6 billion in 1985, and aggregate net financial transfers in 1984–5, while positive, were only two-thirds of the 1980–2 level in nominal terms.

As no additional net transfers of resources came forward in the early 1980s, international reserves were gradually run down in the expectation that the crisis was temporary. This expectation was shared by African policy-makers and the IMF/World Bank institutions alike. However, the situation became unsustainable. International reserves were running out,[25] and other capital flows, including capital flight, worsened the situation even further from 1984.

Material imports had to be cut down and the balance of trade turned positive from 1984. Due to the deficit on the services account, the overall balance of trade and services remained negative, but deficits were significantly reduced. Net financial transfers started a relative revival in nominal terms in 1985, but parallel with this, debt service payments continued their increase. Furthermore, the barter terms of trade fell drastically in 1986.

Table 1.8 External economic shocks – interest rate and terms of trade, 1980–7

	1980	1981	1982	1983	1984	1985	1986	1987
Actual interest payments (current US$ billion)[a]	3.3	4.2	4.5	4.0	4.8	4.7	4.1	3.5
Average interest rate of new borrowing commitments (per cent)[b]	7.2	8.3	7.5	7.1	5.4	5.9	4.9	4.2
'Loss' due to interest rate increase (current US$ billion)[b]	2.8	3.7	3.9	3.4	3.9	3.9	3.2	2.6
Fall in terms of trade (per cent)[c]	0.0	−0.5	5.2	5.0	3.5	8.2	30.2	29.8
'Loss' due to fall in terms of trade (current US$ billion)[d]	0.0	−0.2	2.5	2.0	1.4	3.4	10.2	11.2
Total 'external loss':[e]								
– in current US$ billions	2.8	4.0	6.4	5.4	5.3	7.3	13.4	13.8
– as share of GDP (per cent)	1.3	1.9	3.2	2.8	2.7	3.7	8.7	9.6
– as share of current account deficit (per cent)	80.0	24.8	37.4	51.4	176.7	1,825.0[f]	252.8	212.3
– as share of fiscal deficit (per cent)	20.7	24.1	37.7	37.9	42.6	50.9	103.9	133.8
– as share of aggregate net financial transfers (per cent)	25.5	36.4	58.2	67.5	88.3	91.3	95.7	86.3

Source: World Bank (1988d, 1989a, 1989d, 1990a and 1990c) and Tables 1.4, 1.5 and 1.7.
Notes:
a Sum of actual interest payments on short- and long-term debt and IMF charges from World Bank (1990c) except for 1981–2 which are from World Bank (1989a).
b It is assumed that actual annual interest payments during 1980–7 roughly correspond to the average annual interest rate of new borrowing commitments in each year. The 'loss' is calculated by comparing with the average real interest rate for the period 1974–9, which according to World Bank (1990a:15) was 0.97 per cent.
c As compared to the 1980 terms of trade level.
d The loss or 'income effect' of changes in the terms of trade was calculated by multiplying the value of exports of goods and non-factor services (in constant 1980 US$) by the percentage change in the terms of trade index. Terms of trade losses in 1980 US$ were subsequently converted to current US$ by use of GDP deflator (US$ series).
e See World Bank (1989a:20) for GDP in current prices and Tables 1.4, 1.5 and 1.7 for the other data.
f Recall that the current account deficit was very small in 1985.

The purchasing power of exports (in constant 1980 prices) fell even more from 1980 to 1985 than the terms of trade index as export volumes fell as well.[26] However, while the purchasing power fall between 1980 and 1985 was at a rate of 5.5 per cent per year, the drop in 1986 was almost 25 per cent.[27] Therefore, while economic stabilization seemed underway in 1985,[28] sustained recovery was quickly truncated.

It is difficult to assess the impact of external factors on the economic performance of the sub-Saharan countries. Yet some very tentative calculations have been carried out to compile Table 1.8, showing the estimated loss due to the relatively high rate of interest and the falling terms of trade faced by sub-Saharan Africa during the period 1980–7. No attempt has been made to separate out cyclical and structural components of the terms-of-trade trend, and a detailed analysis of the factors underlying this trend is also beyond the scope of this volume.

Table 1.8 shows that losses increased steadily from a level of 1.3 per cent of GDP in 1980 to 9.6 per cent of GDP in 1987. This is well above the negative overall resource balance of 3.3 per cent of GDP in 1987. Furthermore, had the terms of trade not changed and had the level of interest remained at previous levels sub-Saharan Africa would *ceteris paribus* have had a considerable current account surplus from 1984 onwards. Aggregate net financial transfers remained positive during the 1980–7 period and continue to play an important role in SSA. Nevertheless, the losses due to the interest rate and terms-of-trade shocks escalated from an equivalent of 25 to around 90 per cent of these transfers. Finally, losses due to just these two external shocks grew from around 21 per cent of the fiscal deficit in 1980 to well above the total deficit in 1987.

It is in the above context useful to recall the results of an econometric study by Wheeler (1984) on the relative importance of internal and external factors as sources of stagnation in SSA during the 1970s. In a preliminary survey Wheeler found an extremely close relationship between movements in export prices and average economic performance throughout the post-independence period in SSA. He subsequently studied the performance of twenty-five SSA countries against two groups of explanatory variables from 1970 to 1981. In the first group, exogenous factors such as rainfall, violence, terms of trade, foreign aid, remittances from migrant workers, stability in export earnings and export diversification were included. In the second group of policy variables, one finds the real effective exchange rate, an indicator of import allocation practices and a measure of the ability to preserve balance in the trade accounts.

The results obtained are strong (Wheeler 1984:14). An eight-variable model accounts for nearly 90 per cent of the variation in growth rates for the twenty-five countries in the sample. Furthermore, in allocating the 'blame' for the disappointing growth record, the four exogenous variables as a group enjoy a dominant position. Wheeler's study is an interesting analytic contribution, and it was carried out before the current crisis. His investigation therefore implies that while the sources of the crisis are of both domestic and external nature in a complex interrelationship, external factors are dominant.[29]

In a more recent article with a more limited scope than Wheeler's contribution, Svedberg (1991) tries to provide some broad explanations for the sluggish export performance of thirty-three SSA countries during the period 1970–85. In a decomposition model the income terms of trade or real exports is split up into changes in export volume and barter terms of trade. Svedberg finds that the export performance of all countries in the region, with the exception of the five oil exporters, were affected negatively over the years 1970–85 by external forces in the form of deteriorating barter terms of trade. However, Svedberg underlines that external factors were not any less unfavourable in the earlier period 1954–69, where SSA countries did much better in terms of export volume growth than more recently.[30]

Svedberg has therefore identified a significant fall in the efficacy of domestic economic policy in affecting export volume performance. However, Ndulu (1990:6) points out that Svedberg's conclusions on the relative importance of internal and external factors in explaining the decline in exports cannot be extended beyond 1985. In a similar decomposition exercise for the period of 1980–8, Ndulu shows that a much more significant role can be attributed to the deteriorating barter terms of trade for this period than previously. Furthermore, Svedberg neither untangles the relative role of external and internal influences on the export volume performance nor identifies the specific internal economic and non-economic factors at play. Import compression caused by external factors has been influencial in affecting export volumes negatively,[31] and non-economic variables like weather and military strife, which have played an increasing role during the 1980s, can hardly be attributed to domestic economic policy failure.

Conclusions as regards policy action in particular country circumstances should not, of course, be drawn without more elaborate analyses of the temporary and permanent nature of the changes in the terms of trade, but the sheer magnitude of the negative external factors remains very illuminative. Furthermore, the importance of the external factors is not only due to their size. The unprecedented degree of fluctuation in external resource flows, as well as in other economic variables, should not be overlooked.

Thus, it is difficult to avoid the conclusion that external factors played a decisive role in the African crisis during the 1980s. In other words, external shocks, in the form of drastically-diminished financial transfers and very unfavourable developments in terms of trade sent African economies on a steep downward spiral, which inexperienced governments, subject to pressure from many sides, had difficulties dealing with.[32] In reality, very few countries would have been able to manage external shocks of the above dimensions.

GETTING THE ISSUES RIGHT

It follows from the above review, that economic policies pursued in SSA have not brought about the structural transformation and development set up as goals at independence. SSA economies remain dependent, fragile and very vulnerable to unforeseen events. Growth has been driven largely by external factors, and import starvation impairs capacity utilization in a critical manner. Exogenous shocks related to trade, aid and debt flows, coupled with domestic economic imbalances, have resulted in widespread human suffering and increased national as well as household vulnerability to further shocks.

Analysing the sources of crisis and their relative impact on internal and external balances will no doubt remain an issue, as it provides the necessary background to allocating 'blame', which may have important economic as well as political and moral implications.[33] While 'blame' in the case of the present crisis is in large measure due to external factors, this is not to say that internal factors did not contribute and that domestic adjustment is not required – on the contrary. This volume examines the frameworks within which such adjustment can be analysed, putting at the same time the issues identified below into a clearer perspective.

Macroeconomic policies and management have been deficient and are part of the problem of SSA. Adjustment will therefore have to take place one way or the other. This matter, which will be further pursued in Chapter 2, implies that it is clearly desirable from an overall point of view, if African policy-makers play an active rather than a passive role. The sooner active adjustment is initiated the better because all indications are that the present crisis is not a temporary one.

Public sectors over-expanded in many African countries and incentives were no doubt twisted in undesirable and unproductive ways in the first twenty-five years of the post-independence period. Overvalued exchange rates implied a critical bias against tradables. Interest rates and producer prices were in many cases kept unrealistically low. The real issue is not whether prices should be 'right', but what the right prices are, and how a reorientation can and should take place.

It is also clear that public sectors became less capable of acting in a decisive manner in view of resource constraints and the dimensions of external problems. Yet, there are various ways of achieving balance, and it is also a matter of good policy to foresee unfavourable events and take the necessary steps.[34] The distinction between external and internal factors is 'blurred', and the issues of 'adjustment when and to what' is, as Streeten (1987a) notes, linked to questions like adjustment for what purpose, adjustment of what, by whom and how.

It could be argued that the fundamental objective is to ensure adjustment takes place in a planned and orderly manner so that disorderly adjustment, which is harmful to national development goals and priorities, is avoided. Nevertheless, strategic priorities in such matters as trade policy may differ among the various national and international entities pursuing adjustment. Streeten (1987a:1470) is certainly right when he stresses that whatever the technical intricacies of the adjustment process, it is useful to bear its overall purposes and more specific intermediate objectives in mind.

Greater efficiency in resource use, as well as improved incentive systems and the establishment of sustainable macroeconomic balances, are important objectives. Long-run development and growth is also important and the ultimate goal is, as previously noted, that of diminishing poverty. Trade-offs and tensions are common, however. Thus, there is a need for as high a degree of consistency as possible in the design of adjustment programmes and the set of policies included.

In designing adjustment programmes, the nature of the African economies clearly matters and will remain an issue. The picture which emerges is one of countries with a low capacity to adjust to shocks in a flexible, automatic and orderly manner. More specifically, African economies face structural constraints of significant dimensions, and the degree of flexibility is limited. The substitutability of traded for non-traded goods is generally quite low, and import demand is inelastic due to the structure of commercial production as well as the import licensing system of many SSA countries.[35]

Furthermore, the responsiveness of producers to prices is constrained by a range of non-price factors, implying low supply elasticities.[36] Debate on the Marshall-Lerner conditions will continue, in particular since adjustment will take time.[37] Similarly, interest rates may have only a limited impact on savings and investment as well as the demand for money.[38] In addition, even if savings could be increased, this would not solve the problems due to foreign exchange constraints for which local savings cannot in all cases substitute.

There is no general agreement that all of the above characteristics and constraints are valid and important. Some would argue, for example, that the degree of flexibility is indeed larger than normally assumed and that markets clear faster than often thought.[39] Such differences in views, combined with diverging overall development objectives, imply that different policy packages are recommended. Some emphasize market-based approaches as they find policy-induced inflexibilities are of particular significance; others would attribute a more prominent role to government.

Nevertheless, increased flexibility is desirable, and structural constraints are in the final analysis subject to change. The issue is, how to bring this about. Furthermore, it is not subject to doubt that African countries have to import, invest, diversify and export more, to make room as well for increased utilization of already existing capacity. The question is what is to be done to bring this about.[40] The fallacy of composition issue normally discussed under issues of trade strategy is looming in the background here.

It is not an issue that adjustment may hurt and that austerity may be required. African countries will have to increase savings if growth is to become sustainable. Nevertheless, most Africans are practising austerity already, and indiscriminate cuts may have counterproductive effects. The distributional issue is not just a moral one of who is hurt, but distributional issues are treated in very different ways in the analytical frameworks to be reviewed.

Increasing the availability of foreign exchange appears, as already noted, necessary if adjustment is to become successful, implying *inter alia*, that installed capacity is utilized better. Considering the present external environment, which is not particularly favourable to African exports, there is a case for continued policy dialogue with outside donors. Whatever the causes of the present crisis, it would seem that

African countries have little alternative but to seek assistance from wherever it may come.

Yet, it should not be forgotten that donor assistance implies rigidities and opportunity costs of their own. Such financing is often tied to investment projects, which may not be appropriate, considering the pressing constraints African countries face. Rehabilitation has recently become a catchword in a number of African countries and international organizations. The genuine issue is rehabilitation of what? New investment to remove key bottle-necks may in many cases be more appropriate than rehabilitating loss-generating entities and projects.

Considering the rather gloomy economic situation reviewed on pages 7–25, one is reminded by Corden (in Scott and Lal 1990:19) of Ian Little's reference to 'import starved' countries which may 'always be hovering on the point of crisis'. It is against this worrisome perspective that this book will examine (i) whether the basic characteristics of the economies of sub-Saharan Africa are adequately considered within the various formal, analytical models proposed and in use in practical policy-making, and (ii) how the issues identified in this section are approached and analysed.

2

MACROECONOMIC CONSISTENCY AND ADJUSTMENT POLICIES

Planned and orderly adjustment is desirable when imbalances, such as those reviewed in Chapter 1 and reflected in *inter alia* slowing growth, a growing external deficit and inflationary pressures appear. There are, however, various ways of interpreting the underlying but inter-linked reasons for faltering economic performance, and they lead to markedly different policy conclusions. Furthermore, adjustment policies depend not only on the particular combination of problems at hand, but also on which problems are assigned priority (that is, on the objectives pursued) and on the perceived nature of the economy (that is, on how policies are thought to work). Finally, in the short run, some parameters may be taken as given, which are in the longer run subject to manipulation through policy.

Consistency is a first and basic requirement in all macroeconomic analysis. Thus, it is useful to elaborate on what macroeconomists mean by balances. Consequently, Chapter 2 is devoted to setting out more precisely a macroeconomic accounting framework and provides a general overview of macroeconomic adjustment issues, including an identification of the kinds of policies which may be needed for stabilization and structural adjustment. It is stressed from the outset that the balances to be reviewed are not all independent. Nevertheless, they highlight in an illustrative manner that economists approach stabilization and adjustment problems from very different perspectives. It is obvious that complete macro models are desirable in actual policy analysis, but they are often not the most constructive peda-gogical tools in coming to grips with the essence of the issues at stake.

The starting point is the economy-wide identities known from national accounts, and which are organized around the three concepts of production, income and expenditure.[1] These three notions are interlinked, since budget constraints must be adhered to by all sectors (or agents in the economy). This implies that for any sector, income from production plus net transfers is equal to expenditures plus savings, and that savings plus borrowing is equal to physical and financial asset acquisition. For the economy as a whole, the value of production must equal the value of incomes generated.

SECTOR AND BUDGET CONSTRAINTS

It is assumed that there are four sectors in the economy, that is, the private non-financial sector, government,[2] the domestic monetary system (for simplicity assumed to consist of the central bank only)[3] and the foreign sector. These would be, as Easterly (1989:3) points out, the minimum elements of a sector-based macroeconomic consistency framework.[4] The individual sectoral accounts and budget constraints are presented below in current domestic prices.[5]

The *private sector* receives a gross income (Y_p) in the form of wages (W) and profits (π) (that is, a share of total value added), net transfers and interest income from the government (NTR_{gp}) and net transfers from the external foreign sector (NTR_{fp}). This private gross income is used to pay for consumption of domestic and imported goods (C_p), direct taxes (T_d) and interest on private foreign debt (INP_{pf}) as well as to cover savings (S_p). That is:

$$Y_p = C_p + T_d + INP_{pf} + S_p$$

Private savings (S_p) plus borrowing equal net private asset accumulation. Private assets are held in the form of physical capital, accumulating through private investments (I_p), money (M), net private lending to government (NPB_g), and net foreign assets (NFA_p). Private borrowing occurs through increased domestic credit to the private sector from the banking system (ΔDC_p) or as loans from the public and external sectors (included here via changes in NPB_g and NFA_p).[6] That is:

$$S_p + \Delta DC_p = I_p + \Delta M + \Delta NPB_g + \Delta NFA_p$$

It follows from the above two equations that the private sector budget constraint can be expressed in the following way:

$$S_p - I_p = Y_p - C_p - T_d - INP_{pf} - I_p$$

$$= \Delta M + \Delta NPB_g + \Delta NFA_p - \Delta DC_p \qquad (2.1)$$

Government gross revenue (Y_g) is received in the form of indirect taxes less subsidies ($T_t - Sb$) plus the operating surpluses of government-owned enterprises (OS_g) as direct taxes (T_d) and as net transfers from the foreign sector (NTR_{fg}). Revenue is used to pay for government consumption (C_g), and to cover net transfers to the private sector (NTR_{gp}), interest payments to the foreign sector (INP_{gf}) and government savings (S_g). That is:

$$Y_g = C_g + NTR_{gp} + INP_{gf} + S_g$$

Government savings (S_g) plus borrowing equal net public asset accumulation. Public assets are held in the form of physical capital, accumulating through public investments (I_g) and net foreign assets (NFA_g) Government borrowing occurs through increased domestic credit to the public sector from the monetary system (ΔDC_g) or in the form of loans from the private sector (ΔNPB_g). Loans from the external sector are included via changes in NFA_g. That is:

$$S_g + \Delta DC_g + \Delta NPB_g = I_g + \Delta NFA_g$$

It follows from the above two equations that the government budget constraint can be expressed in the following way:

$$S_g - I_g = Y_g - C_g - I_g - NTR_{gp} - INP_{gf}$$

$$= \Delta NFA_g - \Delta NPB_g - \Delta DC_g \qquad (2.2)$$

The domestic *monetary system* has neither current income nor savings. It performs an intermediary role. Assets include credit to the private and government sectors (DC_p and DC_g) and international reserves (R). Liabilities include money (M). The balance constraint is:

$$\Delta DC_p + \Delta DC_g + \Delta R = \Delta M \qquad (2.3)$$

The *foreign sector* receives revenue in the form of payments for imports (Z), which is exported to the domestic economy, and as interest payments from the domestic private and public sectors (INP_{pf} and INP_{gf}). These receipts are used on exports (X) from the

31

domestic economy and net transfers to the domestic government and private sectors (NTR_{fg} and NTR_{fp}) as well as for foreign savings (S_f). That is:

$$Z + INP_{gf} + INP_{pf} = X + NTR_{fg} + NTR_{fp} + S_f$$

Foreign savings are equal to the net accumulation of assets against the domestic economy.[7] Assets held by the foreign sector are equivalent to the sum of foreign liabilities of the domestic economy. That is:

$$S_f = -\left(\Delta NFA_p + \Delta NFA_g + \Delta R\right)$$

An increase in these liabilities (corresponding to a positive balance on the capital account of the balance of payments of the domestic economy) will finance a deficit (CA) on the current account balance.

It follows from the above two equations (and the way the current account is defined) that the foreign sector budget constraint can be expressed in the following way:

$$CA = X - Z - INP_{pf} - INP_{gf} + NTR_{fp} + NTR_{fg}$$

$$= \Delta NFA_p + \Delta NFA_g + \Delta R \qquad (2.4)$$

Adding up equations 2.1–2.4 (and taking into account how Y_p and Y_g were defined) gives:

$$W + \pi + OS_g + T_i - Sb = C_p + I_p + C_g + I_g - Z + X$$

This can be rewritten as the well-known national income identity:

$$Y = C + I + X - Z \qquad (2.5)$$

where Y is the national income at market prices, $C = C_p + C_g$ and $I = I_p + I_g$.

The above balance equations must always hold. Thus, they have important implications which, if interpreted with due care, illuminate many of the adjustment issues faced by sub-Saharan African economies. These implications are set out in the following sections through manipulation of the original identities. Shortcomings of the framework are highlighted in the concluding section.

NATIONAL BALANCE, ABSORPTION AND ECONOMIC POLICY

Equation 2.5, the overall national income account showing how the domestic product is expended, can also be presented (or interpreted) in the following way:

$$C + I = Y + Z - X \qquad (2.6)$$

This demonstrates that the amount of goods and services absorbed in the economy ($C + I$, which can be denoted A) come from either domestic production (Y) or from the external sector. Accordingly, policies to affect the size and composition of A must aim at affecting Y, $X - Z$ or $C + I$ directly or indirectly. To highlight the relationship between domestic production, the external resource balance $X - Z$ and absorption, the following equation is illustrative:

$$X - Z = Y - A \qquad (2.7)$$

It can be seen that, if the resource (or trade) balance ($X - Z$) *vis-à-vis* the foreign sector is negative, more is absorbed than domestically produced, that is, more is imported (consumed and/or invested) than exported.

In the case of SSA, it was usual practice in the early post-independence period after 1960 to assume that absorption ought to be as high as possible relative to Y in order to promote growth and development.[8] This assumption has been challenged during the 1980s. Critics point out that while high absorption may be required to transform backward economies, this is at most a necessary, but not a sufficient condition. Reference to inadequate and excessive consumption patterns and investments with lower than expected returns abound. These internal sources of the crisis, which reflect either government or private sector imbalance, or some combination hereof, will be discussed on pages 43–50.

Equation 2.7 also demonstrates that external shocks can be an important source of crisis and imbalance. If import capacity suddenly drops, due to, for example, a drastic change in terms of trade, the shock must *ceteris paribus* be absorbed by the domestic balance ($Y - A$). That is, A must fall or Y increase, unless the foreign sector comes to the rescue with additional loans and net transfers. Whether the original source of imbalance is internal or external makes no difference to the need for adjustment *per se*.

Nevertheless, the original source of imbalance (that is, the nature of the economic shock) may be of significant importance to the design of the actual adjustment package. Similarly, the policy response required will depend on whether the duration of the crisis is expected to be temporary or of a longer-term nature. In the sub-Saharan Africa context there is, as pointed out in Chapter 1, reason to expect that the latter is the case.

Maintaining balance-of-payments deficits indefinitely or for very long periods of time is impossible. The economy has in some way to adjust to the deficit. This adjustment process could in theory be left to take place automatically through changes in relative prices, and adjustment in the money supply via linkages with the trade balance. This adjustment process is not very attractive in sub-Saharan Africa. The automatic process may work, but only very slowly, and a protracted recession may be required to achieve the necessary cut in prices. Furthermore, the distributional consequences of such a process can be unacceptable. The alternative is to carry out deliberate policy changes that move the economy towards the balance desired.

Two main categories of adjustment policies, which focus, respectively, on the demand- and the supply-side of the economy, can be pursued if absorption is deemed too high relative to Y.

Demand-side policies (that is, expenditure-changing fiscal and monetary policies) are mainly assigned with the intention of solving the imbalance between demand and supply by reducing aggregate private and public demand (that is, $C + I$), including demand for tradables as well as non-tradables.[9] Hence, this type of policy is commonly represented by a leftward shift in the demand schedule in an aggregate demand–supply diagram with output Y along the x-axis and the price level P along the y-axis.[10]

If the economy is characterized by 'overheating' (that is, excess demand) internally, and deficits externally (that is, an unsustainable balance-of-payments deficit), monetary and fiscal policies may in some cases be effective on their own.[11] Demand management has the added advantage of being a policy measure with relatively immediate effects. However, in sub-Saharan Africa, external imbalance is combined with internal recession and inflation. Even if demand-cutting policies succeed in eliminating excess demand, inflation will not necessarily go away.[12] Furthermore, to the extent that absorption is reduced, costs are attached.

These costs can be of an immediate or longer-term nature depending on whether cuts affect present consumption (C) or investment (I).

The longer-term effect of demand-restraint on growth will depend on the profitability of the investments being cancelled. Cutting unprofitable projects imply in fact a net gain, but cutting export-oriented projects or activities that make these profitable may in the circumstances of SSA be harmful. Whether C or I should be cut involve difficult intertemporal choices, and it is obvious that it may, for political reasons, often be easier to cut investment.

In sum, expenditure-reducing policies will not on their own produce desired results in sub-Saharan Africa. They must be combined with *supply-side measures*, which increase the supply of goods and services the economy produces at any given level of aggregate demand. In other words, the elimination of excess demand should also be pursued by policies that shift the aggregate supply curve, for any given price level, to the right.[13] It follows that the use of supply-side (or structural) policies place more emphasis on growth. The concrete measures can be classified according to whether they aim at improving efficiency in the use of existing resources and capacity, or alternatively at expanding the economy's productive capacity.

Orthodox approaches to adjustment in sub-Saharan Africa and elsewhere emphasize the existence of a wide range of *market distortions* that drive a wedge between prices and marginal costs.[14] Such distortions may arise because of imperfect competition, but can also be government-induced. Price controls, taxes, subsidies and trade restrictions have, it is argued, led to an inefficient allocation of resources. The removal of such distortions (that is, 'getting prices right') is recommended as a way of shifting the aggregate supply curve outwards and increase output, without reducing consumption, through reductions in the incremental capital-output ratio. Thus, efficiency-focused policies are not intended as 'belt-tightening' as was the case with demand-side measures. Finally, policies pursued to improve efficiency also aim at improving the balance of payments through 'switching', which increases Y relatively more than absorption. Positive spin-offs in terms of bringing inflation under control are expected as well.

From a structuralist perspective the removal of market distortions may or may not contribute to improved efficiency and long-term growth, and it is indeed argued below that more efficient prices could play a role in sub-Saharan Africa. However, the fundamental bottlenecks to increased supply remain imbedded in economic, social, political and institutional characteristics. Shifting the aggregate supply curve outwards with a given productive capacity requires in the

35

structuralist perspective more basic changes in the economy than simply the removal of distortions.

'Artificial' barriers to foreign trade in the form of tariffs, quotas and other restrictions as well as price controls are in the orthodox approach examples of policies which have in sub-Saharan Africa led to very significant efficiency losses. Measures aiming at trade liberalization internally, as well as externally, have, in conjunction with changes in the exchange rate, without exception been both a precondition and performance criteria for continued support from the IMF and World Bank during the 1980s in sub-Saharan Africa. A review of the extensive literature on trade, development and price liberalization is beyond the scope of this book.[15] Nevertheless, a few major points are pertinent.

Balassa (1989) argues forcefully that trade liberalization (including in particular the removal of quantitative restrictions and selective import tariffs) are required to improve efficiency. It is, however, necessary to consider that the economies of sub-Saharan Africa face very severe foreign exchange constraints, and that governments have few alternative sources of income. Removing import restrictions will, at least in the short run, add an extra drain on foreign exchange. This can make it impossible to manage the balance of payments. A compensating devaluation (of an assumed overvalued exchange rate) is generally proposed to counteract this effect and safeguard the balance of payments.

However, a nominal devaluation may or may not be successful (as discussed below). Furthermore, governments, who manage to depreciate the real exchange rate, lose revenue obtained through the implicit export tax, which overvalued exchange rates amount to. Liberalization also carries an inherent risk of opening up for consumer-type imports, which have no or little impact on output and growth. The process of de-industrialization, initiated in the 1980s and referred to in Chapter 1, may, in other words, be reinforced.

Hence, there is ample reason to argue that the liberalization approach is likely to be more productive, if emphasis is on streamlining and increasing the efficiency of management systems rather than on outright decontrol.[16] Attempts to rationalize import protection systems by eliminating quantitative import restrictions could also be combined with increased, but uniform, tariff levels. Furthermore, while not always efficient, there may be a need to avoid the collapse of import-substituting industries, some of which have strategic importance or genuine prospects for becoming internationally competitive.

Prospects for increasing exports are rather bleak for sub-Saharan Africa. While the reason for adjusting previous import substituting policies is often that they were not efficient, export promotion must also be efficient. This may not be the case if a large number of countries pursue similar policies at the same time (that is, the so-called 'fallacy of composition' argument). Export promotion policies must therefore be designed with great care, and linking them with import liberalization may not always be justified. Yet, notwithstanding unfavourable global trends and the harmful effects of international market conditions, and notwithstanding the 'fallacy of composition argument', the need for increased export earnings as such is not in question. Careful use of existing comparative advantages as well as the identification and development of new areas of competence should be indispensable measures of an adjustment package.

Internal price de-control is a common component of most orthodox stabilization and structural adjustment packages, promoted with the aim of increasing efficiency in the allocation of resources. There is, as Green (in Commander 1989:39) points out, no particular reason for getting producer prices 'wrong'. And 'getting prices right' is potentially important, since producer prices have clearly been too low in many African countries. However, outright price liberalization will no doubt create undesirable transition problems due to the imperfect nature of output markets and the widespread disruption of production and trade channels. Furthermore, it is no simple matter to say 'what the right prices are' in sub-Saharan Africa. Low elasticities of supply abound, as pointed out by Cleaver (1985), and 'better prices' are not by themselves enough and may, without accompanying measures, make things even worse.[17]

Not only producer but also factor prices have been subjected to scrutiny in structural adjustment programmes on the grounds that distorted factor prices lead to inappropriate technology choices. Controlled wages in the 'modern' sector in general, and in the public sector in particular, are in the standard analysis said to be kept much too high, creating unnecessary unemployment. Cutting real wages will, it is argued, lead to the adoption of more labour-intensive production techniques and more employment. Wage indexation should also be removed as it fuels inflation. This may be correct in some cases, but it is by no means certain what the effect of wage cuts will be due to the composite nature of the economy.

Labour market segmentation implies that higher 'modern sector' wages might even boost total employment in the economy at large.

While wages set 'too high' in the modern sector may reduce employment here, the 'informal' sector, characterized by wages set by demand and supply, could get a competitive edge as they face lower labour costs, and shifting market shares towards the labour intensive 'informal sector' could increase total employment. Cutting wages may also have implications for both efficiency of the labour input as well as the demand for labour-intensive consumer goods.[18] Various other considerations such as, for example, the assumptions regarding the nature of the production function underlying the orthodox policy recommendations, have also been subjected to criticism.[19]

In other words, many of the distortions in sub-Saharan Africa are inherent in the rather inflexible nature of the economy, the segmentation of markets and the fact that factors of production do not move freely. In such an environment the removal of 'distortions' has complex effects, and long periods of time may be required for the adjustment process to work. The second-best issue looms in the background here. The removal of some distortions in an economy with many distortions may not result in an increase in overall efficiency, and it is simply out of the question in sub-Saharan Africa as elsewhere that all 'distortions' can be removed in one stroke. Finally, account must, of course, be taken of the fact that policies are at times pursued to achieve objectives other than economic efficiency.

Supply-side policies aiming at expanding the *productive capacity* of the economy focus on the balance between savings and investment as well as on the nature and quality of the capital stock added. This dimension will be further reviewed on pages 43–5. It is sufficient to note here that IMF/World Bank-supported stabilization and structural adjustment programmes in sub-Saharan Africa have so far concentrated on improving the fiscal position of the public sector, on rationalizing investment priorities and on promoting private sector savings. Interest policies have been assigned a key role in this context.

Reference was made above to the key importance attached to *exchange rate policies* in orthodox approaches. It is indeed relevant to note that balance-of-payments crises have been a major motivating factor in the macroeconomic adjustment efforts in sub-Saharan Africa during the 1980s. The analysis of this policy instrument is complicated as it affects at the same time aggregate domestic demand as well as supply. There are, in other words, aspects of supply-side, structural policy as well as demand-side, absorptive effects, inherent in the use of this instrument.

Debate on the exchange rate as policy instrument hinges, in the formulation of Ahamed (1986:95), on three questions: (i) what does a nominal devaluation mean for the trade balance, (ii) how will a devaluation affect domestic economic activity, and (iii) can a nominal devaluation bring about a real devaluation? It may, in considering these questions, be useful to recall that there are a number of different processes through which exchange rate action can help restore a sustainable balance of payments position. In accordance with Johnson (in Frenkel and Johnson 1976), these processes correspond with, respectively, the elasticities, the absorption and the monetary approach to the balance of payments.

The *elasticities approach* focuses on the effects on imports and exports of a devaluation. A devaluation will increase the domestic currency value of imports and decrease the foreign price of exports. If import demand is price responsive, imports fall, and if foreign demand for domestic exports is elastic, export earnings increase, so the balance of trade improves. However, if foreign demand is inelastic, exports earnings may fall. The overall result is a consequence of the combined effect on the change in import and export demand. It can be shown that if the sum of the elasticities of demand for imports and exports is greater than one, a devaluation will improve the current account.

For this so-called Marshall-Lerner condition to hold formally, initial balance in the trade account is also assumed, and the elasticities of supply of exports and imports must be infinite.[20] That these conditions hold in the case of sub-Saharan Africa cannot be taken for granted. With regard to imports, demand elasticities tend to be low due to the heavy dependence on imported inputs, which must be paid for in scarce foreign currency. In addition, even if export demand is assumed to be rather elastic, many SSA countries produce goods for which the supply elasticity is not infinite due to the underlying structural characteristics of the economies. Thus, a devaluation may, particularly in the short run, cause results which are unexpected from an orthodox perspective.

A weakness of the elasticities approach is that it focuses exclusively on the trade balance and ignores other likely effects on the domestic economy of the exchange rate devaluation. This can be illustrated by noting from equation 2.7 that an improvement in the trade balance implies a decrease in absorption A and/or an increase in output Y. This leads to considering the *absorption approach*. In this context it is customary to distinguish between the effects of a nominal devaluation on, respectively, the demand for, and domestic supply of, traded as well as non-traded goods.

The concept of 'switching' occupies the centre-stage since a devaluation is intended to shift the pattern of domestic demand from tradables towards non-tradables and the output pattern from non-tradables towards tradables.[21] The increase in international competitiveness is to take place through the increase in prices of traded goods relative to the prices of non-traded goods. However, switching along this line of thinking is dependent on a series of critical price and wage relationships, which are, in the final analysis, the outcome of complex economic and political forces and institutional constraints.

The orthodox presumption that a devaluation typically improves international competitiveness and is expansionary has therefore come under serious challenge from various corners, including in particular a number of structuralist economists. They argue that short-, medium- and long-term effects must be distinguished, and that devaluation may lead to increases in unemployment and stagflation in the short run.[22] As an illustration it can be noted that, if exports (denoted in foreign currency) do not respond to better prices due to low supply elasticities, and if imports (denoted in foreign currency) also remain unaltered because of heavy import dependence, then the trade deficit denoted in local currency widens.

This will immediately exert a depressive effect on the economy since an increase in the trade deficit $X - Z$ will lower output Y as is evident from equation 2.5. Similarly, even if producers are willing and capable of increasing production of traded output, it cannot be taken for granted that price increases following a devaluation are in fact passed on to them. Account must in any case be taken of the possibility that imported inflation following the devaluation may spark off a contractionary shift in supply.

Furthermore, if a devaluation raises prices, but nominal wages lag behind, the result is a distributional shift from wage- to profit-earners. This may easily cause a fall in demand for non-traded goods and an increase in import demand due to differences in the propensities to consume. Also the real balance effect following the unavoidable initial price increase may lower demand, as expenditure is reduced to raise money balances back to desired levels. Finally, a devaluation can contribute to fiscal problems as public debt service will increase.

In summary, the short-term impact of a devaluation on output hinges on whether the negative effects on aggregate demand are outweighed by the positive impact on supply. This in turn depends on whether output is close to full capacity output or not, and on possible short-term supply constraints. In this, relative price elasticities of imports and exports and the shares of tradable and non-tradable goods in total production obviously matter. Contraction is more likely when the economy is highly dependent on imported inputs for which no domestic substitutes exist.[23]

To be effective the nominal devaluation will have to bring about a real devaluation, but this may or may not happen. If output is below full capacity and markets clear through the price mechanism (that is, prices are flexible), there are reasons to be hopeful that the standard interpretation applies.[24] However, inflation may modify the end result. A devaluation will at least in the short run tend to be inflationary, through the increase in import costs, and this impact may be substantial in the very open import dependent economies such as those of sub-Saharan Africa. If in addition mark-up pricing is characteristic and nominal wages are pushed up as the cost of living increase (through indexation or income bargaining processes), an inflationary process is initiated and the real exchange rate will appreciate again.

It is clear that the above inflationary result depends on an accommodating change in the money supply. This has led analysts with a *monetary approach* to inflation and balance-of-payments deficits to focus attention on the money supply as the fundamental cause and key policy instrument. This is in contrast with structuralist analysis which perceives the increased money supply as a symptom rather than a fundamental cause of inflation and balance-of-payments deficits. The monetary approach will be further reviewed and assessed on pages 50–4 and throughout Chapter 3.

A final comment on trade policies, which affect M and Z through quantitative restrictions and tariffs or subsidies, may be useful. The imposition of an import tariff/export subsidy scheme is conceptually equivalent to a devaluation.[25] Thus, the serious external imbalances in sub-Saharan Africa, involving the necessary expenditure-switching, could in theory be corrected through trade policy without recourse to exchange rate adjustments. Yet, intensified use of trade policy measures is highly circumscribed in sub-Saharan Africa at present. Years of import substitution and inadequate price policies have created a situation where administrative controls have in many cases become widespread, complex and dislocating. Increasing tariffs is, in other words, simply out of the question, in view of the need for greater efficiency in the allocation of resources. Similarly, export subsidies are not very high on the agenda due to the budget constraints faced by governments.

Real exchange rates in sub-Saharan Africa became, during the 1970s and first part of the 1980s, seriously overvalued in the sense that the nominal exchange rate would have to devalue considerably just to maintain the existing trade position if import protection were removed. It is extremely difficult to manage a very open small economy in such a situation. Active exchange rate management has consequently come more in focus as a policy tool in much of sub-Saharan Africa, and the importance of pursuing an effective price policy, avoiding the development of parallel markets over which the governments have no effective control, has been recognized.

Furthermore, sub-Saharan Africa must adjust in a situation of macroeconomic disequilibrium, where severe constraints and inflexibilities of a structural nature are faced. The results of devaluation and price liberalization on the balance of payments, output and inflation depend on the ability of African governments to pursue at the same time a variety of complementary policies.[26] In other words, realism, not optimism, is called for.

Expenditure-switching type policies theoretically entail less loss of output than pure expenditure-reducing policies. They are also likely to take somewhat longer to achieve results, given the structural characteristics of the African economies. To be successful, they will have to be supplemented with a variety of structural supply-side measures, such as selective investments, possibly in the public sector. Demand expansion may be necessary to make the economy more flexible and in a position to respond to improved incentives to export and overcome barriers around foreign export markets.

Nevertheless, such measures have often been opposed by outside agencies such as the IMF on the grounds that priority attention must be given to reducing the money supply and absorption (in general and in the public sector in particular).[27] This, in combination with a degree of confidence that removing price distortions (including the exchange rate overvaluation) will lead to switching and an efficient allocation of resources, lie at the core of, respectively, monetarist and neo-classical lines of thought which have inspired the IMF approach to stabilization.

The IMF framework will be reviewed in Chapter 3, but before this, further background is provided on pages 43–54 on pertinent issues related to domestic financial policy, the role of government, the private sector and fiscal policy, as well as monetary policy and external capital movements.

SAVINGS AND INVESTMENT

To draw attention to the suggestion that domestic 'savings may be too low', the resource balance equation (2.7) can be shown as follows:

$$X - Z = (Y - C) - I = S - I \qquad (2.8)$$

Savings are crucial, as investment (which is either private or public) is financed by domestic savings (private or public) or comes out of a negative resource balance. This can be seen by noting that:

$$I_p + I_g = S_p + S_g - (X - Z) \qquad (2.9)$$

If domestic savings are negative then the external resource balance will, at aggregate level, finance the whole of domestic investment as well as the excess of consumption over output.[28]

Savings also have a direct relationship to the balance of payments. By use of equations 2.1, 2.2 and 2.3 it follows that:

$$(S_p - I_p) + (S_g - I_g) = \Delta NFA + \Delta R \qquad (2.10)$$

As the current account balance (see equation 2.4) is equal to the right-hand side of equation 2.10, this implies that an improvement in the current account can only take place if private savings rise relative to investment, or government savings improve.

Domestic savings are thus important to the balance of payments as well as to investment and growth through expansion of capacity. Yet if private investment is emphasized, measures to increase profitability may be required. Leaving this to market forces alone will not be sufficient in sub-Saharan Africa.[29] Furthermore, the productive capacity of the economy depends not only on the quantity but also on the nature and quality of investment, and growth hinges on installed capacity as well as its utilization.

Equation 2.10 also illustrates a point made earlier in a slightly different way. If the original source of imbalance is not 'too low savings', but an external shock, it must nevertheless be absorbed; either by increasing savings or lowering investment (assuming that external debt is not allowed to build up or foreign exchange transfers do not make up the shock). Consequently, movements in external factors should be kept close to the centre of analysis to keep matters in perspective.

Financial policies and liberalization in general, and interest rate increase (that is, a change to a positive real interest rate) in particular, have been regular components of adjustment programmes. The justification is both to mobilize more private savings and to rationalize the use of domestic credit (by 'getting the price of credit right'). There are, it is argued, considerable financial repression costs attached to keeping real interest rates low, as in sub-Saharan Africa. These include that incentives are twisted against holding financial as opposed to real assets and an inducement to capital flight. Moreover, negative real interest rates create an excess demand for funds which lead to inefficient credit allocation. Finally, negative real interest rates promote investment in inappropriate capital-intensive technology and the development of financial intermediation is discouraged.

As regards the volume of savings, it is relevant to recall the empirical evidence, which indicates that the effect of variations in interest rates on savings can be quite small.[30] In addition, the very high real interest rates which may be required to have an impact on savings, can have adverse effects of their own. They are contractionary as investment is discouraged, and interest rate increases also contribute to inflation and a worsening of the public debt service burden.

It is also far from clear that high interest rates will always improve the allocation of credit, since portfolio shifts can confuse the interest rate/savings linkage. Wealth-holders may shift from relatively efficient informal credit markets to inefficient official banks when the latter raise deposit rates, to the detriment of lending for working and long-term capital. In addition, credit rationing does not occur because of government-induced distortions alone, but as an inherent characteristic of credit market organization in developing countries. Rationing of credit will therefore continue to exist, and there is no guarantee that those with the more profitable investments will enjoy priority access to credit just because official deposit rates are increased.

Financial reform may, for some of the reasons listed above, be important in contributing to the deepening of financial markets as an indispensable component of the development process. However, outright liberalization is not the most adequate approach. There is a considerable role for government to play. The financial system is in many cases very unstable due to the imbalances created by external shocks, and intricate linkages exist with public sector policies and the balance of payments through international capital movements.

It is widely agreed that liberalization of the capital account 'up front' before other adjustment policies are put in place may cause undue harm if the country is experiencing internal and external macroeconomic imbalances such as unsustainable fiscal and balance-of-payments deficits. Liberalization of capital movements will, due to the lack of confidence in the exchange rate, lead to capital flight. Finally, if expectations cannot be changed easily, a very large increase in interest rates may be required to reverse the capital flow.

Hence, the timing and sequencing of adjustment attempts are critical, and it should in this context be remembered that private savings and capital movements often fluctuate for reasons which have little to do with developments in financial markets. An extreme example of this is the political unrest in several parts of Africa. The initiation of adjustment programmes could lead to some aid-financed foreign exchange transfers, but private flows and investment will not be resumed unless profitable investment opportunities exist and there is confidence that additional policy measures will be taken as required.

GOVERNMENT AND FISCAL POLICY

Rapid increases in government fiscal deficits have, as mentioned in Chapter 1, been an important source of macroeconomic imbalances in sub-Saharan Africa. It is even argued by some analysts that the key to successful stabilization is a lower fiscal deficit.[31] It was furthermore pointed out in the last section, that even if fiscal deficits are not the original source of imbalance, an improvement in the current external balance can only take place if private savings rise relative to private investment or public savings increase relative to public investment. In this section an attempt is made to outline the links between government and other sectors of the economy.

The overall government budget constraint (equation 2.2) shows that a fiscal deficit can be financed in three ways: (i) by running down foreign assets (that is, increasing foreign public borrowing through ΔNFA_g or decreasing international reserves through ΔR), (ii) an increase in net public borrowing from the private sector (ΔNPB_g) or (iii) through increased domestic credit from the monetary system (ΔDC_g). It follows that if public sector borrowings from the external sector and the monetary system are restricted, then such ceilings may affect the overall fiscal deficit. However, financing from these different sources to close the public sector financing requirement will have dissimilar impacts on inflation, balance of payments and output.

Another way of putting the above observations (corresponding to the presentation on pages 50–4) is to note that the fiscal budget deficit

$(S_g - I_g)$ can be written in the following way by use of equations 2.1 and 2.2:

$$S_g - I_g = (I_p - S_p) + \Delta NFA + (\Delta M - \Delta DC) \qquad (2.11)$$

It is clear that the fiscal deficit is financed by private savings greater than private investment, a decrease in net foreign assets (that is, increasing foreign indebtedness) or an increase in domestic credit which exceeds the flow demand for money.

In case additional foreign borrowing can be obtained through official debt renegotiations, new loans or aid, this adds new real resources to the economy through a decrease in NFA.[32] In such cases a planned fiscal deficit can be closed and will add no excess demand inflation as domestic absorption does not exceed available resources.[33] However, unless domestic production (Y) increases quickly and exports (X) increase relatively more than imports (Z), the current account will deteriorate as total absorption increases (see page 33, equation 2.7).

Similarly, if borrowing from the private sector is available to finance the fiscal deficit, little excess demand inflation will occur, assuming that total absorption remains unaltered;[34] but the composition of domestic consumption and investment between the private sector and government will be affected. Interest rates will increase and may crowd out private investment (I_p) or force the private sector to borrow from the external sector by decreasing NFA. The effect on the current account of public borrowing from the private sector to close the fiscal deficit will depend on the relative effect of public *vis-à-vis* private absorption on domestic production, exports and imports.

It follows that if no further loans from the foreign and private sectors are available, a ceiling on domestic credit to the public sector will fix the overall fiscal deficit from the financing side. Government will in such cases have no option but to adjust by increasing revenue or decreasing expenditures. Such efforts have therefore been made in sub-Saharan Africa and were referred to in Chapter 1.

Nevertheless, it may not be feasible or even desirable to close the whole of the remaining fiscal deficit through fiscal policy alone. The magnitude of external shocks has been very considerable, and the high interest rates have become a substantial burden on fiscal outlays. The management capacity of governments is weak and it has become abundantly clear that some expenditure components are difficult to handle and tax collection systems have shown little flexibility. Attention must also be paid to the crowding-in effects of public on private sector investment. Some monetization of the deficit (that is, an expansion of domestic credit to the government by the monetary system through an expansion of money supply) is therefore justified.

If output is close to capacity limits, closing the public sector financing requirement through monetization implies that a part of the fiscal deficit is transferred to the private sector through the inflation tax mechanism. When the monetary system provides domestic credit to government, in excess of the flow demand for money, the private sector will dispose of excess money, total demand will exceed real resources available and inflation ensue. This diminishes the value of money balances of the private sector whose savings are 'forced' to increase.[35]

Not all money-financed deficits need to be inflationary. Some increase in money demand might occur for other reasons, such as real growth or because of an expansion of the monetized sector of the economy. That is, if output is far from capacity limits, money-financed deficits may, if used with due care and kept within safe limits, be a way of stimulating economic development.[36] In this manner the original expansion of the money supply is absorbed without causing inflation. Deficit financing is even more effective and less dangerous if combined with other supply-side policies.

The effect on the current account may not be significant in the short run as private savings (S_p) make up for the decrease in public savings (see page 43, equation 2.10), but in the longer run inflation causes the real exchange rate to appreciate. Furthermore, the inflation tax can only close the fiscal deficit in the short run. The approach cannot be sustained if the rate of increase of revenue collection lags behind inflation. This is likely to be the case in sub-Saharan Africa. The need for fiscal reforms becomes in this way unavoidable.

The above observations show that there are different ways in which the government can close (or lower) a fiscal deficit, which have dissimilar effects on money supply and other macroeconomic variables. Borrowing from the monetary system (that is, the central bank) or from abroad implies an immediate expansion in money supply and as such is more likely to be inflationary. This is not the case for borrowing from the private sector, but in this case the overall expansionary impact on output of the fiscal deficit may be lower.

The effects on output of government spending and revenue have been the subject of considerable controversy.[37] It is not the direct effects of changes in public expenditures and revenue,[38] but the indirect effects via possible crowding out of the private sector which have generated disagreement. This touches, of course, on the very sensitive matter of the relative roles of the private and public sector in development, which has generated some of the most difficult tensions among sub-Saharan African countries and international organizations such as the IMF and the World Bank. Crowding out concerns the effectiveness of fiscal policy in stimulating aggregate demand, and there are indeed several ways public spending increases can affect private sector spending.

Total private spending may first of all be affected by government expenditures to the extent that they are financed by reducing present or future private disposable income (that is, S_p in equation 2.11 is increased).[39] Furthermore, domestic borrowing from the private sector may lead to rising interest rates affecting interest-sensitive components of demand, including in particular private investments (that is, I_p in equation 2.11).[40] Even if no interest increases occur, the financing of additional public spending might still affect the availability of financing for individuals in the private sector who may reduce spending to accumulate cash.[41] Similarly, increases in the price level following increased government spending reduces the real value of money balances. This can lead to lower spending to re-establish money holdings at desired levels. Finally, some public expenditure may be a substitute for private expenditure, which will allow the private sector to save more.

Government spending (consumption and investment) can also crowd in private investment in situations where debt-ridden countries confront a serious constraint on fiscal outlays.[42] Public sector activities can increase the profitability of private investments, or increase demand for output from the private sector, and it is far from settled that private investment would in fact come forward easily in the absence of public action in SSA. It may be lack of profitable investment opportunities or 'market failure' rather than government induced distortions, that is the fundamental constraint on private investment and savings. The fact that considerable additional savings have been 'forced' out of the private sector through the inflation tax mechanism provides at least a sign of caution.

The crowding-in argument can be illustrated by reference to equation 2.11. If a high I_g (or even a high C_g), implying a low S_g, increases the profitability of private investment, then it may call forward a higher S_p which can make I_p higher than it would otherwise be. That is, cutting down I_g may have undesirable effects on medium-term growth as well as on short-run balances through the effect on S_g.

It should be stressed though, that the present dilemma in sub-Saharan Africa is not just one of 'choosing' between private and public services and investments and considering the relationship with private savings and investment. A very considerable part of the public sector's financing needs exist as a backlog because of previous overspending, in many cases promoted by foreign agencies. This 'overhang' limits the real resources presently available for public services and investment and makes it difficult to activate the 'crowding in effects'.

There are, therefore, very significant potential advantages of increased foreign resource inflows and a reduction in interest payments to the external sector in the sub-Saharan context. In other words, the importance of the external sector and the need for integrating external shocks into the analysis cannot be underestimated. There is, as a corollary, no doubt that better debt management, including rescheduling and regularization of arrears and co-ordinated external financing, should be emphasized in adjustment programmes. The same accounts for debt forgiveness despite the moral hazard involved.

While it is fairly easy to outline the various modes of financing a government deficit, the above review demonstrates that the public sector deficit can only with great care be used as an indicator of the fiscal impact on aggregate demand. Composition and not just size matters. It follows that the common procedure of redressing a fiscal imbalance through across-the-board cuts in budget allocations is unwise. Deficits do not have comparable short- and long-term impacts, neither on production efficiency nor on distribution (personal, functional as well as regional). If cuts in public expenditures are inevitable, as they no doubt are in view of the size of present imbalances, considerable attention must be paid to the kind of cuts demanded.[43]

It may well be counterproductive, as Helleiner (1986b:76) points out, to push private sector expansion too fast or too far. Public restraint is often required, but revenue raising from the private sector may also be relevant as a way to budgetary balance restoration. It follows that the limits of these two different, but at times complementary, approaches must be identified, rather than assumed. Parallel with this, institutional reforms and rationalization in such areas as public budget planning and implementation; the use of the budget as a tool of economic management; the effectiveness and desirability of input and consumer subsidies; the choice of investment projects; the management of civil service reforms; the administrative and financial performance of public enterprises; and the importance of maintenance should be pursued continuously.

It is no longer controversial that all of these areas offer possibilities for improvement in efficiency and may contribute to a better mobilization of resources. Yet there are few generally valid answers as to how this should be done in practice. Differences of view on the respective roles of the government and the private sector and the effectiveness of the market mechanism are major stumbling blocks when it comes to formulating concrete proposals for improvement at the operational level. The debates over privatization and user fees are just two examples hereof.

MONETARY BALANCE AND POLICY

Using equation 2.4, the resource balance $(X - Z)$ can also be expressed as follows, putting the external monetary balance in focus:[44]

$$X - Z = (INP - NTR) + \Delta NFA + \Delta R \qquad (2.12)$$

This reveals that if 'interest payments are too high', as in sub-Saharan Africa, a continued real resource inflow (that is, $Z > X$) is only possible if (i) net transfers (including foreign aid) outweigh the burden of interest payments (that is, $NTR > INP$), (ii) additional foreign borrowing is feasible (that is, $\Delta NFA < 0$) or (iii) international reserves can be run down (that is, $\Delta R < 0$).[45] Hence, the role of external financing and dependence upon foreign donors and capital markets can become critical. The accumulation of arrears (usually by the government) and debt rescheduling are included in the above flows. However, it is often for practical purposes necessary to consider them explicitly. In fact, during the 1980s the availability of foreign exchange became in the majority of African countries exceedingly dependent on this kind of exceptional financing.[46]

The above observations in large measure explain the increased role in sub-Saharan Africa of agencies like the IMF and the World Bank, and why increased aid and debt reduction have come to be seen as indispensable components of adjustment programmes.[47] This is reinforced by the fact that availability of foreign assistance could go part of the way in easing some of the short-run costs and difficulties of adjustment referred to on pages 33–42, until possible medium-term benefits appear in the form of increased export earnings. Whether the necessary assistance will be forthcoming remains, however, an open question. There is a real danger that 'SAA will not avoid sliding down a slippery slope',[48] since the resource gap may have to be closed by cutting down imports.

While real resource transfers to SSA ought to be increased, not all resource flows have similar applicability. It is, for example, uncertain to what extent non-concessional resource flows are likely to be desirable in the short run. It may, due to the strings attached, turn out to be difficult to direct such resources towards relieving crucial bottle-necks in activities with high rates of return. Similarly, most aid continues to be tied to specific projects which are not always the most appropriate seen from a macroeconomic stabilization and structural point of view. The difficulties in increasing private external capital inflows and investment were already referred to on pages 43–5.

The adjustment problems become even more complex when capital flight occurs. This phenomenon appears when the private sector decides (and is able) to send an increasing share of its savings (S_p) abroad. This is done, rather than investing locally I_p, holding more financial assets in the form of money (M) or loans to the government (NBP_g), or repaying credits extended by the monetary system (DC_p). Capital flight may be reflected as an increase in net foreign assets held by the private sector or as a fall in private foreign borrowing (that is, an increase in NFA_p). Yet, different kinds of flows can be involved, and it may be recalled from equation 2.1 that $S_p + \Delta DC_p = I_p + \Delta M + \Delta NPB_g + \Delta NFA_p$.

Assume (i) there is no change in the relationship between the flow demand for money and changes in domestic credit to the private sector ($\Delta M + \Delta DC_p = 0$), and (ii) that private savings and investment (that is, $S_p - I_p$) remain unaltered. In such a case, the balancing change of capital flight is a decrease in private lending to the government (ΔNPB_g), equivalent to the increase in net foreign assets of the private sector (ΔNFA_p). The consequence of capital flight financed in this manner is therefore that the public borrowing requirement is no longer satisfied. This must, as shown on pages 45–50, lead to a deteriorating balance of payments (if additional foreign borrowing is resorted to), to increasing inflation (if the public deficit is monetized) or to fiscal contraction (through decreased public consumption and investment or increased revenue).

Additional capital flight can be financed through a decrease in cash balances (ΔM), and/or an increase in monetary credit to the private sector (ΔDC_p). This will deepen the fiscal crisis of the government even further. The private sector may finally decide to increase its foreign assets (ΔNFA_p), rather than investing domestically (I_p). Depending on the rate of return to the economy of private domestic investment, the opportunity cost of the private sector's holding of foreign assets may turn out to be substantial. Overall, the economic and social costs of capital flight may indeed be high as discussed on pages 45–50.

Policies to deal with foreign capital movements (and external monetary imbalance) come partly under the heading of financial policies. Administrative exchange controls can be tried to stop capital flight, but they are generally difficult to implement and are often costly in efficiency terms. It can be tried to increase the interest rate to turn the capital flow, but increases may have to be very high in sub-Saharan Africa, given existing uncertainties regarding future policies and political circumstances. Finally, it must be kept in mind that financial policies interact in intricate ways with fiscal and monetary (that is, expenditure-changing) policies as well as with trade and exchange-rate (that is, expenditure-switching) structural policies.

It follows from the above review that the resource balance $(X - Z)$ is related to domestic monetary changes, but it is useful to specify the relationship explicitly. Recall that $X - Z = Y - A$ (from equation 2.7) and that $\Delta R = \Delta M - \Delta DC$ (from equation 2.3). If these two expressions are substituted into the foreign sector budget constraint (equation 2.4) it appears that:

$$(Y + NTR - \Delta NFA - INP) - A = \Delta M - \Delta DC \qquad (2.13)$$

That is, the amount by which domestic absorption exceeds available resources *ex ante* is the same as the amount by which the increase in domestic credit exceeds the increase in the demand for money. This leads to the interpretation that an imbalance between absorption and domestic production, causing inflation, is due to 'too liberal credit expansion'. This has, in turn, led to the suggestion that the imposition of an overall credit ceiling may be a useful tool in re-establishing sustainable internal and external balances. Also, separate ceilings for government/public and private sector credit have been included in adjustment programmes in order to control the public sector deficit and provide more 'room' for the private sector.

If domestic sources of credit expansion (including some, but not necessarily all of the public budget deficit and credit to the private sector) are excessive relative to growth in the demand for money, spending will be stimulated and inflation will ensue until balance is restored *ex post*. Inflation can certainly be fuelled by excessive credit expansion as well as by external sources of imbalance. The real issue, however, is how 'safe' limits for credit expansion can be established and implemented, taking into consideration the need for internal domestic monetary balance as well as the need for recovery of domestic production.

The interrelationship between external reserves (that is, the current account) and domestic monetary developments was expressed in equation 2.3 from which it follows that:

$$\Delta R = \Delta M - (\Delta DC_p + \Delta DC_g) = (\Delta M - \Delta DC_p) - \Delta DC_g \quad (2.14)$$

That is, if domestic credit (to the private and public sectors) expands faster than the domestic money supply, external reserves will fall. Alternatively, if domestic credit expansion to the public sector (which increases the monetary system's assets against the public sector) expands faster than the net change in the monetary system's asset position *vis-à-vis* the private sector, international reserves must fall.

Excessive credit expansion appears again as the 'villain in the play'. Not only is it the 'cause' of excessive domestic demand and inflation, but also falling international reserves (that is, a deteriorating balance of payments) are traced to this 'source'. Excessive credit expansion can certainly contribute to weaken the external balance as may external sources, which are often more important. The underlying issue is once again how 'safe' limits can be established for the expansion of credit, taking into consideration the need for external balance as well as the need for recovery of domestic production.

It is not the use of credit ceilings (and reserve ratios) *per se*, which is doubtful, in particular since other monetary policy instruments such as open market operations and the discount rate are seriously circumscribed due to the underdeveloped nature of financial markets in SSA. However, focusing on credit expansion is in many ways a superficial approach. Monetary expansion is a symptom rather than a real underlying cause for an existing imbalance. The fiscal deficit and the processes which determine it may be at the core of the matter, but so may external shocks or changes in the investment and savings behaviour of the private sector (formal as well as informal).

The role of monetary policy is twofold. Monetary policy can be seen as a stabilization device through its impact on aggregate demand caused by regulation of interest rates as well as the availability of credit. However, monetary policy also has a role in promoting growth. In other words, if credit ceilings are used they must be set at levels that are consistent with balance of payments and inflation targets as well as the working capital requirements of the economy. For economies which have undergone prolonged deterioration of physical and institutional infrastructure as in SSA, working capital needs for a given level of economic activity may rise well above normal levels. Furthermore, the imposition of credit ceilings have to take account of the fact that exogenous factors of both a positive and negative nature are at work.[49]

If it is assumed that Y, ΔNFA, INP and NTR, as well as ΔM, can be controlled, then a reduction in domestic credit will translate itself into a balance-of-payments improvement through the reduction in absorption – prices must adjust, and output will remain at full capacity. However, output may not be at capacity limits to start with; credit ceilings may be set too low and without the necessary flexibility built in; and prices may be inflexible (or sticky) downwards. These factors vary, but matter, in the imperfect credit markets of sub-Saharan African countries, and the same accounts for international movements in foreign assets, the sensitivity of investment to changes in interest and the availability of credit.[50]

SUMMING UP

Chapter 2 has outlined the minimum elements of a sector-based macroeconomic consistency framework, and identified the kinds of policies which may be required for stabilization and adjustment purposes. Typical links, which may exist in the sub-Saharan context between economic policies and ultimate objectives such as growth, balance of payments and inflation, were also reviewed. This is useful as background to subsequent parts of this monograph where existing analytical adjustment frameworks and models are reviewed. The applicability and relevance of these analytical models depend in the final analysis on their ability to address the adjustment issues raised in Chapters 1 and 2. In summing up this overview of macroeconomic adjustment issues four points are highlighted.

First, a sector-based macroeconomic accounting framework is a very useful analytical tool to present the raw material available to assess the state of the economy, and it serves as an indispensable reading guide and quantitative basis for macroeconomic analysis and modelling. Existing data may be deficient and unsatisfactory, but it is all that is available. By integrating it within a consistent framework and reconciling separate accounts, further vital insights may be gained.

Second, the design of an accounting framework (with its particular identification of sectors, regions and economic agents) reflects how the analyst perceives the fundamental structure of the economy. Yet, however integrated and consistent the framework may be, it is not an economic model and provides no insights into the causal relations in the economy. Understanding obtained on this basis is therefore suggestive, not conclusive, as regards the underlying economic problems and proposed policy measures.

If imbalances exist *ex ante* they will by their very nature be closed *ex post*. The accounting framework can check whether desirable or projected scenarios are feasible and show how past imbalances were in fact closed. But the accounting framework cannot explain the very process (or set of actions) by which imbalances were or will be closed, and whether deliberate policy action could affect the outcome.

That is, the accounting framework cannot show how the economy really functions. For this a fully specified behavioural model with its particular interpretation of reality and the interplay of exogenous, endogenous and policy variables is required. It must in this context be kept in mind, that accounting frameworks share all the drawbacks of social accounting matrices. That is, they represent a linear, fixed-coefficient world. They therefore fail to convey possibilities for substitution, productivity growth and changes in institutional behaviour. Nevertheless, checking consistency of behavioural models and the projections they give rise to is not an unimportant task.

Third, critical institutional characteristics were not captured in the formal consistency framework presented here. Only a superficial interpretation of the consistency relationships is therefore possible. Further disaggregation, without going to the extreme, cannot be avoided if more meaningful generalizations are to be generated. It is in this context necessary to take account of the fact that the private sector consists of households as well as various groups of enterprises and that financial relationships exist in both formal and informal markets.

Fourth, while there is indeed need for adjustment in sub-Saharan Africa, there is, in continuation of point three, good reason to be sceptical about sweeping conclusions about the general efficacy of macroeconomic policy measures. The impact of policies vary according to the particular characteristics of the environment in which they are applied. It is for this reason that orthodox, as well as structuralist, views on how the economies of sub-Saharan Africa work were put forward. The next step will be to see how these views fit with the macroeconomic models that are used in the design of stabilization and structural adjustment programmes.

3

FINANCIAL PROGRAMMING
AND STABILIZATION

The approach of the International Monetary Fund (IMF) to economic stabilization is generally referred to as 'financial programming'. It is claimed by the IMF (1987:1–2) that this method evolved gradually over the years, taking into consideration (i) the major institutional and structural developments in the economies which have requested IMF assistance, (ii) the considerable changes in the international economy and (iii) progress in the study of macroeconomic and international issues. However, very little has in fact changed in the basic IMF framework over the past thirty years or so.[1]

There are several interlinked debates on the IMF approach.[2] These debates have often been translated to the ideological level by IMF critics as well as proponents. This has unfortunately made a largely negative contribution to understanding the issues at stake or how they might be resolved.[3] Furthermore, the IMF and the World Bank tend to set the rules for internal debates in terms of their own predilections and models. This may not be desirable on several grounds. The present chapter therefore aims at presenting as concisely as possible the IMF framework including *inter alia* an identification of key assumptions, more specific targets and policy instruments. An attempt will be made to assess the theoretical adequacy of the IMF approach in the sub-Saharan context, and some common misunderstandings will be clarified.

Doing this in a balanced manner is difficult for several reasons. In particular, financial programming is based largely on oral tradition. There is little readily accessible written material on the theoretical underpinnings of the IMF model and on the interaction among various policy measures in achieving the ultimate objectives of an adjustment programme.[4] Despite this, there is among some IMF and World Bank staff a tendency to assume that their approach is well known and overlook that African government officials at large and other outsiders may not quite as easily comprehend what is going on in a particular programming exercise. This does not, of course, exclude the fact that small technocratic elites are becoming increasingly knowledgeable of IMF views and negotiating tactics.[5]

The IMF was founded together with the World Bank (formally the International Bank for Reconstruction and Development, IBRD) at the Bretton Woods Conference in July 1944 by the delegates of forty-four nations, but now it has more than 150 member nations. It was no coincidence that, rather than one international economic and financial institution, two were established. The founding fathers of the Bretton Woods Institutions were consciously trying to establish a division of labour among the two, and those who have worked with the Fund and the Bank professionally find them very different.[6]

The IMF, with a staff of some 1,700, was not originally designed as a lending (or development finance) institution, and this is still not its primary purpose. It was set up to promote international monetary co-operation by providing a machinery for consultation and collaboration. Members of the IMF have agreed to a code of conduct, which implies that they are required to allow their currency to be exchanged for foreign currencies freely and that the IMF must be informed of changes in financial and monetary policies that will affect fellow members. Furthermore, member states must, to the extent possible, modify these policies on the advice of the IMF to accommodate the needs of the entire membership.[7]

Until 1973 the IMF monitored members' compliance with their obligations within a fixed exchange system, but since then IMF surveillance has been concerned more generally with economic policies that influence the balance of payments in the now legalized flexible exchange rate environment. Surveillance includes a system of regular annual consultations with member governments and aims at promoting orderly exchange relations.[8] However, the Articles of Agreement, which established the IMF, also specify that the Fund is 'to facilitate the expansion and balanced growth of international trade and to contribute thereby to the promotion and maintenance of high levels of employment and real income'. The Articles clearly support liberal trade and payments practices, and it is declared policy in adjustment programmes to open up the economy, liberalize economic activities, establish realistic prices and reduce controls.

To help members abide by the code of conduct, the IMF 'administers a pool of money' (Driscoll 1989:3) from which members can borrow when they are in balance-of-payments trouble. This provides them, as stated in the Articles of Agreement Art. I (v), with the opportunity of correcting maladjustments without resorting to measures destructive to national or international prosperity. Originally the amounts involved were relatively small, but temporary surges in IMF financing have occurred. This happened, for example, during the Suez crisis and after the oil shocks of the 1970s. The IMF also played a role in the debt crisis of the 1980s.[9]

While the IMF may, under special circumstances, borrow from official entities, it mainly draws its financial resources, presently valued at over US $120 billion, from the quota subscriptions (or membership fees) of its member countries. These quotas, of which 25 per cent are paid in international reserve assets and the rest in the currency of the member country, are roughly proportionate with the economic size of member countries. Thus, countries with a higher gross domestic product (GDP) pay more than poorer countries. The basic stand-by 'drawing rights' of member countries are also quota related, but once a country needs to draw more than the reserve tranche (equal to 25 per cent of its quota) policy conditionalities are imposed.

The basic facility of the IMF includes the reserve tranche plus four credit tranches, which are each equal to 25 per cent of the quota, so the country has access to 125 per cent of its own quota. An extended credit facility makes it possible to borrow up to 140 per cent of the quota. Enlarged possibilities give access to additional amounts, and the IMF has recently introduced as well a structural adjustment facility (SAF) and an enhanced structural adjustment facility (ESAF), with a view to the particular problems facing the African continent.

It should be recalled that the IMF mandate is in general limited to the financing of temporary balance-of-payments disequilibria in attempts to stabilize the economy. When balance-of-payments troubles are not of a temporary nature, they must be 'rendered so by corrective policy measures' (that is, supply-side structural policies).[10] It is regularly argued by IMF staff that such measures are beyond the purview of the IMF as they will have a gestation period that far exceeds the permissible time-frame for IMF support. They are, it is held, within the competence of the IMF's sister institution, the World Bank.[11]

The IMF has generally insisted that stabilization must occur before structural reform is attempted.[12] However, more recent statements seem to indicate a growing recognition by the Fund that, to the extent that efforts to channel resources away from inefficient uses are impeded by institutional rigidities, structural reform can play a critical role in achieving balance-of-payments viability and growth.[13]

58

The original dividing line between the IMF and the World Bank implied that IMF received guidance from the World Bank on development issues. In turn, the World Bank followed IMF advice on domestic macroeconomic and exchange rate policies, adjustment of temporary balance-of-payments disequilibria and stabilization programmes. This distinction became, however, blurred during the turbulent years after the breakdown of the Bretton Woods par value system from 1968 to 1973, and the origin of the debt crisis.

The above lack of clarity between the respective perspectives of the IMF and the World Bank is reinforced by the more recent 'special' IMF facilities (as well as World Bank balance-of-payments support) to help low-income developing countries. The future of these facilities is still under debate, and is by no means certain, but their mere existence and use make it indispensable for IMF analysts to start facing supply-side issues. The same accounts for debt rescheduling in a number of countries undertaken under the auspices of the IMF. This has forced the IMF into assessments of the medium- and long-term prospects for the countries concerned. The IMF has, in other words, become, *de facto*, involved in development finance.

THE 'EMPTY' FRAMEWORK

Any IMF financial programming exercise revolves around the macroeconomic accounts reviewed in Chapter 2. Equations 2.5 (national balance), 2.4 (external balance), 2.3 (monetary balance) and 2.2 (fiscal balance) have been singled out as particularly important. The order in which these balances are listed here is not accidental. Early IMF work on balance-of-payments issues was framed within the absorption approach associated with Alexander (1952 and 1959). This approach, which combines equations 2.4 and 2.5, played a key role in the design of early Fund-supported programmes.[14] It also changed the thinking on balance-of-payments issues in a way that put focus on policy issues, as already demonstrated on pages 33–45.[15]

Towards the end of the 1950s, the absorption approach became, however, integrated with the view that the balance of payments is also (and, according to some interpretations, principally) a monetary phenomenon. Focus was, in other words, put on the relation between the money supply and the external sector (that is, the monetary balance equation 2.3), which was 'added' to the first two balance equations (that is, equations 2.4 and 2.5).

Attention was finally drawn to the role of government deficits as a source of domestic credit expansion. This has, as already demonstrated, been a prevalent characteristic of developments in sub-Saharan Africa. The way in which government deficits are financed matter for the money supply and the private sector. The policy issues reviewed on pages 45–50 therefore become important. Government deficits may be a source of excessive credit expansion, and the government deficit can also be viewed as an important policy instrument. Thus, equation 2.2 is 'added', and in summary form, the set of four identities can be presented as follows:[16]

- national balance: $\quad Y = (C + I) + X - Z$
- external balance: $\quad \Delta R + \Delta NFA = (X - Z) - (INP - NTR)$
- monetary balance: $\quad \Delta M = \Delta R + \Delta DC$
- fiscal balance: $\quad S_g - I_g = \Delta NFA_g - \Delta NPB_g - \Delta DC_g$

The above set of balance equations overlap in several ways. For example, the entries common to the national and the external and fiscal accounts are respectively the trade balance and public consumption and investment. The external balance shares the change in international reserves with the monetary balance, and the change in government-held foreign assets with the fiscal balance. Finally, the monetary and the fiscal accounts have in common domestic credit extended to government.

The above set of equations (and the various underlying definitions), which are singled out for further study in the IMF framework, is just a sub-set of the whole set of balances that make up the national accounts.[17] Furthermore, the sub-set of balances do not amount to a model as no behavioural relationships have been specified. *Ex ante* gaps (that is, differences among the 'intentions' or 'plans' of the various sectors at the beginning of a period under study) must close during the period so that they are in balance *ex post*. The identities do not, however, give any clue as to how this adjustment process takes place. For this, it is necessary to specify the causal links in the economy. Finally, and more specifically, the above set of equations do not necessarily imply that the balance of payments is essentially a monetary phenomenon; they are just an 'empty' framework.

THE POLAK MODEL

The first transformation of the above 'empty' framework into an analytic model took place in an article by Polak (1957). The economy that Polak, who had Dutch predecessors, sought to model is a small, open economy operating under a system of fixed nominal exchange rates. In line with the IMF mandate, an improvement in the balance of payments and an acceptable inflation rate were established as key objectives. In the IMF interpretation, these goals form the basis for 'the promotion and maintenance of high levels of employment and real income', listed as objectives in the Articles of the IMF and referred to in the introduction above.

What had struck Polak was the lack of an adequate theoretical basis to handle questions regarding the effects of specified monetary changes on income and the balance of payments. He therefore tried to integrate monetary and credit factors with the absorption approach to the balance of payments, which was used by the IMF as a frame of reference at the time. Thus, Polak suggested explicit links between the monetary and the external sector with the objective of arriving at a formal relationship between the domestic component of the money stock (that is, domestic credit) and changes in international reserves, which could be fruitfully employed for policy. Polak's result was powerful and it continues to form the theoretical basis on which financial programming exercises are carried out in the operational wing of the IMF.[18]

The Polak model was kept in nominal terms and there is consequently no explicit distinction made between price and real income changes. The two key behavioural assumptions include that the demand for money (M_d), which is assumed to depend on a limited number of variables, is stable, and that imports (Z) is a fraction (m) of nominal income (Y).[19] Furthermore, the money supply (M_s) is endogenously determined as the sum of domestic credit (DC) and foreign reserves (R) of the domestic banking system (that is, the identity reflected in equation 2.3). Finally, the balance-of-payments identity (equation 2.4) links changes in the international reserves with the current account and changes in foreign assets (that is, $\Delta R = X - Z - INP + NTR - \Delta NFA$). Changes in the international reserves can, for simplicity, be written $\Delta R = X - Z + \Delta F$, where ΔF represents net non-trade related foreign currency inflows (obtained by a decrease in NFA – that is, by borrowing or through net transfers minus interest payments).

The demand for money obviously depends on a number of variables such as income, the interest rate paid on bank deposits and other financial assets, expected inflation, and so on. However, Polak chose as a first 'worthwhile' step the restrictive relationship that money demand depends on nominal income only, and combined this with an assumption that money circulates at constant velocity (v).[20] Savings and investment are not considered explicitly and there is no capital market. This implies that the money supply can no longer serve as policy instrument as in the standard Keynesian closed-economy model,[21] and that all savings by assumption are immediately invested.[22] Polak finally assumed that X and ΔF are given exogenously.

On the above basis, the structure of the Polak model can be presented as follows:

$$M_d v = Y \tag{3.1}$$

$$Z = mY \tag{3.2}$$

$$\Delta M_s = \Delta R + \Delta DC \tag{3.3}$$

$$\Delta R = \overline{X} - Z + \Delta\overline{F} \tag{3.4}$$

Assuming the money market eventually clears (that is, $\Delta M_s = \Delta M_d$), the model can be solved for the endogenous variables and their evolution over time. Polak used his 'system' to reach a series of conclusions about the effects of changes in the two main autonomous variables, exports (X) and domestic credit (DC). Autonomous changes in imports (Z) were shown to have effects which are equivalent to that of export changes at the level of abstraction 'on which we operate here'.[23]

In deriving his results, Polak lags imports by one period so Z at time t (Z_t) is equal to mY_{t-1}.[24] Polak also distinguishes carefully among lasting increases in the value of exports and the rate of credit expansion, on the one side, and discontinuous changes in the autonomous variables, on the other.[25] Focus in what follows is for illustrative purposes on a discontinuous expansion in domestic credit as the relevant instrument for monetary policy. This is followed by some observations about measures directed towards increasing exports or decreasing imports.

The transmission mechanism through which an increase in domestic credit works is first to increase the money supply by the same amount (equation 3.3). This increases income (equation 3.1) as the whole amount is spent by borrowers (for example, in connection with government deficit spending).[26] Most of the additional expenditure will be directed toward domestic goods and services, and if there is excess capacity the increase in money demand may increase real output with prices rising little or not at all.

If no excess capacity exists, or supply bottle-necks constrain output, the rise in money income will merely reflect price increases. The increase in money income will, however, increase imports (equation 3.2), and the balance of payments deteriorates (equation 3.4) with a resulting fall in international reserves. It is clear that no account is taken of the fact that credit expansion may be linked through policy with investment and capital accumulation, which might have positive effects of their own.

The above process will go on in standard multiplier fashion and it can be shown that the initial expansion in the money supply through domestic credit is eventually exactly offset by the sum of the negative changes in international reserves. Hence, the money stock returns to its original level. This implies (through equations 3.1 and 3.2) that nominal income and imports will also return to their previous levels after an initial rise. The only lasting consequence of the credit expansion is, in other words, a fall in the international reserves caused by the temporary increase in imports.[27]

What Polak's model does is to focus on the links between changes in the domestic money supply and changes in the external account. If a balance-of-payments target (ΔR) is set, a corresponding maximum 'permissible' expansion in domestic credit extended by the monetary system can be estimated. If credit expansion by the monetary system exceeds the value the economy can 'afford', the only consequence will be declining international reserves, that is, the ΔR target will not be met. The policy conclusion is that improving the external balance implies domestic credit restraint. It becomes, in this way, obvious why such great emphasis is placed by the IMF on controlling domestic credit expansion by the monetary system.

As regards measures towards increasing exports (or decreasing imports), it has already been noted that a discontinuous change will have no lasting impact on income, imports or international reserves (that is, balance of payments). A lasting increase in exports will increase income, but as imports are also stimulated, there will be no change in the international reserves.[28] This does not mean, however, that measures directed towards exports or imports should be ruled out in Polak's view. Their temporary effects, combined with other policy measures, may be of great importance in restoring a country's reserve position.

THE MONETARY APPROACH

The Polak model and the work of other IMF staff played a significant role in the development of the monetary approach to the balance of payments (MABOP). This approach has been identified as the 'theory' underlying IMF supported programmes,[29] but this remains a controversial point. Polak stressed in his original article that his model was not to be seen as an alternative to Keynesian economics.[30] On the contrary, Polak (1957:11) argued that 'by focusing on the monetary side of the same circular process, we can approach the problem from another angle, which makes it more tractable in many situations'.

Furthermore, a more recent contribution from the IMF concludes that identifying 'IMF theory' with MABOP is outright erroneous.[31] It is accepted that MABOP is a central part of the theoretical underpinnings of IMF-supported programmes, and that the framework reviewed above serves to highlight the essential theoretical features of any programme designed for a small open economy operating under a fixed exchange rate. However, the actual design of a programme is said to be far more pragmatic, as there are 'various possible interpretations of the theoretical mechanisms forming the adjustment process, and consequently a variety of theoretical models can be used as the framework for constructing adjustment programs' (IMF 1987:2).

Nevertheless, the significance accorded to monetary phenomena is very much different when it comes to the 'Chicago' version of the monetary approach to the balance of payments, which follows the Polak model in chronological time. Leading exponents of this approach (including, in particular, Frenkel and Johnson 1976) have been highly critical of the Keynesian approach (or the elasticity approach as they term it). They suggest that 'the balance of payments is essentially a monetary phenomenon', and as a corollary draw the conclusion that balance-of-payments problems must necessarily be corrected through appropriate monetary policy.

Frenkel and Johnson (1976) also point out that the domestic banking system (that is, the central bank) cannot, over the longer run, sterilize the impact of the current account balance on the domestic money supply (equation 3.4). It follows that the money supply cannot be used as a policy instrument. Finally, Frenkel and Johnson (1976:22) suggest to put focus on 'behavioral determinants directly relevant to the money account, rather than an analysis in terms of the behavioral relations directly relevant to the other accounts and only indirectly to the money account via the budget constraint'. Since the money account is 'determined' by the excess flow demand for money, it is clear why the balance of payments is regarded as a monetary phenomenon and why this approach is referred to as 'the monetary approach'.

A simple model along the 'Chicago' line of thinking was developed by Johnson (in Frenkel and Johnson 1976) and, to illustrate the differences from the Polak model, it is summarized below using a similar notation as above, unless otherwise indicated. In Johnson's model, nominal and real variables are separated explicitly through the introduction of the domestic price level P_d. This implies that nominal income Y may be written as $P_d y$ where y is real income. It is furthermore assumed that the law of one price holds so the rate of inflation in the domestic economy is equal to the rate of inflation in the rest of the world.[32] Consequently, the domestic price level is determined by foreign prices through purchasing power parity, and P_d is equal to the foreign price level P_f times e, where e is the exchange rate (that is, the domestic currency price of a unit of foreign currency).

The demand for money M_d is in the monetary model a stable function (f) of real output and the level of interest. To keep the model as simple as possible, the interest rate is ignored. Money supply M_s is determined endogenously as the sum of foreign reserves R and domestic credit DC, whereas real output y is set solely by an aggregate neo-classical supply function and as such is independent of the level of aggregate demand. Therefore $y = \bar{y}$, so y is an exogenous variable, which may, however, be growing over time. Finally, the money market is assumed to be in continuous equilibrium, that is, $M_s = M_d = M$, where M is the money stock. Consequently, the minimum version of the 'Chicago' version of the monetary approach can be set out as follows:[33]

$$y = \bar{y} \tag{3.5}$$

$$Y = P_d \bar{y} \tag{3.6}$$

$$P_d = e P_f \tag{3.7}$$

$$M_d = P_d f(\bar{y}) \tag{3.8}$$

$$M_s = R + DC \tag{3.9}$$

$$M_s = M_d = M \tag{3.10}$$

It follows that foreign reserves R may be written as $R = P_d f(y) - DC$. By differentiating with respect to time (t) it appears that changes in foreign reserves are linked to changes in domestic credit as follows:

$$\frac{dR}{dt} = f(y) \, \frac{dP_d}{dt} + P_d \frac{\delta f(y)}{\delta y} \, \frac{dy}{dt} - \frac{dDC}{dt} \qquad (3.11)$$

That is, the rate of change of international reserves is equal to the difference between the rate of change of the money demand and the rate of change of domestic credit expansion, which are effectively independent of each other due to the assumptions listed above. If it is assumed that the foreign price level, the exchange rate and real output remain constant, equation 3.11 reduces to:

$$\frac{dR}{dt} = - \frac{dDC}{dt} \qquad (3.12)$$

This is the fundamental result of the 'Chicago' version of the monetary approach to the balance of payments. Under fixed exchange rates the money supply is endogenous, and any increase due to an expansion in domestic credit will automatically lead to a decrease in foreign reserves on a 'one-for-one basis'. If the economy is growing, the demand for money is also growing, so domestic credit can expand without causing balance-of-payments problems. But if the rate of domestic credit expansion exceeds the positive flow demand for money, the balance of payments will deteriorate and foreign reserves fall. Similarly, if the rate of domestic credit expansion falls short of the rate of increase of money demand, the balance of payments will improve and foreign reserves increase. A good balance-of-payments performance depends on controlling domestic credit expansion.

These central conclusions as to the impact of domestic credit expansion were also reached by Polak, but there are nevertheless key differences between the two models. If the 'law of one price' holds and real output is exogenous, the Polak model breaks down, as there is no mechanism to dispose of the excess money supply generated by the credit expansion. In the 'Chicago version' of the monetary approach to the balance of payments, the transmission mechanism, through which a domestic credit expansion works, is much more direct and speedy. Increases in DC increases the money supply as in the Polak model, but demand for goods and services is stimulated directly (without the intermediating increase in nominal income) and imports react instantaneously. Consequently, unlike the Polak version, it is assumed that the basic monetary relationship holds continuously. Monetary flows are in equilibrium at all times and any excess supply of money is constantly eliminated.

If there is an imbalance between absorption and domestic output (reflected in a balance-of-payments deficit), this must in the 'Chicago' model correspond to too liberal credit expansion. The way to solve the problem is to limit domestic credit expansion. The same conclusion was reached by Polak for the long run, but in his model the end state was reached through a process where real income as well as prices might be affected in addition to the balance of payments. That is, the possibility for short-run disequilibria is not ruled out in the Polak model. It follows that if an import function is specified in the 'Chicago model', this must be done differently from the Polak model in such a way that imports react passively to eliminate any disequilibrium in the money market.

In the 'Chicago model', an additional policy instrument, the exchange rate, which was not considered formally in the Polak model, appears.[34] According to standard Keynesian analysis, a devaluation can, if the Marshall-Lerner conditions hold, improve the current account permanently.[35] However, this does not happen within the monetary model outlined above. Here an exchange rate devaluation has only a temporary impact. Starting from external balance, the argument is that in the short run a devaluation improves the competitive position *vis-à-vis* the foreign sector. This causes a surplus in the trade balance and therefore an increase in foreign reserves. This increase also makes the money supply grow (via equation 3.9). Assuming this increase is not sterilized, and as people will strive to maintain their money balances, excess demand for goods and services will drive up prices and imports until the surplus on the current account is eliminated.

Starting from external imbalance, as in sub-Saharan Africa, the demand for money is smaller (or growing at a lower rate) than the supply of money. The increase in the demand for money following the increase in the domestic price level, which comes after a devaluation, will eliminate temporarily the imbalance between money demand and money supply. This impact will, on the other hand, only be lasting if domestic credit expansion is eventually limited to the level, which is consistent with growth in money demand reflecting exogenous increases in real output. A devaluation may thus be required to stop the outflow of foreign reserves, but unless action is also taken on what the 'Chicago' approach considers the essential cause of the external imbalance, i.e., the excess of credit expansion over money demand, adjustment will not be permanent.

The assumptions that all goods are tradables, and that the law of one price holds are not critical for the qualitative conclusions reached by the monetary approach. Dornbusch (in Frenkel and Johnson 1976: 168) has demonstrated that if real balances are unrelated with expenditure, the effects of a devaluation will continue to be negligible in the medium- to long-run even if non-tradable goods are introduced in the model. That is, the only way to reduce a balance-of-payments problem under a fixed exchange rate system is to lower the rate of domestic credit expansion.

Similarly, if the law of one price does not hold, the rate of price increases in the domestic economy will end up being equal to that of the rate of rest of the world, even if domestic credit is restricted. If foreign prices are growing faster than domestic prices and the exchange rate is fixed, then the relative price of foreign goods to domestic goods will keep rising. However, if the Marshall-Lerner condition is fulfilled, a current account surplus must develop, which causes an increase in the money supply. This forces domestic prices up in line with foreign prices in the monetary model.

It is clear from the above review that the monetary model is very similar in its objectives and conclusions to that of Polak. Nevertheless, monetary phenomena are much more in focus and their importance is highlighted, even to the extent that output adjustments are neglected through the assumption that real output is exogenous. The transmission mechanism of the Polak model, where balance of payments, output and inflation are all affected by imbalances in monetary flows, appears more realistic than that of the 'Chicago' monetary model. But, as pointed out by Chand (1989:488), the response coefficients, which have been estimated from historical data, are not sufficiently stable for use in forecasting or financial programming. The assumption that the money market is in continuous equilibrium is therefore maintained in the current financial programming model of the IMF.

FINANCIAL PROGRAMMING IN THEORY

There is, as mentioned above, little readily-accessible written material on the financial programming model of the IMF. A fairly consistent picture can, nevertheless, be put together from a review of Chand

(1989), Guitián (in Corbo, Goldstein and Khan 1987), IMF (1987), Khan, Montiel and Haque (1986 and 1990) and Robichek (1985).[36]

Many of the elements of the present IMF framework have already been discussed above and can therefore be stated rather briefly. Real output y is assumed exogenously determined, but may be growing over time. Nominal output Y is given as $P\bar{y}$. The nominal exchange rate e is introduced by assuming that the domestic price level P is a weighted average of the price for domestic goods P_d and the exogenous international price $\bar{P}_f$ (measured in foreign currency) for imported goods.[37] The share of imports in the price index is denoted θ so the share of domestic goods is $(1 - \theta)$. Therefore, $P = (1 - \theta)P_d + \theta e \bar{P}_f$ where $e\bar{P}_f$ is the international price level measured in domestic currency. In line with Khan, Montiel and Haque (1986:17) it is also assumed that foreign prices remain stable (that is, $\Delta \bar{P}_f = 0$) and that $P_d = 1$ initially. This implies that $e\bar{P}_f$ and P are also equal to unity.

Money demand M_d is positively related to changes in the domestic price level P, and real output y and the velocity of money v are assumed constant.[38] The money supply M_s is determined endogenously as the sum of the stock of international reserves R and domestic credit DC. Domestic credit consists of credit to the government (DC_g) and credit to the private sector (DC_p). The stock of international reserves in domestic currency R is equal to the exchange rate (e) times the stock of international reserves in foreign currency $(\tilde{R})$. The money market is assumed to be in flow equilibrium, which implies that people will, during the period under consideration, succeed in adding to their money balances at the desired rate. Hence, the stock of money (M) equals money demanded and supplied.

Exports and other net foreign currency inflows, which can be disaggregated into flows to the government and to the private sector respectively, are assumed exogenously determined. It is stressed that it is now the foreign currency value of exports $(\tilde{X})$ and other net inflows $(\Delta \tilde{F})$ that are given exogenously. Exports X and other net foreign currency inflows ΔF denominated in domestic currency (and obtained by multiplying the foreign currency values by e) may therefore change due to changes in the exchange rate. Imports could, for simplicity, be assumed a linear function of nominal output as in the Polak model, but a slightly more complicated linear import function, which makes imports Z dependent not only on real output (that is, y), but also on changes in relative prices (that is, on $e\bar{P}_f / P_d$), is used here.[39] As is the case for the first behavioural equation (that is, the money demand function), it is not so much the particular specification chosen, but the stability of the import function that is essential.

Finally, from the balance of payments identity, it follows that the change in foreign reserves R (in domestic currency) equals the sum of the surplus/deficit on the trade balance (that is, $X - Z$) and other net non-trade related foreign currency flows to the private sector and government, respectively ΔF_p and ΔF_g.[40] The theoretical core of the IMF financial programming model can, based on these preliminaries, be summarized as follows:

$$y = \overline{y} \tag{3.13}$$

$$Y = P\overline{y} \tag{3.14}$$

$$P = (1 - \theta)P_d + \theta e \overline{P_f} \tag{3.15}$$

$$M_d v = P\overline{y} \tag{3.16}$$

$$M_s = R + DC \tag{3.17}$$

$$DC = DC_g + DC_p \tag{3.18}$$

$$R = e\widetilde{R} \tag{3.19}$$

$$M_d = M_s = M \tag{3.20}$$

$$X = e\widetilde{X} \tag{3.21}$$

$$\Delta F = \Delta F_g + \Delta F_p = e \Delta \widetilde{F} \tag{3.22}$$

$$\Delta F_g = e \Delta \widetilde{F_g} \tag{3.23}$$

$$\Delta F_p = e \Delta \widetilde{F_p} \tag{3.24}$$

$$(S_g - I_g) = -(\Delta F_g + \Delta DC_g) \tag{3.25}$$

$$Z = e\widetilde{Z} \tag{3.26}$$

$$\widetilde{Z} = \overline{P_f} Z_q \tag{3.27}$$

$$Z_q = \alpha_0 + \alpha_1 \overline{y} - \alpha_2 (e \overline{P_f} / P_d) \tag{3.28}$$

$$\Delta R = X - Z + \Delta F \tag{3.29}$$

The above framework can be reduced to two linear equations in ΔR and ΔP_d that reflect changes in international reserves and the domestic price level. These are the two main targets in IMF-supported stabilization programmes. The nominal exchange rate (e), and the amount of domestic credit outstanding (DC), is assumed under the control of the policy-making authority. The policy instruments in the model are therefore Δe and ΔDC, which is equal to $\Delta DC_g + \Delta DC_p$.

The reduction is carried out by taking first differences and substituting into equations 3.20 and 3.29.[41] Equations 3.14, 3.15 and 3.16 imply that:[42]

$$\Delta M_d = \frac{1}{v}\,\bar{y}\,(1-\theta)\,\Delta P_d + \frac{1}{v}\,\bar{y}\,\bar{P}_f\theta\Delta\,e + \frac{1}{v}\,P_{-1}\Delta\bar{y} \qquad (3.30)$$

Changes in the money supply occur following changes in the international reserves and domestic credit. Taking account of equations 3.17 and 3.18 and remembering that changes in the domestic value of foreign reserves may develop due to changes in the exchange rate (that is, a valuation change equal to the stock of foreign reserves in foreign currency held in the previous period $\tilde{R}_{-1}$ times the exchange rate change Δe), the following expression for the flow supply of money appears:

$$\Delta M_s = \Delta R + \Delta e\tilde{R} + (\Delta DC_g + \Delta DC_p) \qquad (3.31)$$

Substituting equations 3.30 and 3.31 into the equilibrium condition 3.20 and rearranging the following expression for ΔR as a function of the second target ΔP_d (together with a set of parameters and predetermined, exogenous and endogenous variables, as well as the two policy instruments, Δe and ΔDC) appears:

$$\Delta R = \frac{1}{v}\,P_{-1}\Delta\bar{y} + \left(\frac{1}{v}\,\bar{y}\,\bar{P}_f\,\theta - \tilde{R}_{-1}\right)\Delta\,e - \Delta DC + \frac{1}{v}\,\bar{y}\,(1-\theta)\,\Delta P_d$$
$$(3.32)$$

Since real output is determined outside the model, this expression can be abbreviated to $\Delta R = (\gamma_0 + \gamma_1\,\Delta e - \Delta DC) + \gamma_2\,\Delta P_d$, where γ_0 and γ_2 are positive. It is, furthermore, assumed that γ_1 is positive. Equations 3.21–3.24 imply that:[43]

$$X + \Delta F = (\tilde{X} + \Delta\tilde{F}_g + \Delta\tilde{F}_p)\,e_{-1} + (\tilde{X} + \Delta\tilde{F}_g + \Delta\tilde{F}_p)\,\Delta\,e \quad (3.33)$$

From the import equations 3.26–3.28 it follows that:[44]

$$Z = Z_{-1} + \alpha_1 \Delta \bar{y} + \alpha_2 \Delta P_d + (Z_{-1} - \alpha_2) \Delta e \bar{P_f} \qquad (3.34)$$

Substituting equations 3.33 and 3.34 into equation 3.29 and re-arranging, the following expression for ΔR as a function of the second target ΔP_d (together with a set of parameters and predetermined, exogenous and endogenous variables as well as the two policy instruments) appears:

$$\Delta R = (\tilde{X} + \Delta \tilde{F}) \, e_{-1} - Z_{-1} - \alpha_1 \Delta \bar{y}$$
$$+ [\tilde{X} + \Delta \tilde{F} - (Z_{-1} - \alpha_2)\bar{P_f}] \, \Delta e - \alpha_2 \Delta P_d \qquad (3.35)$$

This expression can be abbreviated to $\Delta R = (\rho_0 + \rho_1 \Delta e) - \rho_2 \Delta P_d$. It can be noted that ρ_0 is the change in the balance of payments, which result when domestic prices and the exchange rate are maintained unchanged. The sign may vary. The second parameter ρ_1 expresses the change in the balance of payments following changes in the exchange rate. Assuming a devaluation (that is, $\Delta e > 0$) improves the balance of payments, ρ_1 is positive. Finally, $\rho_2 (= \alpha_2)$ is positive, since the response of imports to relative price changes was assumed positive.

It follows from the above, that the two expressions in equation 3.32 and 3.35, linking ΔR and ΔP_d can be represented as straight lines in a $(\Delta P_d, \Delta R)$ space with respectively positive and negative slopes. Their intersection represents the chosen combination of the two main targets. The values of the policy instruments can, once the targets ΔR and ΔP_d have been established, be derived by solving equations 3.32 and 3.35 for Δe and ΔDC as follows:

$$\Delta e = -\frac{\rho_0}{\rho_1} + \frac{1}{\rho_1} \Delta R + \frac{\rho_2}{\rho_1} \Delta P_d \qquad (3.36)$$

$$\Delta DC = \left(\gamma_0 - \gamma_1 \frac{\rho_0}{\rho_1} \right) + \left(\frac{\gamma_1}{\rho_1} - 1 \right) \Delta R + \left(\frac{\rho_2}{\rho_1} \gamma_1 + \gamma_2 \right) \Delta P_d \qquad (3.37)$$

If a third target is established for credit to the private sector, in addition to the targets for the balance of payments and domestic inflation, the second policy instrument becomes ΔDC_g, that is, changes in the domestic credit to the government, rather than ΔDC. Once ΔDC_g has been calculated following the procedure used above, the corresponding fiscal balance can be found from equation 3.25.

FINANCIAL PROGRAMMING IN PRACTICE

Following the review of the theoretical underpinnings of IMF-supported adjustment programmes, this section describes briefly the actual process of formulating an IMF financial stabilization programme. The process normally follows the same outline, but there always are local variations in the computational/negotiating procedure. These differences are not in focus in what follows, but they are duly acknowledged. The programming exercises have, in the case of sub-Saharan African countries in need of balance-of-payments support during the 1980s, been undertaken within the context of so-called policy framework papers (PFPs). These PFPs are considered by the executive boards of the IMF and the World Bank before any assistance is approved.

The PFP describes the medium-term objectives of the country in question, the particular balance-of-payments and development problems faced, the policies to be followed in pursuing the stated objectives and the result of financial and growth projections. It is the adjusting country that has the formal responsibility for preparing the PFP, but this is in practice done with extensive help from the professional staff of the IMF, the World Bank and other agencies involved.

The first step in financial programming is to choose the target variables. A desired level of international reserves (R) is typically the principal target, but also inflation (ΔP_d) and additional credit extended to the private sector (ΔDC_p) appear. The second step is to generate projections for the exogenous variables, including real output (y), exports of goods and services (X) and other net foreign currency flows (ΔF), which must of course be broken down into the various non-trade related components of the balance of payments, that is, interest and other transfer payments as well as capital flows of a non-compensatory nature.

The above information makes it possible in a third step to make a first assessment of the value of imports (Z), which is consistent with the targeted change in international reserves (or rather, the desired improvement in the balance of payments). If this import value appears reasonable, based on past experience and overall needs, there is in fact no need for macroeconomic adjustment. Such a finding has not been the usual result in the case of sub-Saharan Africa during the 1980s. On the contrary, the imputed import value has normally been much smaller than that estimated on the basis of past import trends.

It has therefore been necessary to consider how the gap should be closed, and the fourth step in the financial programming procedure is to assess whether a devaluation is called for or not. This is in principle done by solving equation 3.36, but additional judgements as to the possible effects of the devaluation on exogenous variables (in particular, exports, real output and capital flows) may also have to be considered here. If a devaluation is deemed desirable, it becomes necessary to recalculate the imputed import value with the new exchange rate.

Whether or not exchange rate action is recommended, domestic credit expansion must be consistent with the targets set for inflation and changes in international reserves. Thus, the fifth step in the programming procedure is to establish the demand for money based on equations 3.13–3.16, which can be solved using the targeted price level and the constant money velocity. A certain flexibility is sometimes allowed for, and the constant velocity assumption is usually, but not always, taken as a dictum. Based on the level of demand for money, it is analysed whether action is needed on the interest rate to attempt to affect money demand and velocity. If so, the money demand level is revised before determining in a sixth step the overall permissible domestic credit expansion (that is, ΔDC – equation 3.37 refers).

This permissible level of credit expansion is compared with the demand for domestic credit in the seventh step. Given that domestic credit to the private sector is often implicitly or explicitly targeted, focus in this step is on the painstaking analysis of public finance trends. In practice, the analysis encompasses projections of government revenue, current and capital expenditure, as well as the possible alternative sources of financing a public sector deficit. Any gap emerging at this stage signals that the government borrowing requirements exceed the amount 'permitted' by the targeted change in international reserves and domestic credit expansion. Hence, this gap must be closed.

There are various ways of doing this. The targets concerning changes in international reserves can be lowered if the level of international reserves permits. If this is not the case, as in sub-Saharan Africa, fiscal policy (that is, demand restraint and/or revenue raising measures), together with supply-side policies to affect real output (that is, y) and financial policies to affect money demand, come into the picture. These possibilities are consequently the subject of the eighth step, which involves complex and often rather tense negotiations between IMF (and the World Bank) on the one side, and the country in need of adjustment on the other.

Once the negotiation process about these complementary policy measures is completed, the consistency of the overall programme is tested in a ninth step. Final agreement on the implementation of the programme and the performance criteria to be used in monitoring is reached in step ten and formally expressed in a letter of intent from the government to the IMF. It follows that the basic performance criteria must, according to the IMF approach, embrace ceilings on total domestic credit expansion and the fiscal deficit (including ceilings on domestic credit to government and foreign borrowing which are the main financing sources of fiscal deficits). Furthermore, action on the exchange rate is a potential but, in theory, not unavoidable, measure. A final performance criteria generally introduced, refers to increased exchange and trade liberalization, and incomes policy criteria are also common.[45] However, in these respects the IMF is moving outside the narrow confines of the monetary model underlying the core of its policy prescriptions.

DISCUSSION

The stated objectives of the IMF are geared towards the achievement of a viable balance-of-payments position within a relatively short-time horizon, together with acceptable levels of inflation during the adjustment process. Adjustment programmes are designed and policy measures undertaken with these overall targets in mind. Policy action should, at the same time, contribute to the promotion and maintenance of high levels of employment and real income which, in accordance with the Articles of Agreement establishing the IMF, are primary objectives of economic policy.

While the IMF (1987:1) makes the point that the conception and structure of IMF-supported adjustment programmes have gradually evolved and expanded over time, this chapter has shown that the core of the IMF theoretical framework has remained largely unchanged since the late 1950s. If prices are taken as given, the exchange rate is assumed not to change and imports are a function of nominal income, the financial programming model is actually identical to the Polak model.

Furthermore, the financial programming model remains static, and it does not take account of uncertainty and expectations. Similarly, the model fails to incorporate many of the more recent developments in macroeconomic theory, including issues related to the intertemporal nature of the current account, the role of risk and self-insurance in portfolio choices, the role of time consistency and pre-commitments in economic policy, the economics of contracts and reputation, the economics of equilibrium real exchange rates, the 'Lucas rational expectations critique' and the theory of speculative attacks and de-valuation crises.[46]

It was a stated objective of Polak to keep his model simple, and it is an advantage that the IMF framework uses monetary data, which are generally up to date, and that the policy implications concern variables over which the government would appear to have at least some degree of control. Furthermore, the above-mentioned developments in mainstream theory are on the whole very abstract and difficult to introduce into the IMF policy-making framework at operational levels. Thus, they have been of no practical use so far. Nevertheless, simplicity in combination with data of often poor quality and elegant programming techniques can be deceptive, as the underlying causal factors are much more complex than it appears from the model.

The IMF is not monetarist in the strict sense of the word and does not see balance of payments and inflation as purely monetary phenomena. On the other hand, the IMF model is monetary, and it is based on the critical assumption that real output is exogenously determined. The IMF model is internally consistent, but it explains no real variables. Neither production functions nor sectoral articulation are present. The productive capacity of the economy is assumed fixed, output variation is ignored, and the impact of credit controls (that is, how monetary variables interact with real variables) is not specified.

Rather, IMF conclusions on how domestic credit restraint affects monetary targets are based on an assumed stability in the demand for money function, together with the even more critical assumption that changes in domestic credit changes international reserves only. The Polak model cannot be used to investigate supply-side issues, an aspect which has so far led the IMF to focus particularly on demand restraint in attempts to establish macroeconomic balances in an orderly manner.

Yet, output depends on a range of variables, and working capital provided by the monetary system is an essential component of the production process. A credit squeeze may affect output as well as demand and absorption. This is highlighted by the relative insignificance of consumer credit in sub-Saharan Africa and the fact that adjustment programmes based on the IMF model are vulnerable to forecasting errors. Given the widely-reported tendency of the IMF to underestimate inflation, this implies that the credit squeeze may become even more counter-productive than the use of credit ceilings *per se* need imply.

If the burden of credit adjustment falls solely on the public sector, it could be argued that there may be little impact on output, but the underlying crowding out hypothesis must be subjected to empirical testing under the particular circumstances of the adjusting country before the IMF policy conclusions become convincing. It is, in this regard, not altogether clear that government expenditures are as easy to control in sub-Saharan Africa as the IMF model seems to imply. It may in practice be difficult to reduce the budget deficit.

Limiting demand may also by itself bring about lower domestic production rather than reduced absorption in the absence of effective policies to counteract the contractionary impact of stabilization measures. A devaluation may eventually help through expenditure-switching, but this policy measure is bound to take at best some time to have a positive impact on production as already discussed in Chapter 2, and will in the short run contribute to inflationary pressures. The consistency of economic policies with overall objectives must be carefully analysed rather than assumed. Also the possibility of 'overkill' remains a critical issue.

The IMF tends to be more optimistic as regards price elasticities than seems warranted in the sub-Saharan African context, and prices are in the IMF model assumed to be determined by the 'law of one price' for traded goods, and non-traded goods prices are established from the demand-side in a flexible market-clearing and perfect competition manner. Mark-up pricing and rigid wages are not even considered as possibilities. Consequently, no account is taken in the model of structural constraints, widespread fragmentation and severe inflexibilities, which are important given the relatively short-time horizon of the IMF programmes.

Polak (1957) as well as IMF (1987) makes it clear that the IMF is fully aware that the velocity of money is not constant at all times, and that action on domestic credit may have an effect on interest rates, consumption-savings decisions, prices and the exchange rate and not just on the level of international reserves. Dynamics and lags are in fact explicitly discussed and can in practice be handled through forecasting and estimations of the basic equations referred to above. It is even argued (IMF 1987:13) that, in the actual formulation of Fund-supported programmes, the implications of policies for both output and the price level are 'carefully analysed'. This statement is, however, contentious.

IMF missions to sub-Saharan African countries do not seem to have adapted their approach significantly in response to diverse economic situations.[47] The IMF may recognize the need for supply-side actions and structural reforms, but these measures are seen as subsequent steps outside the purview of the IMF. The above reservations, including the possible feedback among real income, prices and the monetary sector have, for sure, not led to any theoretical redesign of the operational IMF model, within which the full employment, supply-determined output and flex-price assumptions are maintained.

The monetary model of the IMF has led many IMF staff to identifying policy failure in the form of excessive expansion of the money supply (that is, domestic credit expansion plus foreign credit) over money demand as the key mover (or cause) behind external and internal domestic economic imbalances. The nature of economic shocks may vary, however, and in the case of sub-Saharan Africa, it is loss of import capacity and reduction of supply and not overheating of demand, which has been predominant during the 1980s. External shocks have, as already pointed out in Chapter 1, made sound macroeconomic management exceedingly difficult. The IMF approach was originally intended to deal with temporary crises, but it is by now obvious that the African crisis is of a more permanent nature. All this points to the need for supply expansion and growth rather than demand contraction as the basic approach.

4

GROWTH PROGRAMMING
AND ADJUSTMENT

The theoretical core of the Revised Minimum Standard Model
(RMSM), which is the most widely-used economy-wide numerical
programming model within the World Bank,[1] is very different in
approach from that of the 'financial programming' undertaken by the
IMF. In the World Bank model, which is a variant of the two-gap
growth model (or the Harrod-Domar model for the open economy),
the financing needs for developmental purposes are in focus together
with 'real' variables and relationships.

The RMSM relates investment, imports and savings with output or
disposable income, and the World Bank emphasizes growth and
supply-side issues in attempts to establish economic balances in an
orderly manner. The World Bank approach therefore involves 'grapp-
ling' more directly with micro- and macroeconomic structural and
institutional issues, and World Bank imposed conditionality has consequently tended to be more detailed than that of the IMF. It is for
this reason that the World Bank has in some cases been perceived by
African governments and policy-makers as even more intrusive than
the IMF.

The World Bank was, as mentioned in Chapter 3, established at the
Bretton Woods Conference in 1944 together with the IMF. Objectives
were in the very beginning geared towards the reconstruction of
post-war Western Europe. As soon as this region achieved a degree
of economic self-sufficiency, attention turned, however, to the longer-
term task of financing economic growth and social development in
the developing countries, mainly in the form of specific investment
projects.

The World Bank is the major multilateral agency for channelling
financial resources to the developing countries and is basically an
investment bank. While the IMF is relatively small, the structure of

the World Bank is complex, including a number of affiliates such as the International Development Association (IDA).[2] The range of expertise of its 6,500 staff members goes well beyond the narrow focus on economists and financial specialists, characteristic of the IMF. The Bank is owned by its 155 member countries with equity shares valued in June 1990 at little more than US $125 billion.[3]

The IBRD obtains the larger share of its funds by market borrowing through the issue of bonds, but other funds are also available as some 7 per cent of capital subscriptions had actually been paid in 1991. The IDA is largely financed by grants from donor countries. The World Bank is therefore a major borrower in world capital markets, and since it is backed by the industrialized countries it has been able to maintain the triple A rating. This implies that the Bank is able to obtain loans at low rates of interest, which in turn makes it possible to extend loans to credit-worthy developing countries at favourable terms.[4] Besides financial assistance, the World Bank also extends technical assistance, both in the form of general policy advice and in connection with the implementation of specific projects.

The policies of the World Bank, its mode of operation and the composition of its projects, have changed over the years, reflecting developments in the world economy at large, the shifting priorities of its member governments, the accumulated growth experience in the developing countries and the evolution in development thinking and theory.[5] After the successful reconstruction of Western Europe, the World Bank in its second decennium mainly financed infrastructural projects such as roads and harbours in developing countries, and loan disbursements grew in a relatively steady manner.

The 1970s were a period of rapid expansion with significant growth in World Bank disbursements in real terms based on a policy agenda of redistribution with growth, poverty alleviation and the provision of basic needs such as employment, housing, education and health services. Yet, the dominant mode of operation remained the project loan, where funds are made available for specific capital investments in accordance with the well defined 'project cycle' of identification, preparation, implementation and evaluation, in which cost-benefit analysis has played a major role in the analysis and appraisal of projects.[6]

Nevertheless, the range of activities of the World Bank is much broader than its lending operations, and the overall economic performance of its clients has always been an important subject in World Bank work.[7] Macroeconomic and sectoral studies are a regular feature, and the World Bank has a widely-recognized analytic capacity in the field of development planning and policy analysis.[8] The wider economic environment has important implications for the degree of success of discrete development projects. The changes in the world economy during the turbulent years of the 1970s and the increasing economic difficulties of the developing countries led the World Bank to recognize that it could not continue relying exclusively on the project mode of operation in its lending activities.

The prospects of a deteriorating economic environment suggested that the Bank would find it increasingly difficult to identify sufficient sound projects, undermining the rationale behind its operations and thus threaten its very existence.[9] As a consequence, non-project structural adjustment lending was initiated and policy dialogue and conditionality moved to the centre of attention, although project-lending continues to be the major channel of lending. In fact, ceilings of 25 per cent in the case of IBRD, and 24–28 per cent for IDA, effectively limit the amount of resources which the World Bank can extend for adjustment purposes.

The reorientation of the lending activities of the World Bank into general balance-of-payments support has, together with the changes in the international monetary system and the role of the IMF, contributed to blurring the original well-defined division of labour between the two Bretton Woods institutions. The uncertainty has created considerable tension in the past, and friction remains.[10] Improved IMF/World Bank co-ordination is now pursued in the context of preparing the policy framework papers (PFPs), the fielding of joint missions, and so on, and loan conditions of the two institutions are also generally in line with each other in formal agreements.[11] Yet, the PFPs have often been less than satisfactory, loaded with an excess of unrealistic statements, and the closer co-ordination and collaboration of the IMF and the World Bank at operational level is bound to continue creating difficulties. This underlines the need for exploring their different theoretical approaches to adjustment.

ACCOUNTING FRAMEWORK

It may be recalled from Chapter 3 that the 'empty framework' of the IMF financial programming model concentrates on monetary variables, and four key national accounts identities were listed on page 60. The overall national balance identity, stating that gross domestic product at market prices (Y) can be expressed as the sum of domestic consumption (C), and investment (I) plus exports (X) and minus imports (Z), also appears in the World Bank framework. However, contrary to the IMF approach, where the balance of payments, monetary and fiscal accounts were subsequently added, focus in the Bank model is on the resource gaps in the economy.

Thus, the two additional identities included by the World Bank are the identities discussed on pages 43–5 on savings and investment. Following Addison (1989:2), the basic identities in the 'empty' Bank framework are the following in their aggregated form, noting that Addison ignores interest payments (INP) and net transfers (NTR):[12]

- production-expenditure balance: $Y = C + I + X - Z$
- income-savings balance: $Y = C + S$
- savings-and trade gaps: $I - S = Z - X$

Income is used for consumption or savings, and it is clear that investment (I) must come out of either domestic savings (S) or a negative resource (trade) balance *vis-à-vis* the foreign sector.

In other words, if domestic savings are inadequate to realize a targeted level of investment, imports (Z) must be larger than exports (X). This implies that foreign real resources must be made available for use in the domestic economy. If international reserves are limited, external financial borrowing is called for. This is highlighted by equation 2.10, which stated that $S - I = \Delta NFA + \Delta R$, and $- \Delta NFA$ is, as already noted on page 51, equivalent to the additional foreign borrowing by the private and public sectors (that is, ΔNFB).

GROWTH AND RESOURCE GAP MODELS

The study of the process of growth has been central to the analysis of development.[13] One is reminded by Lewis (1954:155) that

the central problem in the theory of economic development is to understand the process by which a community which was previously saving and investing 4 or 5 per cent of its national income or less converts itself to an economy where voluntary savings are much higher.

This focus on rapid capital accumulation, characteristic for the early decades of work within the field of development economics, meant that the aggregate growth theory developed by Harrod (1939) and Domar (1946) became a natural first building block in the World Bank approach to economic development.

In a closed economy, real output y is equal to $C + I$ and equilibrium in the final goods market requires that planned investment (I) is equal to planned savings (S). Assuming that S is a stable share (s) of real income:

$$I = sy \qquad (4.1)$$

As I is equal to ΔK (where K is the capital stock), it follows by dividing with K that the growth rate of the capital stock ($g = \Delta K / K$) is equal to the savings rate (s) divided by the capital-output ratio ($k = K/y$). Assuming k is constant (determined historically or by technological factors), the growth in real output ($\Delta y/y$) will be the same as growth in the capital stock. Therefore:[14]

$$g = \frac{\Delta K}{K} = \frac{\Delta y}{y} = \frac{s}{k} \qquad (4.2)$$

Equation 4.2 is a simplified version of the Harrod-Domar equation, stating that the rate of growth is determined jointly by the savings rate and the capital-output ratio. It puts focus on capital accumulation as the key constraint on development.[15] In order to grow, economies must save and invest a certain share of real output y. The more that is saved the more can be invested and the larger the growth rate will be. The actual rate also depends, of course, on the productivity of capital, that is, the inverse of k.

It follows that the Harrod-Domar equation 4.2 can be used ('passively') to determine the rate of output growth based on the available level of savings and investments. But it can also be used as a planning tool to establish how much savings and investment is required to raise the rate of growth and attain a certain desired target. A 'savings gap' is said to exist when domestic savings are lower than the investment required to achieve the output growth target.[16] As $\Delta y/y = \Delta K/K$ and $\Delta K = I$, it follows that a targeted increase in real output Δy^* can be expressed in the following way:

$$\Delta y^* = \frac{I}{k} \qquad (4.3)$$

Once Δy^* is fixed it follows that y is determined as well, since $y = y_{-1} + \Delta y^*$. Using this, together with $S - I = \Delta NFA + \Delta R$ and $- \Delta NFA = \Delta NFB$, establishes the expression in equation 4.4 for the additional foreign borrowing needed to close a 'savings gap'. The expression takes due account of the savings rate of the economy and any restrictions on changes in international reserves. It can be seen that ΔNFB is a function of predetermined or targeted variables together with the parameters k and s, which are assumed known.

$$\Delta NFB = k\Delta y^* - sy + \Delta R = (\Delta R - sy_{-1}) + (k - s)\Delta y^* \quad (4.4)$$

The savings constraint approach was fundamental in early World Bank work on the post-war reconstruction of Western Europe and provided, in fact, the main theoretical rationale for the massive American capital injection into Europe under the Marshall Plan. The early approach to development in developing countries was built on much the same lines of thought with foreign capital as a 'gap-filler' or supplement to national savings. This implies that no difference was assumed to exist in the effect on growth between an increase in savings and a similar increase in foreign capital inflows.

A second theoretical building block was added in the 1960s with the development of the two-gap models.[17] These fix-price models include the possibility of a savings constraint, but in addition a lack of foreign exchange may act as a separate and independent constraint on economic growth. The rationale behind this innovation was that developing countries may need foreign exchange not only to supplement domestic savings (which in the closed economy model sets the investment limit), but also to finance imports.

Rapid growth presupposes the availability of capital and intermediate goods, and in a poor country, such goods (for which it is assumed that no domestic substitutes exist) will have to be imported. A stable relationship links imports with real output, expressed as $Z = my$, where m is the propensity to import. More complex functions can be justified and specified with different import propensities for imported capital goods and consumer goods for which no local substitutes exist. A common specification is $Z = m_1 I + m_2 y$.

At the heart of the two-gap model one finds a hypothesis of an economy characterized by structural rigidities which is, as already shown, a relevant starting point in relation to analyses of the sub-Saharan economies. Those who make decisions over savings, investment, exports and imports are different people. In addition, the existing economic structure may make it impossible for the economy to provide, at least in the short- to medium-run, the composition of output that is required to realize the growth target. The higher the target and the slower the reallocation of resources, the more likely it is that bottle-necks will appear.

If the feasible growth of exports (X), international reserves (R) and access to additional foreign exchange (ΔF) are limited,[18] there is no guarantee that the *ex ante* capital inflow implied by the 'savings gap' will automatically correspond to the difference between the necessary level of imports (determined by the productive system and the composition of consumer demand) and the feasible export level. That is, a 'foreign exchange (or trade) gap' may exist.

Provided savings and foreign exchange (or exports) cannot substitute each other, the two gaps can be binding independently. When the 'trade gap' binds, shortages of imported goods make it impossible for the economy to transform all potential savings into investment. In such cases, additional savings are no guarantee for growth. The 'savings' and 'trade' gaps are, of course, identical *ex post* as the necessary adjustments in macroeconomic variables will take place one way or the other.

The additional foreign borrowing by the private and public sectors needed to close the 'trade gap' can, with due account for any restrictions on changes in international reserves, be estimated in much the same way as the 'savings gap'. Using for illustrative purposes $Z = m_1 I + m_2 y$ as the specification for imports, and ignoring INP and NTR for the time being, $\Delta NFA + \Delta R = X - m_1 I - m_2 y$ (or $\Delta NFB = m_1 I + m_2 y - X + \Delta R$). In addition, equation 4.3 implies that $I = k\,\Delta y^*$. Therefore:

$$\Delta NFB = m_1 k \Delta y^* + m_2 y - X + \Delta R$$

$$= (\Delta R - X + m_2 y_{-1}) + (m_1 k + m_2) \Delta y^* \quad (4.5)$$

Equations 4.4 and 4.5 reflect two different relationships between the targeted increase in real output and the additional borrowing needed to close the 'savings' and the 'trade' gap. The two gaps will only exceptionally be of the same size. In fact, in a (Δy^*, ΔNFB) space they could be represented by two straight lines with positive slopes ($k - s$) and ($m_1 k + m_2$).[19]

The issue of which constraint is most likely to be binding over what range will not be pursued further here. It is clear, however, that this has significant importance since the model implies that the productivity of foreign exchange can differ, depending on the binding constraint. The impact on growth of additional foreign exchange will for all realistic values of the parameters be greater if the 'trade gap' binds rather than the 'savings gap'.[20]

It can also be recalled from Chapter 3 that the change in net non-trade-related foreign currency inflows (denominated ΔF and in the IMF model assumed given exogenously) are not only a result of the possibility of increasing foreign debt by running down NFA (that is, increasing NFB). Net transfers and interest payments from the current account were also included in ΔF. In actual programming this must be taken into account. In addition, while exports can for simplicity be assumed exogenously determined, government policy may have some influence. Hence, the export level may have to be specified as, for example, $X_t = X_0 (1 + \varepsilon)^t$, where ε is a parameter summarizing the effect of government policy on exports and t is time.

The introduction of the trade in addition to the savings gap is but one of many possible structural constraints or variables which could be included explicitly in the analysis. Actually, Chenery and Strout (1966:681) state:

> The impact of external resources on the growth of an economy can be judged by their contribution to the mobilization and allocation of all productive resources. Three types of resources should be distinguished: (i) the supply of skills and organizational ability; (ii) the supply of domestic savings; and (iii) the supply of imported commodities and services.

That is, in the original Chenery and Strout model, not only the savings and foreign exchange constraints, but also the various variables which determine the absorptive capacity of the aid-receiving economy were considered.

Chenery and Strout cannot be held responsible for all of the applications of their theoretical model, but the savings and foreign exchange constraints have been the crucial constraints in the World Bank RMSM. That is, point (i) in the Chenery and Strout list of three has 'fallen out'. Also, structuralist economists at the Economic Commission for Latin America (ECLA), whose contributions will be reviewed in Chapter 6, have assigned primary importance to shortage of foreign exchange, perceived as a factor of 'strangulation' in the development process.

REVISED MINIMUM STANDARD MODEL

The Revised Minimum Standard Model (RMSM) was originally constructed in the early 1970s, after Chenery joined the World Bank as Chief Economist, to ensure a consistent approach to World Bank projections. The primary purpose was similar to that of the two-gap model, that is, to show what levels of investment, imports and external borrowing will be required for a targeted real output. The number of variables was deliberately minimized, partly because of the generally poor quality of data in developing countries, partly to allow the model to be easily adapted to particular country circumstances. As the RMSM model stands today, however, it is not all that limited in size. It contains some 430 variables,[21] but a basic core can be identified,[22] using the macroeconomic accounting framework in Chapter 2, together with the additional notation introduced in Chapter 3.

Real output growth is a targeted variable in the RMSM, so Δy^* is set by the government. The incremental capital-output ratio (ICOR) or k links output growth and investment as in the Harrod–Domar specification. It is also assumed that exports are determined exogenously, independent of actual output y. The import function can, as already mentioned, be specified in various ways depending on what 'drives' the need for imports, and the RMSM actually includes several import categories.[23] In what follows, to simplify the exposition it will be assumed that imports are a stable function of actual output, so $Z = my$ where m is the marginal (and average) propensity to import. Finally, consumption (or savings) is determined as a residual from the national accounting identity $y = C + I + X - Z$.

With the above introductory comments, the theoretical core of the RMSM model is complete and can be set out as follows in the form of four equations:[24]

$$\Delta y = \Delta y^* \tag{4.6}$$

That is, $y = y^* = y_{-1} + \Delta y^*$. This highlights that the RMSM postulates full use of available capacity, that is, actual output is equal to potential output.

$$I = k\,\Delta y^* \tag{4.7}$$

$$X = \overline{X} \tag{4.8}$$

$$Z = my \tag{4.9}$$

The RMSM model is in actual practice closed by suppressing the 'savings gap' and calculating C (or C_p, assuming C_g is controlled by government) from the overall national income account balance.[25] This amounts, in fact, to running the model as a one-gap (trade) model.

Therefore:

$$C = y - I - \overline{X} + Z$$

It may, for obvious reasons, be unrealistic to assume that consumption can be determined in the above manner. It is totally devoid of behavioural insight into the consumption/savings processes, and the residual value of C may make neither economic nor political sense.

Another approach where the 'trade gap' is suppressed is suggested by Khan, Montiel and Haque (1986 and 1990). They specify private consumption endogenously as $C_p = (1 - s)(y - T)$, where $y - T$ is disposable real income, and treat C_g as an exogenous policy instrument along with T (or better, treating the fiscal deficit as a policy variable). To close the model, they designate the change in international reserves (ΔR) as an additional target variable (ΔR^*) and let government set ΔF (that is, the foreign capital inflow consisting of both foreign borrowing, from the capital account, and interest payments and net transfers from the current account) at the level required to establish overall balance.

Therefore, their model specification continues from equation 4.9 as follows:

$$C_p = (1 - s)(y - T) \tag{4.10}$$

$$C = (C_p + C_g) = y - I - \overline{X} + Z \tag{4.11}$$

$$\Delta R = \Delta R^* \tag{4.12}$$

And the closure mechanism implies:

$$\Delta F = Z - \overline{X} + \Delta R^*$$

Suppressing the 'trade gap' in the above manner, and assuming that ΔF is controlled by government rather than being a constraint, is also questionable – a reality of which African policy-makers have become painstakingly aware during the 1980s as already pointed out in Chapter 1.

The RMSM was originally designed as a two-gap structural model in which both the trade and the savings gap might be binding, so suppressing either one of these constraints (without at least specifying the process by which this takes place) is clearly unsatisfactory. To avoid the problem of overdetermination caused by the introduction of a restriction on ΔF, the World Bank has experimented with changes in the parameters (that is, k, s and m) to obtain consistent projections.

The two-gap nature of the model can also be maintained by introducing additional policy variables. For the reasons discussed in Chapter 2, the exchange rate is a candidate, and action in this field is a common (expenditure-switching) policy instrument in World-Bank-supported structural adjustment packages.[26] One of the several possible ways of completing the model is therefore to let ΔF be determined by exogenous factors beyond government control (so $\Delta F = \Delta \overline{F}$); modify the import function 4.9 so Z becomes dependent upon e (for example, by introducing an exchange rate sensitive element ze, where z is the effect on imports of changing the exchange rate);[27] and use the balance-of-payments identity. That is:

$$\Delta F = \Delta \overline{F} \qquad (4.13)$$

$$Z = my - ze \qquad ('4.9')$$

$$\Delta R^* = \overline{X} - Z + \Delta \overline{F} \qquad (4.14)$$

In this way the model is complete. Substituting equation '4.9' into 4.14, recalling that $y^* = y_{-1} + \Delta y^*$, and rearranging the following expression for ΔR^*, as a function of the output target, together with predetermined, exogenous and endogenous variables and the policy instrument e, appears:

$$\Delta R^* = \Delta \overline{F} - my^* + ze + \overline{X} \qquad (4.15)$$

This shows that given the output target, the balance-of-payments target can be attained by manipulation of the exchange rate e, whose equilibrium value can be determined by rearranging the equation. Similarly, by substituting into equation 4.11 and rearranging, the output target is given by:

$$\Delta y^* = \frac{1}{k - s - m} [(s + m)y_{-1} + (1 - s) T - C_g - \overline{X} - ze] \qquad (4.16)$$

This equation implies that taxes and public expenditures can be manipulated in such a way, that not only the balance-of-payments target (that is, ΔR^*) but also the output target Δy^*, can be realized.

T and C_g are not, however, independent policy variables. Once T is fixed, the value of C_g must be set at a level that satisfies equation 4.16.

The above extension of the RMSM will be convenient in Chapter 5 and shows that the core RMSM model can be expanded in a rather straightforward manner without impairing its two-gap nature. In other words, suppressing one or the other gap, as is usually done in practice, is not a theoretical necessity.

GROWTH PROGRAMMING IN PRACTICE

The actual use of the theoretical approach to growth programming summarized above depends in various critical ways on the country, the purpose and the issues of the analysis as well as the availability of data.[28] There is no clear-cut programming procedure as to how the World Bank RMSM approach is implemented in practice, and there is very little published material on this topic. A number of observations on the necessary steps in compiling a consistent projection for use in policy dialogue can, however, be made. They are synthesized in this section.

Any programming exercise starts by specifying the desired targets or objectives to be achieved by the adjustment programme. This implies that Δy^* must be set. There are, in principle, two ways of arriving at Δy^*. The first is to choose a target level of growth in real output (adequately disaggregated by sector), and subsequently determine the level of investment and external borrowing needed. The targeting of Δy^* could also be approached from the side of expectations relating to the availability of savings and foreign exchange and then, in turn, determine the feasible level of growth. In what follows, the first approach will be assumed. At the initial stage a balance-of-payments target (that is, ΔR^*) could also be specified, but this is left for later stages in line with the presentation of the RMSM seen on pages 86–90.

The second step in the growth programming exercise normally involves estimation of the marginal capital-output ratio (k) and the marginal propensity to import (m), together with a projection of exports, which must be set from outside the model. It is in practice tempting to be over-optimistic at this stage, and policy-makers' desire to avoid facing existing trade-offs have clearly influenced many of the analyses undertaken. However, for the projection to be meaningful, realism rather than wishful thinking is called for. This includes a careful assessment of past performance of the economy as well as informed judgements about the impact of policy measures included in the adjustment programme.

Before any conclusions are drawn, due account must be taken of an in-depth analysis of market demand for the particular products produced by the country under study and the effect of the policy package on the competitiveness of local producers. It should also be kept in mind that X can only increase more than real output growth, if it is possible to run down inventories or if consumption or investment can be relinquished.

The simple formulation of the RMSM leaves out many key variables, such as the degree of capacity utilization. In an elegant reappraisal of the two-gap model, Bacha (1984) emphasizes the restrictiveness of the assumed, but somewhat 'hidden', full-capacity assumption in gap models, and underlines the need to distinguish between potential and actual output. Effective demand problems may be part of the universe of open developing economies, which implies that a current account deficit may not always be due to a particular developing country 'living beyond its means'.

More specifically, setting k at a low level permits the attainment of a relatively high level of growth. But the implicit assumption made, that capacity utilization can and will in fact increase as a consequence of efficiency-seeking policies without supplementary investments, must be considered cautiously.

Parallel with the estimation of the parameters of the RMSM and the projection of X, the required level of the endogenous variables, that is, investment (I) and imports (Z), must be calculated. In this third programming step disaggregation is obviously called for. Investment could, for example, be disaggregated into three sectors (agriculture, industry and other sectors) but other possibilities, including regional disaggregation, exist, and imports must at least be divided into capital, intermediate and consumer goods.

On the above basis, the feasible level of consumption can in a fourth step be calculated from the national account balance. This may lead to a level which is unsustainable from an economic or political point of view. The savings rate, determined on the basis of historical data, can be used as an indicator of the feasibility of the projection developed in the above manner, but in the case of inconsistency, targets or policy instruments must be adjusted. To assess whether inconsistency prevails, an explicit consumption (or savings function) can be introduced into the model, specifying a minimum marginal consumption (or maximum marginal savings) relationship with disposable income. Disposable income can, for example, be expressed as $C_p = (1 - \bar{s})(y - T)$, where T is the level of taxes, assumed to be under the control of the government, and $\bar{s}$ is the maximum savings rate. The introduction of a separate consumption function implies, however, that the model becomes overdetermined, since C as a function of y may not correspond with the residual determined from the national accounting identity.

The problem of overdetermination is, in practice, solved by running through a series of iterations with feasible changes in the parameters of the model (that is, k, s and m), but Addison (1989:8) underlines that the World Bank usually assumes that the adjusting variable will be consumption-related imports. This is a highly questionable procedure in SSA where investment has taken considerable cuts during the crisis as explained in Chapter 1.

The above steps assume the exchange rate and terms of trade do not change, and that the projected real resource balance $(X - Z)$ can be financed without difficulty. The underlying assumption has been that foreign exchange inflows are not constrained in any way. This will rarely be so in practice. Thus, the balance of payments must be brought explicitly into the analysis in a fifth step.

Changes in the terms of trade are taken into account by recognizing the distinction between real output and income. It is also necessary to project all expected current account flows in addition to X and Z (that is, INP and NTR). It must finally be assessed whether the current account is consistent with stock changes in the capital account (that is, additional foreign borrowing) plus any target as regards the level of international reserves.

Accordingly, care must be exercised to distinguish changes, which are certain in the sense that they have been set in motion by events prior to the period under study, or whether they are foreseen to happen as a consequence of the policy measures on the drawing-board. It is, for example, common in SSA that adjustment programmes end up underfinanced as expectations have been too optimistic.

If access to foreign borrowing is insufficient to close the resource gap, there is need for adjusting the original projection. This might, within the expanded RMSM framework set out on pages 86–90, take place through adjustment in the exchange rate, but there is no guarantee that this measure will be sufficient (or strong enough) to bring about the desired balance. In a final step, the growth target (or the various parameters) may therefore have to be adjusted to levels which are consistent with the available amount of foreign exchange, and the whole procedure is run through again to ensure consistency.

DISCUSSION

It has become increasingly obvious during the past two decades that growth in GDP is not equivalent to development. Distributional goals came into focus during the 1970s, and environmental issues and concern about sustainability came in high on the agenda at the end of the 1980s, despite the generally free-market orientation of policy-making during this decade. It is, in other words, no longer contentious that 'development is *both a physical reality and a state of mind* in which society has, through the combination of social, economic, and institutional processes, secured the means of obtaining a better life'.[29]

While the multidimensional nature of the development process is now more widely recognized, growth remains an important means to increase the availability and widen the distribution of basic life-sustaining goods, raise levels of living and expand the range of economic and social choices available to society. There is no guarantee these objectives will automatically come about, but the need for growth sets the background against which the World Bank approach to adjustment in sub-Saharan Africa (and elsewhere) should be gauged.

The World Bank approach to structural adjustment in sub-Saharan Africa reflects the 'requirements' attitude towards economic development, which has been the basis for World Bank work since the institution was formed at the Bretton Woods Conference. The original theoretical underpinnings of this approach can be found in the Harrod–Domar growth models and the two-gap model of Chenery and Strout. Not only World Bank macroeconomic planning exercises, but also numerous development plans in sub-Saharan Africa as well as elsewhere have been built on this foundation during the past decades.

This chapter has reviewed the core version of the Revised Minimum Standard Model (RMSM), which remains the most prominent method of ensuring quantitative consistency in operational World Bank country economic projections.[30] The RMSM focuses on real, rather than monetary, variables, and it can be perceived as primarily a planning and thinking tool, yielding an estimate of the amount of investment and foreign borrowing needed to maintain a targeted real rate of output growth. Provided the resources necessary to fill the estimated gaps are supplied, growth is assumed to ensue automatically in accordance with the above theoretical foundation of the model.

However, various assessments suggest that the main contribution of past RMSM exercises is more related to facilitating communication and refining the intuition of analysts than to the numerical results of actual projections.[31] It certainly remains true that the process of data collection and reconciliation, together with discussion of the results, can help in demonstrating inconsistencies, provide an order of magnitude, allow the disentangling of simultaneous influences on policy choice, and be used to create proxy measures for variables, not easily observable but important for policy design.[32]

To achieve this kind of result and improve the policy dialogue between the World Bank on the one side, and a developing country on the other, accounting frameworks such as the one described in Chapter 2 will often be sufficient. Yet, the RMSM does carry the potential of bringing the dialogue a few steps further. While remaining simple and easy to use, it demonstrates that the link between savings and growth may not be perfect, and it has helped draw attention to crucial imbalances and structural bottle-necks, which can lead to the under-utilization of domestic factors of production.

Structural change in demand and supply can be handled within the model when adequately disaggregated. Alternative scenarios, providing useful insights into the medium- and long-term growth perspectives of the economy in question, can be constructed without difficulty through the manipulation of the various parameters and exogenous variables of the model. The amount of investment can be controlled through the capital-output relationship, imports can be modified through the import elasticities underlying the propensities to import, and exports can similarly be manipulated from outside the model. Consumption and savings constraints can be handled using maximum and minimum savings and consumption propensities. The model can finally accommodate a variety of disaggregations and can be modified to suit particular country circumstances. In conclusion, the RMSM has been, and continues to be, an important point of departure in analytic work related to the design of structural adjustment programmes.

In spite of attractive characteristics, the two-gap approach and the RMSM model are based on a number of restrictive assumptions. A first and important difficulty with the two-gap model is that it is, in practice, difficult to identify the binding constraint. Still, to estimate savings and/or import functions from historical data, a judgement must be made about which constraint was binding over the relevant time period. A similar assessment is required for the determination of the feasible growth path.[33] Such judgements, which can hardly avoid being subjective, will therefore have a decisive influence on the policy conclusions drawn on the basis of the RMSM.

A second point of weakness is that the World Bank framework has very few behavioural relationships and lacks relative prices and other key reform variables already discussed in Chapter 2. The RMSM does not provide a quantitative structure linking economic policy actions with macroeconomic performance. Consequently, it cannot provide the detailed resource allocation analyses needed in the design and appraisal of structural adjustment packages. The planner can, in the formulation of Addison (1989:25), 'describe the desired changes and trends, but he or she cannot be sure, that these will be consistent with the existing arrangement of price and other incentives in the economy'.

Hence, the planner cannot indicate how prices and policies should be changed, and the implication is, *inter alia*, that all aspects of the growth and development process related with allocative efficiency of domestic resource use cannot be handled within the model. The debate on X-inefficiency, 'rent-seeking' and directly-unproductive activities (DUP), which has been at the centre of much of the policy debate during the 1980s, fall largely outside the formalized World Bank framework.[34] Furthermore, it is difficult to establish meaningful progress indicators in reform programmes because so little can be said about the quantitative impact of policy measures.

Some of the operational shortcomings of the RMSM were precipitated in the theoretical literature on the two-gap model, which appeared after its formulation in the early 1960s. Many, but by no means all, of the critical contributions have come from economists, who have since supported the 'neo-classical counter-revolution' in development theory and policy-making.[35] The central conclusions of the two-gap analysis are that the productivity of foreign exchange may differ, depending on the nature of the binding constraint, and that the foreign exchange constraint is caused by the inflexible nature of the economy, which can only be overcome in the course of the development process. These conclusions were not accepted by the neo-classical school.

The absence of relative prices and the perception of an economy characterized by structural rigidities came in for severe attack. It was argued that there are possibilities for substitution in production and consumption, and that the export pessimism implied in setting X exogenously and independent of the level of real output and economic policy is unwarranted. Also the proposition of the two-gap model that the import content of current production cannot be reduced was refuted, and it was claimed that the parameters of the model (k, m and s) are not sufficiently stable to allow meaningful policy conclusions. In the neo-classical view, domestic savings can substitute foreign savings, and 'allowing' prices (including the exchange rate) to operate in a flexible manner 'removes' the foreign exchange gap as an independent constraint. Inflexibilities are not inherent but a consequence of ill-conceived development strategies and an inadequate exchange rate policy that twist incentives in favour of imported goods and against exports.

The above set of criticisms have led some IMF economists, such as Guitián (in Corbo, Goldstein and Khan 1987:70–1), to claim that there is really no meaningful concept of a foreign exchange constraint, except in the sense of an intertemporal constraint. In other words, an adjustment strategy that makes use of foreign resources basically transfers and adds the imbalances from one period to the next, until no more financing is available. This view can be challenged.[36] Given the current financial position in many African countries, economic reforms alone cannot go very far in restoring growth. Additional finance in the initial years of a reform process are an essential component of a strategy designed to restore long-term growth while maintaining consumption in the interim.[37] In other words, austerity may not be the right approach to adjustment as suggested by the above IMF view.

Firm conclusions relating to the above arguments, and on whether it is the foreign exchange or the savings constraint that is binding in African countries, must in the final analysis rest on empirical testing. Few generally valid results come out of the existing evidence. Nevertheless, the series of studies summarized in Taylor (1988) make it justified to characterize many of the sub-Saharan African economies as externally strangled.[38] The insights of the two-gap model therefore retains analytic relevance.

The neo-classical inspired critique does not, however, stand alone.[39] The procedure used in gap forecasting is often much too mechanistic, relying on a comparative static approach of balancing required and available resources. A certain risk, that modelling is done for modelling's sake, also exists. Some exercises have been poorly specified and are at best costly and irrelevant, and at worst, costly and misleading.[40] 'Gap-filling' is also constrained by the need to fix the size of the parameters of the model. In this way not only important policy variables, but also structural and institutional factors, may be overlooked.

Development implies a need for transformation of economic structures and institutions, but the parameters of the two-gap model are constant. Similarly, within the two-gap framework it will always be rational and profitable to borrow, when the economy is short of foreign exchange. However, the amount of foreign exchange a particular country can use productively, depends on a series of economic and institutional characteristics, not explicitly considered. The absorptive capacity, discussed literally by Chenery and Strout, is one of these. Closing the foreign exchange gap through borrowing and aid does not necessarily carry with it the transfer of technology, which lies at the very core of the growth process.

More specifically, the two-gap model assumes a foreign exchange inflow will always lead to increased investment and more intensive utilization of existing capacity, with subsequent recovery in production and an increase in the growth rate (g). This generates additional domestic savings, and the development process eventually becomes self-sustaining. Foreign borrowing, which helped start this process, is perceived as transitory in nature. The additional domestic savings generated will make it possible, at some future date, to revert the capital flow, so accumulated debt is repaid. There are, however, several ways in which this process may not materialize as expected or projected on the basis of the two-gap model.

First, investment may not be profitable, so actual as opposed to potential output does not grow. Second, the rate of capacity utilization is not unrelated with monetary variables. Inflation can become a problem as capacity utilization increases, which will lead to a deterioration in international competitiveness, unless an appropriate exchange rate policy is followed. However, e is not part of the basic RMSM framework.[41] Third, foreign currency inflows may not be unrelated with domestic savings/consumption decisions. If the additional foreign currency inflow induces increased consumption, the trade-off between investment and consumption can lead to a propensity to invest of foreign capital, which is well below one. This undermines the RMSM projection of increased growth.

Fourth, the elimination of debt and a process of self-sustaining growth assumes both that sufficient production can be exported, and that growth in domestic savings will eventually be higher than the sum of the original loan and interest payments on accumulated debt. In other words, the marginal savings rate must be larger than the average rate, so an increasing share of additional output generated can be channelled to productive investment and savings, to sustain growth and repay debt. External factors such as lagging export demand and substantially-increased international interest rates can, as in SSA, play havoc with this process, putting into doubt the usefulness of non-concessional foreign inflows as a temporary bridge.

It follows from the above discussion that mainstream neo-classical critiques have centred around the alleged non-existence of the foreign exchange constraint. This view is difficult to accept under SSA circumstances. It is more productive to focus on the proposition that closing the savings and trade gaps (which within the two-gap model appears as both a necessary and sufficient condition for sustained growth) is not enough. For example, the effect of foreign borrowing and aid can differ considerably, depending on the circumstances of the particular case and the use made of such assistance.

There is, finally, reason to point out that distributional concerns are absent from the two-gap model, as was also the case in the financial programming framework of the IMF. The political and social consequences of World-Bank-supported adjustment policies cannot be analysed within the present RMSM framework.

5

GROWTH-ORIENTED ADJUSTMENT – AN IMF/WORLD BANK SYNTHESIS?

After nearly a decade of trying to adjust their economies to the deficiencies in domestic policy-making and the severe exogenous shocks reviewed in Chapter 1, the majority of sub-Saharan African countries have yet to return to the standards of living realized more than ten years ago. Consequently, the 1980s can be characterized as 'a lost decade for development'.[1] At the same time, the 1980s witnessed a significant increase in the importance and influence of the World Bank and the IMF on macroeconomic policy formulation and implementation in sub-Saharan Africa.

Initially, the policy stand of the Bretton Woods institutions was very restricted and focused exclusively on stabilization. The above distressing background and a decade of intense debate have implied that growth aspects of adjustment programmes are now receiving increasing attention.[2] Growth is accepted as an indispensable component of an adjustment strategy aiming at reversing the declining trend in economic performance. 'Growth-oriented adjustment' has become a concept, which represents, at least to some extent, a measure of agreement on a solution to the problems of sub-Saharan Africa.[3]

The nature of the African crisis and the experiences gained have, as pointed out in Chapter 3, led to the development of new IMF financial facilities. Also the traditional World Bank focus on project-lending has been changing with the introduction of structural and sectoral adjustment loans. These innovations, together with the changes in the international financial and economic environment, and in the respective roles of the two Bretton Woods institutions, underline the need for greater co-ordination of IMF and World Bank policy advice.

On the other hand, increased collaboration is bound to create difficulties at operational levels as it brings out into the open the differences and deficiencies in the financial programming and revised minimum standard modelling frameworks used by, respectively, IMF and World Bank staff. Consequently, the lack of a common integrated analytical framework, incorporating the most important macroeconomic policy instruments, existing development constraints and standard adjustment targets, has come into focus within the two institutions as well as within the development community at large.

There are several empirical models available that attempt to capture the relationships among the main instruments, constraints and objectives of adjustment programmes.[4] These models tend, however, to be either too complicated or too country-specific to apply across countries. They have, with only rare exceptions, been formulated with reference to the countries of sub-Saharan Africa. They do not, in other words, represent a generalized perception of the underlying reality.

Consequently, Khan and Montiel (1989:280) point to a well-identified need when they argue for the development of an overall conceptual framework that can serve the respective analytic needs of the IMF and the World Bank, and at the same time be tailored to the circumstances and structural characteristics of individual countries. This is, in their view, by 'now clearly one of the main priorities of research on developing countries'. This chapter is devoted to reviewing and assessing the most recent 'insider' proposal for integrating the IMF and World Bank methodologies, formalized by a group of researchers who have, over the past decade, occupied positions in the research departments of both institutions.[5]

A CONCEPTUAL FRAMEWORK

The underlying principle of the Khan, Montiel and Haque (1986 and 1990) and Khan and Montiel (1989) proposal for a common IMF/World Bank conceptual model is in reality very simple. They basically merge the financial programming and the RMSM models into one framework. Given the IMF attention to financial variables and the World Bank focus on real variables, the resulting 'hybrid' model turns out to be internally consistent.

The merged model contains a growth and a monetary building block, which are in accordance with RMSM and financial programming lines of thinking, respectively. These two components jointly determine the growth rate, the balance of payments and domestic prices. The revised model links three of the major objectives of most adjustment programmes directly to a variety of economic policies, behavioural parameters and exogenous variables, including *inter alia* the availability of external financing.

The various components of the model are set out below using by now familiar notation and definitions. In addition, the macroeconomic accounting framework prese[…]·ed in Chapter 2 remains relevant to the analysis.[6] The economy in reference continues to be a small open economy with a fixed nominal exchange rate (e) and, in line with Khan, Montiel and Haque (1986 and 1990), the economy is seen as divided into three sectors: a monetary, an external and a price-output sector.

With reference to the monetary sector, the assumed stability of the relationship between the stock demand (M_d) for money and explanatory variables such as real income, expected inflation and the exchange and interest rates is maintained. For simplicity the specification used here assumes, as on pages 68–73, that money circulates at constant velocity (v). That is, the flow demand for money (ΔM_d) can be expressed as follows:

$$\Delta M_d v = \Delta Y \qquad (5.1)$$

The supply of money (M_s) is determined from the monetary balance set out on pages 50–4 as the sum of international reserves (R), held by the monetary system, plus domestic credit, extended to, respectively, the private sector (DC_p) and government (DC_g). The flow supply of money (ΔM_s) is therefore given by:

$$\Delta M_s = \Delta R + \Delta DC_p + \Delta DC_g \qquad (5.2)$$

The third characteristic of the monetary sector is the equilibrium condition ensuring balance between the flow demand and flow supply of money. That is:

$$\Delta M_d = \Delta M_s = \Delta M \qquad (5.3)$$

By substituting the expressions for the flow demand and flow supply of money into the equilibrium condition and solving for the change in reserves, the fundamental result of the monetary approach to the balance of payments (discussed on pages 64–8) appears. Given the flow demand of money, an increase in the rate of domestic credit expansion will be exactly matched by a deterioration in the balance of payments, so $\Delta R = \Delta M_d - \Delta DC$.[7]

101

The above monetary system is subsequently enlarged with an external sector component starting with the balance-of-payments identity in equation 2.12, recalling that $(INP - NTR) + \Delta NFA = - \Delta F$. Therefore:

$$\Delta R = X - Z + \Delta F \qquad (5.4)$$

Exports and the inflow of non-trade-related foreign exchange (representing changes in net foreign assets, interest payments and net transfers) are assumed exogenously determined. The foreign currency value of exports ($\Delta \tilde{X}$) and non-trade foreign exchange inflows ($\Delta \tilde{F}$) are given exogenously. This implies the local currency value of exports (X) and foreign exchange inflows (ΔF) depend on the exchange rate. In accordance with pages 68–73 the following expressions appear:[8]

$$X = \tilde{X} e_{-1} + \tilde{X} \Delta e \qquad (5.5)$$

$$\Delta F = \Delta \tilde{F} e_{-1} + \Delta \tilde{F} \Delta e \qquad (5.6)$$

Imports are assumed to depend on income and relative prices in a manner similar to that expressed in equations 3.26–3.28,[9] which as already noted in equation 3.34, implies that:

$$Z = Z_{-1} + \alpha_1 \Delta y + \alpha_2 \Delta P_d + (Z_{-1} - \alpha_2) \Delta e P_f \qquad (5.7)$$

The above specification of the external economic relations does not fully capture the importance attached to the exchange rate in many IMF/World Bank-supported adjustment programmes. In these, an active exchange rate policy plays a key role and is supposed to lead directly to both expenditure-switching and mobilization of additional capital inflows, as discussed in Chapter 2. The model could, as demonstrated by Khan and Montiel (1989:289), be improved by assuming that the foreign currency value of the overall trade balance (and not just imports) is a function of changes in the real exchange rate and income to take account of expenditure-switching. However, the lack of an adequate theory of capital flows is a stumbling block in trying to endogenize such flows.

The third and final component of the merged model is the price-output sector. Real output is derived from the Harrod–Domar equation 4.3, but the aggregate price level, to be defined shortly, is introduced explicitly to underline that nominal investment must be deflated.[10] Therefore:

$$\Delta y = \frac{1}{k} \frac{I}{(P_{-1} + \Delta P)} \qquad (5.8)$$

This specification of output growth is commonly used in planning exercises and empirical analyses of growth in developing countries. But equation 5.8 is admittedly rather restrictive. It assumes that actual growth is equal to potential growth due to the assumed full use of installed capacity, and does not allow for productivity changes. The effect of policies directed at increasing the efficiency in the use of productive resources is not captured, and similarly for the potential effects of demand changes.

Investment can be derived from the identities reviewed in Chapter 2. Equation 2.9 shows that $I = S - (X - Z)$. Furthermore, it follows from the definition of the balance of payments (equation 2.12), that the difference between exports and imports $(X - Z)$ is equal to $(INP - NTR) + \Delta NEA + \Delta R$ (or $\Delta R - \Delta F$ as in equation 5.4). In accordance with equation 2.14, ΔR is equal to $\Delta M - \Delta DC$. Therefore, $I = I_p + I_g = S_p + S_g + \Delta F - \Delta M + \Delta DC$.

The above expression could be further detailed by introducing the budget constraints of the private and public sector (that is, equations 2.1 and 2.2), which provide expressions for S_p and S_g. To simplify the presentation, it is assumed that private disposable income amounts to nominal income minus taxes (that is, $Y - T$ or $Y_{-1} + \Delta Y - T$), and that the fiscal balance of the public sector corresponds to taxes minus government consumption and public investment only (that is, $T - C_g - I_g$). Assuming finally that private savings can be specified as a function of disposable income, so $S_p = s(Y_{-1} + \Delta Y - T)$, I can be expressed in the following way:

$$I = s(Y_{-1} + \Delta Y - T) + (T - C_g) + \Delta F - \Delta R \qquad (5.9)$$

With real output determined by the level of investment and the capital-output ratio k, the change in nominal output can be specified as:[11]

$$\Delta Y = \Delta P y_{-1} + P_{-1} \Delta y + \Delta y \Delta P \qquad (5.10)$$

To complete the merged model the aggregate price level must be set. This can be done as on pages 68–73, where P was expressed as a weighted average of the market-determined, flex-price of domestic output (P_d) and the constant price of importables (P_f). The share of importables in the price index is denoted θ, implying that the share of domestic goods is $(1 - \theta)$. Therefore:[12]

$$\Delta P = (1 - \theta) \Delta P_d + \theta \Delta e P_f \qquad (5.11)$$

The merged model contains three targets (ΔR, ΔP_d and Δy), eight endogenous variables (ΔM_d, ΔM_s, ΔF, X, Z, I, ΔY and ΔP), three exogenous variables ($\Delta \widetilde{F}$, $\widetilde{X}$ and P_f), six parameters (v, α_1, α_2, k, s and θ), a number of predetermined variables (e_{-1}, Z_{-1}, P_{-1} and Y_{-1}) together with the policy instruments ΔDC, Δe, T and C_g.

Since there are eleven independent equations in the model, the three targets and eight endogenous variables can be determined as functions of parameters together with predetermined, exogenous and policy variables. Thus, their impact can be assessed. Similarly, with three targets established by the political process, the value of the policy variables leading to the realization of set targets can be calculated.[13] In the remainder of this chapter, focus is on the programming use and policy implications of the model.

POLICY ANALYSIS

When analysing the properties of the merged model, it is useful to start by recalling that the monetary component of the model implies $\Delta R = \Delta M_d - \Delta DC$. Furthermore, from the money demand equation 5.1 $\Delta M_d = (1/v) \Delta Y$. Therefore, $\Delta R = (1/v) \Delta Y - \Delta DC$. Substituting into this expression the breakdown of ΔY given by equation 5.10 and using as well the definition of the aggregate price level in equation 5.11 to obtain an expression containing the policy target variable ΔP_d it appears after some rearranging that:

$$\Delta R = \Delta P_d \frac{1}{v} (1 - \theta)(y_{-1} + \Delta y) + \frac{1}{v} \theta \Delta e P_f (y_{-1} + \Delta y)$$

$$+ \frac{1}{v} P_{-1} \Delta y - \Delta DC \qquad (5.12)$$

Equation 5.12 does not determine unique values for the two policy instruments, ΔDC and Δe. There are three targets and only two instruments. However, by substituting the external sector equations 5.5–5.7 into the balance-of-payments identity 5.4 ($\Delta R = X - Z + \Delta F$), and rearranging, the following additional expression for ΔR appears:

$$\Delta R = [(\widetilde{X} + \Delta \widetilde{F}) e_{-1} - Z_{-1}] - [\alpha_1 \Delta y + \alpha_2 \Delta P_d]$$
$$+ [\widetilde{X} + \Delta \widetilde{F} - (Z_{-1} - \alpha_2) P_f] \Delta e \qquad (5.13)$$

From equation 5.13 it is clear that, with Δy, ΔP_d and ΔR at targeted values, Δe is uniquely determined. Using this equilibrium value in equation 5.12 allows ΔDC to be determined. Furthermore, with Δe and ΔDC known, the value of the final policy instrument (that is, fiscal policy exercised through taxes T or public consumption C_g) can be found from equation 5.9.

Knowing ΔDC (and of course the targeted ΔR) implies that ΔM_s can be derived from equation 5.2. Given monetary equilibrium from equation 5.3 ($\Delta M_s = \Delta M_d = \Delta M$) and a constant velocity of money circulation, equation 5.1 determines ΔY. Knowing as well Δe (together with the targeted domestic price increase) allows ΔP to be determined from equation 5.11. Similarly, ΔF can be determined from equation 5.6. With Δy targeted and ΔP known, I is given by equation 5.8. After these preliminaries, T and C_g can be found from equation 5.9 since all other variables in this equation are known, and s is assumed constant.

In conclusion, once Δy, ΔR and ΔP_d have been targeted, the merged model can be used in its 'programming' mode to determine the values of the policy instruments, Δe, ΔDC and T together with C_g. The expressions for these three instruments, derived in the above manner can be stated as follows:

$$\Delta e = \frac{\Delta R - [(\widetilde{X} + \Delta \widetilde{F}) e_{-1} - Z_{-1}] + [\alpha_1 \Delta y + \alpha_2 \Delta P_d]}{[\widetilde{X} + \Delta \widetilde{F} - (Z_{-1} - \alpha_2)P_f]} \qquad (5.14)$$

$$\Delta DC = (y_{-1} + \Delta y)\left[\Delta P_d \frac{1}{v}(1-\theta) + \frac{1}{v}\theta \Delta eP_f\right] + \frac{1}{v}P_{-1}\Delta y - \Delta R \qquad (5.15)$$

$$C_g - T(1-s) = s(Y_{-1} + \Delta Y) + \Delta F - \Delta M + \Delta DC - k\Delta y(P_{-1} + \Delta P) \qquad (5.16)$$

The merged model can also be used for comparative-static analyses, where the impact of changes in selected policy instruments, the parameters and the exogenous variables on the target variables (that is, balance of payments, inflation and growth) is assessed. This can be done in an illustrative manner by condensing the model into two independent relationships between Δy and ΔP_d, corresponding to, respectively, the real (or growth) and the monetary components of the merged model.[14]

These two relationships can, under various assumptions such as the Marshall-Lerner condition, be drawn as, respectively, a positively (GG)- and a negatively (MM)-sloped line in the $(\Delta y, \Delta P_d)$ space. The intersection of the GG and the MM lines represents the overall macroeconomic equilibrium in the merged model. By considering how the GG and MM lines interact as a consequence of policy and parametric changes, their impact can be assessed in the common IS–LM manner.

Khan, Montiel and Haque (1986 and 1990) provide useful diagrams and Khan and Montiel (1989) prove the policy properties of the merged model algebraically. Their results are set out in Table 5.1, noting that the policy instruments listed include measures common in IMF/World Bank adjustment programmes in sub-Saharan Africa.

Several of the impact effects and underlying economic mechanisms of the merged model are already known from previous chapters. Some brief comments are therefore sufficient to highlight the particular properties of this model.[15]

A decrease in domestic credit leads to an excess flow demand for money (via equations 5.2 and 5.3). At the initial level of output this puts (via equation 5.1) a downward pressure on prices as the money market must clear. However, for a given level of import prices, the domestic price fall improves the balance of payments (via equation 5.7). Therefore, the decrease in domestic credit is followed by an increase in international reserves as in the monetary approach to the balance of payments. Real output subsequently decreases (via equation 5.8–5.9).

Table 5.1 Impact effects of changes in policy instruments, behavioural parameters, and exogenous variables[16]

	Domestic prices (ΔP_d)	Real output (Δy)	Balance of payments (ΔR)
Domestic credit (ΔDC)	+	+	÷
Exchange rate (Δe)	+	÷	+
Government spending (ΔC_g)	+	÷	+/÷
Private savings rate (Δs)	÷	+	+/÷
Capital flows (ΔF)	÷	+	+/÷

Note: +, ÷, +/÷ means that the variable is respectively greater than (>) zero, less than (<) zero, and either greater than (>) or less than (<) zero.

A devaluation increases the overall price level (via equation 5.11) as import prices increase. This in turn affects real output negatively (via equation 5.8). International reserves increase (via equation 5.4), due to the fall in imports, following the increase in import prices and the drop in output.[17] Consequently, the merged model calls attention to the possibility that recession may be the likely result of too restrictive an application of domestic credit policy, and although the stagflationary result of the devaluation is model specific, it is a useful illustration of the potential negative real effects of monetary policies. These are exactly the effects about which many critics of IMF programmes have complained.

In the merged model a decrease in government spending will result in output growth (via equation 5.9), and a decrease in domestic prices.[18] However, the impact on the balance of payments is indeterminate.[19] Reductions in government spending lead to a decrease in domestic absorption, which points to an improvement in the balance of payments. But the increase in real output (caused by the increase in domestic savings due to the increase in public sector savings and the implied channelling of freed credit to the private sector) implies higher import needs. This points to a deterioration in the balance of payments. An overall improvement in the balance of payments cannot therefore be assumed, and will in fact only come about under fairly restrictive assumptions, including a large price drop and that the income effect is relatively unimportant in the trade balance.[20] At least the latter point does not hold in the case of import-strangled sub-Saharan Africa, and also the assumed perfect flexibility in prices is unacceptable.

An increase in the private savings rate (s), achieved through, for example, an increase in interest rates or financial deepening, will (via equation 5.9) affect investment positively, so real output grows. This will put downward pressure on domestic prices, as the increase in output must be accompanied by a decrease in prices to clear the flow money market. The impact on the balance of payments is again difficult to determine as prices and output move in opposite directions, as was the case with fiscal tightening.[21] But the above conclusions about the positive impact on real output assumes private savings are in fact invested and not hoarded. This assumption is critical under the present conditions of sub-Saharan Africa, where the investment climate is extremely troubled.

Finally, an increase in capital inflows will, if they simply go into international reserves, have an impact on the target variables, which is equivalent to an increase in domestic credit. Since it is reasonable to expect that the increase in foreign capital inflows is matched by an increase in imports, no immediate monetary consequences appear.[22] However, assuming consumption of imported goods can be controlled, the increased availability of imports will increase investment and therefore growth (via equations 5.8 and 5.9).[23] This will put a downward pressure on domestic prices, since the money market must clear. But the impact on the balance of payments is once again difficult to determine, as output and domestic prices go in opposite directions.

This ends the summary presentation of the merged model. The model will be critically assessed with reference to sub-Saharan Africa in what follows, but it can already now be noted that some of the above simplifications and conclusions are challenged on pages 110–16. This is so in particular because Khan and Montiel (1989) do not study the effects of a negative external shock and the policies appropriate in such a situation.

Before entering into this, it is useful to outline briefly the results and conclusions of an analysis carried out by Reinhart (1989). His article is relevant partly because it is the only empirical study with direct reference to the merged model offering an indication of some of its more immediate weaknesses, and partly because more empirical testing will in the final analysis be indispensable in assessing the appropriateness of particular theoretical models for growth-oriented adjustment.

AN EMPIRICAL ANALYSIS

Reinhart (1989) tries to assess the usefulness of the merged model for policy analysis by investigating three types of issues:[24] (i) whether the key parameters are stable, (ii) how sensitive the policy implications are to changes in the parameters and (iii) whether some target variables are more vulnerable to forecast errors than others. These questions are raised for a diverse sample of seven developing countries for which relevant time-series data are available. Two countries (Ghana and Tanzania) are part of sub-Saharan Africa.

Relating to the stability of the parameters of the model, several striking conclusions do in fact result from the analysis:

(a) Production functions do not explain much of the variation in actual output. One very likely explanation for this is that the production function traces out the production possibility frontier, but many developing countries are not operating at full capacity. This renders the specification of output growth unstable over time, seriously undermining one of the key components of the merged model.

(b) Savings rates appear relatively stable. This implies there is at least some empirical support for this behavioural equation of the model. Stability might even be improved with the introduction of further variables such as the interest rate, which was left out above to simplify the model.

(c) The fit for the money demand function, as specified in the merged framework, is almost uniformly poor. This indicates, either that the assumed stability in money circulation is empirically unjusti- fied, or that the specification used is much too restrictive. In both cases this is an indication of yet another very weak link in the merged model.

(d) The import and export specifications appeared with the theoreti- cally-expected signs in all seven countries. The specifications of the external sector components do not therefore attract quite the same amount of attention as the shortcomings just mentioned.

Estimations of the parameters of a model are useful in indicating how it fits diverse circumstances. This is, however, only an intermedi- ate step in assessing the value of the model for policy-making purposes. If the multipliers, linking endogenous variables with the policy instruments, are very sensitive to changes in the parameters, the model is not very 'robust', and the degree of precision in forecasting will be low. Two observations on robustness follow from Reinhart's investigation:

(a) The empirical (ir)relevance of the merged model depends very much on whether primary attention is given to inflation or to output and balance of payments. In the former case, the model may in some cases be meaningful. This is not so in the latter case. The reason is that for output growth and the balance of payments the range of multipliers is limited, but for inflation the range is rather broad.

(b) The reliability of the policy implications hinge in a critical manner on the policy instruments under consideration. The impact on all target variables of changes in the exchange rate tends to be little affected by parameter changes, whereas credit and fiscal policies are more sensitive. This implies that the model is only potentially relevant in the assessment of exchange rate policy. It should be stressed, however, that the multipliers associated with the exchange rate tend to be relatively small, suggesting it takes large exchange rate modifications to affect the targets in any significant way.

In conclusion, the theoretical assumptions of the merged model appear, based on the empirical analysis reviewed, very inadequate, and the effects of macroeconomic policies suggested are subject to a large degree of uncertainty. This obviously makes the operational value of the model in designing growth-oriented policies highly circumscribed, not to say largely irrelevant. These issues and problems are further pursued in the next section.

ISSUES AND PROBLEMS

The merged model is, as any theoretical model, naturally based on a number of simplifying assumptions. In follow-up to the empirical testing in the last section, it is illustrative to interpret the integrated model within a broader, more conventional macro-framework to investigate the hardiness of the policy results and pay explicit attention to supply-side issues. These may, as already discussed, be of crucial importance in growth-oriented adjustment in the sub-Saharan context. The model proposed by Vines (1990) is a good starting point in this regard. It is set out below in summary form and in a way which makes it directly comparable with the Khan and Montiel framework.

Like the merged model, the more general model is a one-period static framework for a small open economy, and it contains three well-known policy instruments (e, DC and C_g). Capital flows are ignored together with reserve revaluations. An explicit distinction is made between capacity and actual output denominated respectively $\hat{y}$ and y. Capacity $\hat{y}$ depends, as in the Harrod–Domar model, on the capital stock, and any change in investment causes a change in output, which is α times the change in investment (that is, α is the inverse of the capital-output ratio k).

Unlike the Khan and Montiel model, an explicit investment function makes investment equal to μ times the change in the interest rate r.[25] Furthermore, labour is introduced as an additional factor of production to capture the effect (ε) on aggregate supply of a depreciation of the real exchange rate.[26] It follows that:

$$\Delta \hat{y} = - \alpha \, \mu \, \Delta r - \varepsilon \, (\Delta e - \Delta P_d) \qquad (5.17)$$

Actual output can be derived from the overall national account balance equation 2.5, that is $y = C_p + C_g + I + (X - Z)$. Assuming savings are a constant share s of disposable income, and that taxes a constant share t of y, private consumption (C_p) is equal to $(1 - s)(1 - t)y$. Real government spending (C_g) is under the control of government as a policy instrument, and investment is equal to $-\mu \Delta r$.

The trade balance $(X - Z)$ is assumed to depend positively on the real exchange rate $(\Delta e - \Delta P_d)$ and negatively on output y. In addition, the trade balance worsens following a negative demand shock $\Delta \xi$.[27] The parameter reflecting the effect of the real exchange rate on the trade balance is denominated a, and the propensity to import is b. The national balance equation can be rewritten as follows:

$$\Delta y = (1 - s)(1 - t)\Delta y - \mu \Delta r + \Delta C_g + a(\Delta e - \Delta P_d) - b \Delta y - \Delta \xi$$
$$(5.18)$$

Flow equilibrium in the money market ensures that $M_d = M_s$. Changes in the money supply reflect changes in domestic credit DC and international reserves R. Various specifications of the money demand are possible. In the merged model the simple money demand function where $M_d = (1/v)Py$ was chosen. This can be generalized to take account of the negative effect (ρ) of the interest rate (r) on money demand. Therefore, $(1/v)(\Delta P + \Delta y) - \rho \Delta r = \Delta DC + \Delta R$ or:

$$\Delta r = \frac{1}{\rho}\left[-(\Delta DC + \Delta R) + \frac{1}{v}(\Delta P + \Delta y)\right] \qquad (5.19)$$

By allowing actual output to differ from capacity, it is necessary to introduce an additional equation as compared with the merged model of Khan and Montiel. There is one more variable to determine. This can be done by an aggregate supply relationship, which makes domestic prices an increasing function of the difference between y and $\hat{y}$, with Φ measuring the impact of 'excess demand on prices'. No attempt is made, however, to model the reasons leading to output differing from capacity. Therefore:

$$\Delta P_d = \Phi(\Delta y - \Delta \hat{y}) \qquad (5.20)$$

Furthermore, the aggregate price level is, as in the merged model (equation 5.11), a weighted average of imported and domestic output prices. Assuming the import content θ and foreign prices are constant,

111

and that the initial values of the exchange rate and import and domestic prices are unity, the price determination rule can be expressed as follows:[28]

$$\Delta P = \theta \Delta e + (1 - \theta)\Delta P_d \qquad (5.21)$$

Finally, the balance of payments determines the last equation of the model. Capital flows (that is, ΔF) are ignored, and the determinants of the remaining elements of the balance of payments (that is, the trade balance) were already discussed above. Thus, the change in international reserves can be expressed as follows:

$$\Delta R = a(\Delta e - \Delta P_d) - b\Delta y - \Delta \xi \qquad (5.22)$$

In summary, the general model contains six endogenous variables ($\hat{y}$, y, r, P_d, P and R) and eleven parameters (α, s, t, v, ρ, μ, θ, b, a, Φ and ϵ), in addition to three policy instruments DC, e and C_g and the 'shock' variable ξ. The workings of this model and the interaction among the various sectors of the economy can be illustrated in the IS–LM fashion.[29]

Substituting equation 5.17 into 5.20 the following expression for ΔP_d appears:

$$\Delta P_d = \frac{\Phi}{1 + \Phi\epsilon} (\Delta y - \alpha\mu\Delta r + \epsilon\Delta e) \qquad (5.23)$$

The term $\Phi/(1 + \Phi\epsilon)$ will be denominated Φ', which, given the definition of Φ, is positive. It is also noted that Φ' is less than one. Substituting the expression for ΔP_d into equation 5.18 and rearranging gives the following expression for the IS-curve:

$$\Delta y = k_{is}[(1 - \epsilon\Phi')a\Delta e + \Delta C_g - \Delta\xi - \mu(1 + a\Phi'\alpha)\Delta r] \quad (5.24)$$

where $k_{is} = 1/[s(1 - t) + t + b + a\Phi']$. Note that k_{is} (that is, the generalized output multiplier) and $\mu(1 + a\Phi'\alpha)$ are positive, so the IS-curve has the familiar negative slope in the $(\Delta y, \Delta r)$ space. This can also be seen by rearranging equation 5.24, isolating Δr on the left-hand side as follows:

$$\Delta r = \frac{(1 - \epsilon\Phi')a\Delta e + \Delta C_g - \Delta\xi - \Delta y/k_{is}}{\mu(1 + a\Phi'\alpha)} \qquad (5.25)$$

Since Δy is preceded by a minus sign, the slope of the IS curve is negative. As Φ' grows (that is, the more flexible the domestic prices are) the flatter the IS curve will be.

An expression for the LM-curve can be derived from equation 5.19, using the expressions for ΔP, ΔR and ΔP_d known from equations 5.21, 5.22 and 5.23. This gives:

$$\Delta r = k_{lm} \left\{ \Delta \xi - \Delta DC + \left[\frac{\theta - av + \Phi' \varepsilon (1 - \theta)}{v} + \Phi' \varepsilon a \right] \Delta e \right.$$

$$\left. + \left[\frac{1 + bv + \Phi' - \theta \Phi'}{v} + \Phi' a \right] \Delta y \right\} \tag{5.26}$$

where $k_{lm} = 1/[\rho + \Phi' \alpha \mu (v^{-1} (1 - \theta) + a)]$. Note that k_{lm} (that is, the generalized money demand multiplier) as well as $[(1/v)(1 + bv + \Phi'(1 - \theta)) + \Phi' a]$ are positive, so the LM-curve has the familiar positive slope in the $(\Delta y, \Delta r)$ space due to the plus sign in front of Δy on the right-hand side of equation 5.25.[30] As Φ' grows the LM curve gets steeper.

It is now possible to analyse in a standard comparative-static manner the effects of changes in the three policy instruments and in the parameters. These more detailed analyses will with one exception be left out here. The purpose of this section is to focus on the overall appropriateness of the Khan and Montiel model in the sub-Saharan context. It is for this reason sufficient to trace the effects of, and possible policy responses to, a negative external shock $\Delta \xi$. This is taken to imply that foreign demand for exports from the domestic economy falls.

An external shock will shift both the IS and the LM curves to the left, since $\Delta \xi$ appears in equation 5.25 with a negative sign and in 5.26 with a positive sign. Therefore, such a shock will, as one might expect, lower output. It cannot be concluded, however, what the effect on the interest rate will be, since this will depend on whether the shift in the IS or the LM curve dominates.

In the former case, r will fall leading to an increase in capacity output due to the nature of the investment function, but if the LM shift dominates, capacity output will fall. The effect on domestic prices (see equation 5.20) is a fall in P_d since the drop in actual output will dominate the possible fall in capacity. Also the balance of payments (see equation 5.22) will deteriorate, although the derived positive effect from the drops in y and P_d will make the overall deterioration less than the original shock.[31]

In the merged Khan and Montiel model there is perfect price flexibility (that is, $\Phi = \infty$) and the real exchange rate does not affect capacity (that is, $\varepsilon = 0$). On the other hand, capacity output is endogenous (that is, $\alpha > 0$) through changes in investment. The interest elasticity in the demand for money is ignored, thus $\rho = 0$, and what is saved is assumed to be invested without any difficulties.

Taking account of these assumptions the Khan and Montiel 'adjustment with growth' framework can be presented as follows in the terms of the more general model:[32]

$$\Delta y = \frac{\Delta C_g + a(\Delta e - \Delta P_d) - \Delta \xi}{s(1-t) + t + b - 1/\alpha} \tag{5.27}$$

$$\Delta P = v(\Delta DC + \Delta R) - \Delta y \tag{5.28}$$

$$\Delta P_d = \frac{(\Delta P - \theta \Delta e)}{(1 - \theta)} \tag{5.29}$$

$$\Delta R = a(\Delta e - \Delta P_d) - b\Delta y - \Delta \xi \tag{5.30}$$

Rearranging,[33] this system can be reduced to two equations representing two curves in the $(\Delta y, \Delta P_d)$ space. First, the upward sloping 'real' sector (or capacity) curve can be expressed as follows:[34]

$$\Delta P_d = \frac{1}{a}\{\Delta C_g + a\Delta e - \Delta \xi - [s(1-t) + t + b - 1/\alpha]\Delta y\} \tag{5.31}$$

Second, the downward sloping 'monetary' sector (or price) curve can be expressed as follows:[35]

$$\Delta P_d = \frac{\Delta DC - \Delta \xi + (a - \theta/v)\Delta e - (1/v + b)\Delta y}{(1/v)(1 - \theta) + a} \tag{5.32}$$

In this model an external shock $\Delta \xi$ will shift the capacity curve to the right and the price curve to the left. There is no doubt that the external shock will lower domestic prices. It appears at first sight that the effect on y is indeterminate, depending on which of the shifts in the two curves dominate, but by solving the model algebraically, it can be shown that, while the balance of payments worsens, output increases.[36]

In other words, a reduction in export demand promotes growth within the merged framework as reinterpreted here. This happens because an external shock improves the external resource balance and therefore the availability of real resources, assumed to be invested automatically. The positive effect on output of a negative external shock is an unacceptable result, and contrasts starkly with the above more appealing Keynesian-type conclusion from Vines (1990), where a shock lowers output. This puts the practical relevance of the merged model seriously into question.

The Khan and Montiel model can also be misleading in its conclusions about the appropriate policy response to an external shock. Assume for illustrative purpose that adjustment aims at exactly counteracting the effect of a negative external shock so the overall change in prices, balance of payments and output is nil (that is, $\Delta P = \Delta R = \Delta y = 0$). If the requirements that $\Delta R = 0$ and $\Delta y = 0$ are used in equation 5.30, it can be seen that the real exchange rate $(\Delta e - \Delta P_d)$ must depreciate by $\Delta \xi / a$. This gives a necessary change in domestic prices of $\Delta P_d = \Delta e - \Delta \xi / a$. Substituting into equation 5.29 and using the $\Delta P = 0$, the nominal exchange rate depreciation Δe can be calculated as equal to $(1 - \theta)(\Delta \xi / a)$. This implies that $\Delta P_d = - (\Delta \xi / a) \theta$.

A nominal devaluation of $(1 - \theta)(\Delta \xi / a)$ is therefore in the merged framework part of the adjustment programme. In addition, equations 5.27 and 5.28 show that it is actually the only measure required.[37] This is a very troublesome observation, as it would be exceptional that just one policy measure could in practice achieve at the same time three policy objectives.

The crucial difference between the Khan and Montiel model and the more general framework lies in the simplifying assumptions of the former. In other words, the reason that a nominal devaluation of size $(1 - \theta)(\Delta \xi / a)$ is both a necessary and a sufficient policy measure to achieve the stated adjustment objectives is a consequence of the perfect price flexibility (that is, $\Phi = \infty$), and the fact that Khan and Montiel ignore the effects of the real exchange rate on capacity and of the interest rate on money demand (that is, set ε and ρ equal to 0).

If these restrictive assumptions are dropped, price stickiness implies that the necessary fall in domestic prices following the recommended nominal devaluation can only come about through an expansion in capacity. This is also necessary to counteract the repressive effect on supply of the real exchange rate depreciation. Expansion in capacity requires a fall in interest rates, so domestic credit must rise. Finally, aggregate demand must remain unchanged, so government spending must be reduced to make room for the additional investment, assuming private consumption or imports cannot be affected through s and t on the one side, and b on the other.

The policy package that emanates from the more general model is more complex than the package derived from the perspective of the merged model. Three policies (exchange rate, credit and fiscal) must all be in action to achieve the adjustment objectives specified ($\Delta P = \Delta R = \Delta y = 0$) rather than just one (devaluation). The more general model is certainly vulnerable to criticism. It is debatable, in the sub-Saharan context, to which extent permissive credit policy can influence investment and capacity. Account must also be taken of possible negative effects of contractionary fiscal actions. Still, Vines's framework makes it possible to address supply-side issues, whereas they are simply assumed away in the merged model.

It can furthermore be shown that an adjustment programme, which only consists of a nominal devaluation of size $(1 - \theta) \Delta \xi / a$ referred to above, and which is intended to nullify the effects of an external shock of size $\Delta \xi$, leads to output contraction and price increases when interpreted within the model formulated by Vines.[38] That is, the adjustment suggested by the merged model actually leads to stagflation. Moreover, the impact on the balance of payments and the interest rate cannot be determined. These results obviously conflict with the stated goals of achieving $\Delta P = \Delta R = \Delta y = 0$, and the combination of a possible, but uncertain balance-of-payments impact, with a certain output fall and price increases, is the very essence of the standard critique raised against orthodox adjustment programmes.

CONCLUSION

Khan, Montiel and Haque have offered an interesting merger of the analytically very simple financial programming framework of the IMF and the even simpler RMSM of the World Bank. It may be recalled from Chapter 3 that real output was exogenous in the former model, and what Khan, Montiel and Haque in effect propose is to use the growth rate of the latter as an input into the financial programming framework. At the same time, foreign savings, which were exogenous in the RMSM framework, become partly endogenous.

It is high time that the need for revising the IMF and World Bank programming procedures be faced head on. It is encouraging that attempts like the one examined in this chapter are initiated from within the IMF and the World Bank. A natural first step from this position is, of course, to assess whether the IMF and World Bank frameworks can be combined. The above review demonstrates that this is indeed technically feasible.

Khan, Montiel and Haque (1986 and 1990) stress that their merged model is not intended as the final answer in the search for an integrated framework within which growth-oriented adjustment issues can be analysed. They conclude that while their model is internally consistent, it is still too simple, and is therefore better perceived as a starting point put forward for expository purposes to lay the groundwork for future research. On the other hand, Khan and Montiel (1989:292) conclude that the merged model yields 'useful insights into the relationships among growth, inflation, and the balance of payments that one would need to take into account in designing programmes in which growth is an explicit objective'. This is an overambitious statement, since their composite framework has been built around exactly the same kinds of restrictive assumptions as the RMSM and the financial programming model.

Consequently, a number of critical supply-side issues in structural adjustment remain unaddressed. Adjustment programmes aim *inter alia* at raising efficiency levels, so the ability of the economy to react to 'better prices' (including a better-aligned exchange rate) is an issue that should not be avoided. The same accounts for the impact of other policies such as credit and fiscal policy on actual as opposed to capacity output. The merged model brushes, as it stands, these issues aside.

Khan and Montiel do not provide a proper reply to the stagflation-ary critique of orthodox adjustment programmes, and an appropriate complex policy response to promote 'adjustment with growth' in the face of negative external shocks cannot be identified within their framework. Negative external shocks have been of primary importance in the economic crisis in sub-Saharan Africa. These shortcomings are serious since the very purpose of formulating the merged model was to establish a framework for investigating 'growth-oriented adjustment' issues. In addition, it should not be overlooked that further short-comings may emerge, when the dynamic properties of the model are clarified, and reference is also made to the empirical assessment of the model which was summarized on pages 108–10.

In conclusion, the composite model represents a synthesis in technical terms. However, the merged model does not capture the essence of structural adjustment. The analysis of the impact of an external shock and the formulation of an appropriate policy response to such a shock clearly illustrates the fragility of the merged framework in the particular conditions of sub-Saharan Africa, where the simplifying assumptions of Khan and Montiel simply do not hold. Policy analysis based on the merged framework is therefore 'a bit beside the point'.[39] In other words, contrary to Khan and Montiel's optimistic statement quoted above, the merged model cannot, in its present form, be accepted as a theoretically-useful tool for analysing adjustment with growth issues in sub-Saharan Africa.

The attractiveness of the financial programming framework and the RMSM model is that they require very little data, and that they are relatively easy to understand and utilize. The two sub-models do not contain much in terms of an understanding of the interaction between economic policy and the objectives of adjustment programmes. But the planner does have the option of modifying the exogenous variables based on extra-modular analyses and data. So if used flexibly, and with the necessary care, the two models can at least draw attention to a few important macroeconomic links and possible trade-offs, which policy-makers have to face.

The merged framework adds nothing to the above, since the growth rate of the aggregate RMSM is simply plugged into the financial programming framework without further explanation. This means that the theoretical flexibility of considering alternative growth paths within the latter framework 'evaporates' by being 'tied down' by the former without justifying or considering the underlying behavioural implications in a proper manner. The appealing simplicity and potential flexibility which the two sub-models possess vanish in merging them. That is, even if the merged model is theoretically simple in its 'pure' form, it is still more complex than its two component models. To use even these simpler models in a pragmatic manner has not been without difficulty.

The above problems would become even further apparent if some of the indispensable changes in the underlying behavioural characteristics and the structure of the model were introduced. The merged framework can easily be expanded to include demand and supply of domestic and foreign financial assets, and the interaction of the central bank, the fiscal sector, and the banking system can, of course, be specified. A distinction between growth in productive capacity and growth of output can also be introduced,[40] and it would be desirable to endogenize international capital flows as well.

However, introducing such changes might, as demonstrated, change the policy conclusions in fundamental ways. Furthermore, for practical purposes very simple models are needed. The merged model of Khan, Montiel and Haque is far too complicated. For theoretical as well as purely practical reasons, it is unlikely that the merged model is an operationally-useful synthesis of IMF/World Bank approaches to stabilization and structural adjustment.

6

ALTERNATIVE APPROACHES
AND PERSPECTIVES

The mounting importance of the IMF/World Bank approaches to macroeconomic adjustment, which is evident in the large number of stabilization and structural adjustment programmes presently under implementation in sub-Saharan Africa, should not, and indeed has not, gone unchallenged. For this reason a variety of non-orthodox critiques were already formulated in preceding chapters. Yet no attempt was made to furnish a more coherent examination of existing alternative approaches.

Subsequent to the review of macroeconomic adjustment policies in Chapter 2, focus was deliberately put on the simple macroeconomic models of the IMF and World Bank. These have, after all, occupied the centre stage in operational IMF/World Bank adjustment work and served in defining conditionalities to which sub-Saharan African countries have had to subscribe to obtain badly-needed balance-of-payments and development finance. This is so even if the amount of finance which the IMF and the World Bank provide themselves is limited, as the acceptance of programmes designed with the help of the Bretton Woods institutions is considered an important seal of approval by private lenders, and more importantly in the African context, by public lenders as well.

This chapter is meant to fill the above gap. But it is stressed from the outset that what is intended is not a comprehensive and detailed review. For obvious reasons of space this would be outside the scope of this book. What is aimed for is a succinct, but consistent, outline of the main routes of thought that counterbalance the intellectual and ideological properties of the IMF/World Bank models and adjustment approaches. This is no easy task. Many critics of the IMF/World Bank approaches are eclectic in outlook and cannot be said to adhere to one paradigm only. Furthermore, the literature is immense and of very uneven quality, ranging from highly complex, at times algebraically formulated, analytical pieces of work, to writings which may best be characterized as propaganda with dubious empirical and theoretical foundations.

A considerable part of the criticisms staged against the IMF/World Bank frameworks has been formulated by analysts who may, broadly speaking, be said to subscribe to structuralist theories about development issues. Yet it would be much too narrow a perspective to assume that the debate on structural adjustment in the 1980s is nothing but an extension of the monetarist/structuralist debate of the 1950s.[1] Much has indeed changed on both sides of this divide within the field of development economics.

The original structuralist ideas of the 1940s and 1950s have been considerably revised and are now in several aspects contradicted by the neo-structuralists of the 1980s. On the other hand, the wisdom behind the IMF and World Bank approaches, as they were conceived in the early 1980s, has come under close scrutiny. Traditional critics have maintained that these programmes are badly conceived, unnecessarily austere, poverty promoting and at best ineffective in attaining their stated objectives. Also mainstream economists and staff within the IMF and World Bank have come to question the effectiveness of adjustment programmes as designed so far. Consequently, the IMF and the World Bank have started to modify their earlier positions in a number of ways, in particular on the issue of putting more focus on the human aspects of adjustment.[2]

ADJUSTMENT WITH A HUMAN FACE

Several of the organizations of the United Nations system to which the Bretton Woods institutions are formally attached have over the past decade voiced increasing distress over the design and implementation of orthodox adjustment packages in the sub-Saharan African context as well as elsewhere. Prominent among this group of institutions is UNICEF which, in line with its institutional mandate and concerns with the situation of the world's children, has consistently argued that the experience which most countries have had with adjustment cannot be labelled an unqualified success.[3]

It is readily recognized by UNICEF that it is not adjustment policy as such which is the main cause of the human difficulties and social set-backs, especially of vulnerable groups. The root cause must, in the UNICEF view, be found in the overall economic situation, globally and nationally. It is also repeatedly underlined that, without some form of adjustment, the situation would often be far worse.[4] None the less, standard adjustment policies have, it is held, aggravated the situation of the poor. Alternative adjustment policies, which could take into account the negative social consequences and provide a basis for equitable growth, are required.

Accordingly, UNICEF has called for adjustment with a 'human face', an expression originally coined by Cornia, Jolly and Stewart (1987a). At the heart of their proposal is the notion that, if adjustment is not people-centred, it is wrongly conceived. The human implications for the most vulnerable parts of society must be made an integral part of overall adjustment policies, rather than being ignored altogether or treated as an additional welfare component to be tagged on eventually.

Economic policies should seek to improve the productivity and incomes of the poor directly, and essential services and subsidies should be strengthened rather than discarded outright. Furthermore, since the social sectors are central to the formation of human capital, basic health, education, water, extension services, and so on, should not be viewed as amenity consumer goods only. Unless these are provided, the ability to produce is affected and the future potential for productivity growth is impaired, not to mention social and political stability. This perspective contrasts with the widespread negative effects on social sector budgets and employment which have so far been a consequence of structural adjustment programmes. Well-documented adverse affects on poorer segments of the population (in particular children, poor women and the aged) can no longer be ignored.[5]

It is correct, as argued by the IMF and the World Bank, that many adjustment programmes are intended to move societies towards greater equality by reducing the prevailing 'urban bias'. But even if rural incomes are generally lower than urban incomes, expectations about positive distributional outcomes must be analytically and empirically grounded. There is, in fact, good reason *a priori* to foresee that standard adjustment programmes will increase inequality within the rural sector, and the creation or further deepening of urban poverty is a rather common feature as well. The net effect on poverty and income distribution may therefore be more complex than a simple urban–rural dichotomy seems to indicate.

Distributive concerns are by no means a new topic within the field of development economics. The end of the first United Nations development decade (1960–70), as well as the decade of the 1970s, witnessed an upsurge in theoretical as well as policy literature about poverty, inequality and employment. Seers (1969:3–4) signalled an important redefinition of the development concept when he argued that the questions to ask about a country's development are: 'what has been happening to poverty?', 'what has been happening to unemployment?' and 'what has been happening to inequality?'. The logical conclusion is that if one or two of these central problems have worsened, and especially if all three have, it would be strange to call the result 'development' even if per capita income soars.

The 'trickle down' beliefs of the 1940s and 1950s came under close scrutiny, and disillusion with progress during the 1960s was widespread, despite the historically very impressive growth record. Attention switched to 'human capital' formation; 'basic human needs' came to acquire the status of a new paradigm of development;[6] and 'redistribution with growth' became a cornerstone in the World Bank development approach of the 1970s. The World Bank was in the forefront of much of the new thinking together with organizations such as the International Labour Organization (ILO) and fully supported the emphasis on equitable growth. A more conscious view of the distributional consequences of development aid was taken, and the design of projects was targeted deliberately on poverty groups. In other words, the pendulum of mainstream development thinking had by 1970 swung from its original very restrictive emphasis on economic growth only.[7]

Development theory and practice changed again in the early 1980s, in line with shifts in the political philosophy of major Western countries. The above broader perceptions and views did not retain their dominant position. Distributive concerns became somehow submerged in the adjustment debate. Moreover, the policy packages promoted by the IMF and the World Bank to counter damaging macroeconomic imbalances were focused very narrowly on the economic dimensions of adjustment with little attention to the social sectors or the human dimensions.

This neglect of social issues was reinforced by the limited range of decision-makers and institutions, typically drawn into the formulation of adjustment programmes in sub-Saharan Africa as elsewhere. The vital task of formulating adjustment packages with wide-ranging impact on development performance and perspectives has, in line with the IMF/World Bank style of work, tended to be assigned exclusively to a small group of technical experts and officials in the Ministries of Finance and Planning, who have found it difficult to maintain social issues in focus.

Even if they were supplemented by a few key officials from the more important economic sector ministries, work has generally been carried out under great time pressure and confidentiality, and mainly conducted with visiting groups of specialists from the World Bank and IMF Headquarters with little time to spare for in-depth discussions. It is hardly surprising that the more delicate and decentralized process and sectoral details, which are required to promote equitable adjustment policies, were generally overlooked during the 1980s.

It is troubling, but not surprising, that the IMF pursued the above line of action and attached limited importance to the social and political consequences of adjustment policies until 1986, where policy statements by the managing director signalled more concern with the distributional impact of economic policies. The traditional IMF position is, after all, that the consequences for income distribution of economic policy is the exclusive prerogative of domestic policy-makers.[8] The fact that the World Bank also contributed to the formal neglect of the human dimension issues in the preparation of adjustment programmes is more perplexing, seen against the positions taken during the 1970s.

Consequently, the UNICEF approach is a reminder of the distributive concerns and the development insights of previous decades, and 'adjustment with a human face' therefore adds a poverty alleviation dimension to adjustment in much the same way as 'redistribution with growth' and 'basic needs' added such a dimension to growth.[9] 'Adjustment with a human face' can, in other words, be thought of as the 'basic needs approach' to adjustment. The importance of this dimension is, of course, even more significant now than during the growth experiences of the 1960s and 1970s since output per capita is presently declining in so many African countries. This implies that the absolute incomes of the poor may be falling even in cases where their share of incomes remain constant.

The alternative UNICEF policy package geared towards the goal of a more satisfactory adjustment process consists of five key elements which can briefly be summarized as follows, implicitly comparing with a typical or orthodox IMF/World Bank-supported programme:[10]

(a) *More expansionary (that is, less austere) macroeconomic fiscal, monetary and wage policies* aimed at sustaining levels of production, employment and human needs satisfaction over the adjustment period. The adjustment process is moreover situated in a time horizon which is longer (that is, 5–10 years) than the very short-term perspective originally envisaged by the Bretton Woods institutions. Emphasis is on the crucial importance of massive support from abroad rather than on adjustment in domestic economic policies only. The rationale for providing external support is put in economic as well as political terms.

(b) *Meso and targeted policies that benefit the poor* are not new policy instruments. They are instruments already in use, but which are frequently analysed in terms of their macro impact only, and without systematic regard for their consequences for vulnerable groups and growth. Meso policies should include policies, such as government expenditure, taxation or credit policy, which influence the allocation of incomes and resources within a given macro policy package. The key to appropriate meso policy is to combine macro instruments with selectivity, so distributional concerns are taken account of.[11]

(c) *Sectoral policies aimed at restructuring production* to give greater emphasis to income-generating and productive employment of the poorer sections of the population, including support for small-scale productive activities in the urban informal sector, and among small farmers, women and landless. This in particular includes investment in areas geared towards enhancing the productive capacity of the poor, especially women, in the form of credit and extension schemes, research and development of appropriate technologies, literacy programmes, and so on.

(d) *Restructuring of social expenditures* toward low-cost, basic education, primary health care and other basic mass-coverage services, with a view to improving equity as well as efficiency in service provision. This involves changes both among and within sectors, and protection of basic social services; and the adoption of high impact, cost effective measures, such as essential drugs schemes, are explicitly recommended.

(e) *Compensatory programmes* that provide temporary, but additional and targeted support for poor people affected by adjustment, with a view to protecting basic health and nutritional standards. Examples are income maintenance, through public works programmes, in the form of labour-intensive food-for-work schemes, and nutrition interventions, including school-feeding of high-risk children and other forms of food subsidies to high-risk groups.

Improvements in the modalities of adjustment design are also suggested. The extension of the time perspective of the adjustment process, and mobilization of additional external resources demanded by UNICEF, are aspects which have already been referred to. In addition, improved and continuous monitoring of the human situation (especially of living standards, health and nutrition of low-income groups) is promoted. Similarly, a broadening of the group of national and international analysts and policy-makers involved in formulation work is recommended. Such changes are perceived as necessary measures to focus more attention on the human dimension of the adjustment process, as well as to identify and assess the effectiveness of adjustment programmes, so they can be modified as required.

In summary, the UNICEF 'human face' approach implies that adjustment policies are not merely intended to reduce macroeconomic imbalances, but are seen as an integral part of a longer-term development strategy. As such, the approach takes into account the economic as well as the non-economic fabric of society. Focusing on economic policy and fabric only is, in the 'human face' view, a much too narrow approach, which endangers the future growth potential as well as that of development. Growth is required, but it must be growth of production and incomes among the lower-income groups.

STRUCTURALIST-INSPIRED VIEWS AND MODELS

Since the inception of development economics as a separate branch of economics in the 1940s, standard neo-classically-inspired economic theory has, with the exception of the 1980s, been on the defensive in this terrain.[12] Seers (1963) even suggests that the more able the student of economics is in absorbing the neo-classical doctrine, the more difficult the process of adaptation to the study of development issues will be.[13]

This is admittedly a rather extreme position, but it is clear that the assumptions of perfect competition, well-functioning markets with flexible prices, and free mobility of factors and products, are not in general sustainable in actual Third World economies, and certainly not in low-income sub-Saharan Africa. Therefore, theoretical, as well as applied, development economists have focused much of their attention and professional efforts on trying to identify and understand (and in some cases formalize) non-neo-classical behavioural relations, macro-imbalances and institutional rigidities, that are thought to better reflect the characteristics of Third World economies.

Despite the common perception of the restricted usefulness of orthodox economics, structuralist-inspired views on development and adjustment do not form one consolidated body of theory and policy advice. On the contrary, they comprise a variety of ideas and concepts from a number of different sources, and sub-groups of thought have over the years argued for different mixes of structuralist features. As pointed out by Taylor (1990:2), structuralism is more a programme of research and policy formulation than a well-defined set of rules for putting models together. It is therefore impossible to give a brief and clear-cut definition that would cover satisfactorily all of the differing lines of structuralist-inspired micro- and macro-analysis.

Nevertheless, a review of a selective sample of structuralist-inspired themes and policy concerns is useful to put the IMF and World Bank approaches to stabilization and adjustment in sub-Saharan Africa into perspective.[14] In the following, particular emphasis is put on what may be termed the neo-structuralist school of the 1980s. The point of departure is that structural adjustment is needed in sub-Saharan Africa, and that such adjustment will have to consist, not only of microeconomic changes in production, demand, resource allocation and relative prices, but also in macroeconomic variables such as absorption, income, consumption and investment.

At one end of the structuralist spectrum one finds a body of thought that can be described as 'neo-classical structuralist',[15] since this cluster of ideas is based on an acceptance in principle of the neo-classical model of resource allocation and the fundamental importance attached to the operation of markets. This endorsement of the neo-classical framework is combined, however, with elements of 'elasticity' and/or 'micro-structuralism'. This is done by arguing that substitution possibilities and supply responses are more limited in developing countries than generally assumed, especially in foreign trade and production, and that markets are imperfect, incomplete or outright absent.

Such characteristics are widespread in sub-Saharan Africa, but it should be stressed that policy conclusions which emerge from neo-classical structuralists vary, depending on whether institutional causes or policy choices are identified as the main culprit in obstructing the proper workings of market forces. It is evident, therefore, that neo-classical structuralists are eclectic in their approach. They recognize that it is quite possible that a shift in prices may not necessarily cause a smooth reallocation of resources and a related change in production, which is subject to a range of supply-side constraints. Furthermore, they do not rule out that a range of different prices may exist for essentially the same kinds of products or factors of production.

Yet another aspect of the neo-classical structuralist approach is non-price rationing, and the view that structural changes, which are inherent in the development process, lead to continuing dynamic micro and macro as well as internal and external disequilibria. Market adjustments are constantly trying to catch up with these dynamic processes, but prices are unable to bring about equilibrium between supply and demand. It can, in this regard, be recalled that the RMSM of the World Bank draws on structuralist thinking as discussed in Chapter 4, and Chenery and his various associates (for example, Strout, in Chenery and Strout 1966, and Bruno, in Chenery and Bruno 1962) are outstanding in this group of analysts.[16]

Reference was made in Chapter 2 to development economists such as Faber and Green (1985), Helleiner (1986a), Killick (1984), Loxley (in Helleiner 1986a) and Streeten (1987a, 1987b). This group, together with many others of broadly similar orientation such as Mosley and Toye (1988), can perhaps be said to occupy what, in rather loose terms, might be called the middle ground among structuralists.

While definitely not in agreement on all issues, these economists have maintained positions which are clearly independent of the views of the IMF and the World Bank. Typical arguments include the insistence on the crucial importance of the low capacity of the countries in sub-Saharan Africa to adjust, the potentially-damaging distributional effects of orthodox policies (along the lines of thinking of UNICEF), and the need to adopt a 'real economy approach', where adjustment programmes are primarily aimed at re-orienting the productive system. Also the classic argument about 'overkill' is a recurrent point referred to.

The above group is more outspokenly structuralist in orientation than the neo-classical structuralists, but their views also overlap in some ways with the position taken by proponents of more pragmatic versions of the World Bank approach.[17] The same is not true, however, for the aggregate monetary focused approach of the IMF, which has been a frequent target for criticism. Anyone who has worked with the IMF and World Bank in practice will readily recognize that the two institutions are indeed very different in outlook and approach as well as in their sensitivity to real economy issues.

While the weaknesses of a one-dimensional classification of structuralist-inspired views should not be overlooked, one can at the other end of the structuralist spectrum trace a distinct analytical approach to stabilization and adjustment issues among a group of political economists. Leaving out the strands, who are more adequately covered under the heading of dependency theory, they take as a starting point the existence of disequilibria that work through macroeconomic mechanisms, but whose causes are thought to be embedded in the underlying economic, social and political characteristics of society.

This school of thought includes Taylor and Bacha as prominent members,[18] and is at times labelled 'Latin American structuralism'. This is understandable in view of the inspiration derived from the non-orthodox analyses carried out over the years at the UN Economic Commission for Latin America, known as ECLA or by its Spanish acronym CEPAL.[19] It is indisputable that the distinct political economy nature of this approach, which bears intellectual lineage directly to Marx, is shared with the early structuralist writers. The focus on political and social conflicts over distribution and the attempt to identify the fundamental roots of macroeconomic disequilibria rather than their more immediate and apparent causes is, in other words, the same.

Nevertheless, the original structuralist ideas of the 1940s and 1950s have been revised very considerably, and the macro structuralist nature of this newer body of analysis may as well be traced to Kalecki, Keynes or post-Keynesian academics at Cambridge such as Kaldor.[20] Consequently, it seems more appropriate, as suggested by FitzGerald (1988:29), to perceive this approach as 'analytical structuralism' or use the labels 'neo-structuralism' or 'macro-structuralism' in accordance with, respectively, Taylor (1989a:4) and Robinson (in Chenery and Srinivasan 1989:927).

Much of the macroeconomic debate, inspired by neo-structuralists over the past decade or so, has been carried out under the heading of 'alternative closure rules' of economy-wide models. When aggregate demand and supply or other relations are out of balance *ex ante*, economic adjustments must take place since balance is established *ex post*. The key problem, before appropriate conclusions about the effects of policy changes can be drawn, is to identify the causal factors driving the process towards balance. The adjustment mechanisms must be specified and the equilibrating variables identified in the models (whether one-sector or general equilibrium) that are formulated to try to capture the essential features of the economy.

Neo-classical-inspired models assume that prices are perfectly flexible and all markets clear instantly. In other words, no additional equilibrating variables, but market prices are required. This kind of 'closure' mechanism underlies the IMF model, although a fixed exchange rate is allowed for. Savings and investment are not considered explicitly, but it is assumed that savings are automatically invested, so 'closure' is a smooth and instantaneous process ensured by the operation of the market prices, which are the only signals economic agents need to see.

A second approach is the RMSM of the World Bank. Here the model is closed by determining aggregate consumption as a residual from the overall national income account balance.[21] In this situation it is assumed that governments can intervene effectively to adjust immediately total consumption (or foreign capital inflows) as required. That is, government, rather than prices, assure the establishment of macroeconomic balance, but in both the IMF and the World Bank approaches closure is assumed to come about in a smooth and unproblematic manner. Yet the macroeconomic implications of the two models are quite different. The IMF model is based on a stable demand for money function, and savings are immediately invested. The World Bank RMSM is 'investment-driven' since consumption is adjusted, so the necessary savings are available, given the desired level of investment.[22]

Analytical or neo-structuralists are generally not satisfied with the kind of assumptions underlying the IMF financial programming and World Bank RMSM models. Due to the nature of the closure rules chosen, no room is left for variations in output and unemployment levels, and focus is (with the exception of the foreign exchange constraint in the RMSM) turned away from structural constraints in the economy. Fixed prices and wages, for example, cannot serve as equilibrating variables, so other processes must be at work. The forces that propagate poverty and inequality are conspicuous in their absence. Instead, the maintenance of macro balances is at centre stage.

While macroeconomic balances are important, they are only reflections of more fundamental forces at work, and cannot therefore be the whole of development. Furthermore, in the IMF/World Bank frameworks the domestic sector is supposed to act in a stable manner. When external and internal disequilibria appear, the logical conclusion seems to be that the cause must necessarily lie in fiscal and monetary mismanagement. Yet the behaviour of the private sector is not really explained and specified. The analysis remains, therefore, in the formulation of FitzGerald (1988:2) *ex hypothesi*.

Accordingly, no links exist in the IMF and World Bank models between real and monetary variables. But feedbacks between prices and costs, for inputs as well as working capital and factors of production, can in reality be very important. In addition, output and absorption depend on monetary variables through income-expenditure linkages. Savings and the composition of demand may change through income redistribution processes as different actors do not have the same consumption and savings behaviour. Furthermore, foreign trade, the availability of foreign exchange and the role of the fiscal budget need to be linked more directly to the production process. That is, while neo-structuralists hold that the IMF and World Bank models are internally consistent, they are viewed as an incomplete description of developing economies.

One must, in other words, be clear about the closure rules and the adjacent direction of causality that is built into the macro models. Such rules are hard to derive on the basis of regressions on GDP and in any case may change in the future, which is what concerns policy-makers. An intimate knowledge about the economy under examination is required. In addition, a developing economy has a micro structure that interacts with macro variables. Yet this interaction can easily be concealed in aggregated models. Some disaggregation is often called for. However, it is not the need for consistency as such that is in question. Sectoral and macro constraints must in any case be respected, and balance (or equilibrium) is still well defined in the neo-structuralist approach.[23]

It is against this background that neo-structuralists do not emphasize abstraction, but instead try to include institutional content in their models, which have a focus on practical, socially-relevant policy issues.[24] Strong links between the real and monetary sides of the economy are generally postulated, and there is a preference to work within multi-sectoral frameworks with at least some prices fixed. Two equilibrating mechanisms are common in the writings of macro-structuralists.

The first is a Keynesian multiplier effect by which changes in aggregate demand lead to changes in aggregate supply. This mechanism is possible when supply constraints are absent. Under such circumstances the level of productive activity is set by the level of demand. The model becomes in other words demand driven, since the necessary changes in savings to close any *ex ante* gaps are generated from increased incomes.

The second typical structuralist closure rule involves 'forced saving', which occurs when output is constrained on the supply-side (because of, for example, shortage of capital and imported inputs or fiscal limitations) or when supply elasticities are low. In these cases the economy cannot be driven by demand, and output prices are likely to be market clearing. The structuralists add the key observation that the 'forced saving' process of closing the savings–investment gap is linked to changes in the functional distribution of income rather than to a smooth process of reallocation of resources along neo-classical lines of thinking. Savings rates are assumed to differ among social classes, so the necessary changes in aggregate savings are related to the efforts of the various social classes to increase their respective income shares. The reduced consumption, necessary to close a savings–investment gap, is in other words a result of conflict, and is born by particular social groups rather than being 'spread out' in the economy as a whole.

In practice, closure will, as Taylor (1988:29) points out, probably involve a little of both of the above two mechanisms, but he goes on to stress that it is useful to keep the distinction for analytical purposes. For reasons of space, it is not the intention here to derive and trace the detailed workings of structuralist models. Yet it may be valuable to specify a bit more precisely the key behavioural rules and other assumptions of the model put forward by Taylor·(1989a) to illustrate macro-structuralist reasoning on adjustment problems, and the perceived linkages between nominal macro aggregates and real output and employment.[25]

The first behavioural relationship of Taylor's model is a distinctive structuralist fix-price rule in which prices are defined directly in relation to the production process itself. Prices are not set from the side of demand as in the case of the neo-classical flex-price approach of the IMF financial programming model. More specifically, the overall price level P is determined using a mark-up h defined over prime cost of labour and imported intermediaries. Prime cost per unit of output (B) can be broken down as follows:

$$B = wb + eP_f a \qquad (6.1)$$

where w is the money wage, b the labour–output ratio, e the fixed nominal exchange rate, P_f the price of imported intermediate inputs and a the input–output coefficient for such intermediates.

It is assumed that w is fixed through wage-bargaining processes, and the mark-up rate responds to social conflict over distribution as well as to past inflation experiences. A nominal devaluation (that is, an increase in e) will increase the domestic currency costs of imported goods and drive up B and subsequently the overall domestic price level P, given by:

132

$$P = (1 + b)B$$

This equation shows that the real wage ($z = w/P$) can be stated as:

$$z = \frac{w}{P} = \frac{1}{b}\left(\frac{1}{1+b} - \frac{eP_f a}{P}\right)$$

This implies, *ceteris paribus*, a negative relationship between the real wage (w/P) and the real exchange rate (eP_f/P). A nominal devaluation of e will tend to drive down the real wage through the above mentioned increase in P. Wage-earners will, however, try to counteract this real wage fall with additional inflationary pressures as the consequence.

To take account of the impact of indirect taxation (υ) on final goods' prices, as well as the cost of financing working capital, the price determination equation must be rewritten. This can be done as follows:

$$P = (1 + \upsilon)(1 + b^*)(1 + i\omega)B \qquad (6.2)$$

where b^* is the mark-up over interest-inclusive costs, i is the nominal interest rate and ω the time period over which prime inputs must be financed as working capital. These modifications will, of course, increase the overall domestic price level P. Monetary restraint that drives up the interest rate therefore contributes to inflation, and the same accounts for increased tax rates.

Possible ways of specifying the behaviour of firms and wage-earners, influencing how b^* and w change, is to make these two variables responsive to the level of economic activity. If activity is measured by the output–capital ratio u (that is, the rate of capacity utilization y/K where K is the capital stock),[26] mark-up behaviour can be stated as:

$$\Delta b^* = \alpha(u - \bar{u}) \qquad (6.3)$$

where $\bar{u}$ is the level of activity when the mark-up is held constant by 'satisfied' firms. The sign of α is uncertain.[27] Any reduction in the real wage ($z = w/P$) of workers will lead them to push for increases in the nominal wage w. Wage inflation is also likely to increase with the rate of capacity utilization. This gives the following possible specification for change in w:

133

$$\Delta w = \psi (u - \overline{u}) - \lambda (z - \overline{z}) \qquad (6.4)$$

where ψ and λ can be expected to have positive signs and $\overline{u}$ and $\overline{z}$ are the levels of capacity utilization and real wages at which point no further nominal wage changes are pursued by 'satisfied' wage-earners. There is no reason, *a priori*, to expect that $\overline{u}$ in equation 6.3 and 6.4 are equal to each other since they refer, respectively, to the behaviour of firms and wage-earners, and z and u are not necessarily independent of each other in all cases.

Solving the above set of equations provides the reduced forms for price inflation and growth in the real wage. These expressions are left out here, but they generate quite complex distributional dynamics.[28] A nominal devaluation will contribute to inflation both through the cost increase for imported goods as well as the subsequent upwards pressure on the nominal wage rate. In practice this is recognized by the IMF and World Bank, which often include wage controls as a common measure in their adjustment packages. A restrictive wage policy leads, however, to increased inequality among profit (that is, mark-up) receivers and wage-earners, so attempts to curb inflation through wage controls does not eliminate the underlying social conflict. This is why social classes and productive sectors are identified explicitly in structuralist models, making it possible to decompose production costs and demand and analyse the effect of changes in income distribution on the economy.

Substituting equation 6.1 into equation 6.2, the decomposition of the production costs can be rewritten as follows:

$$Py = wby + eP_f ay + b^* (1 + i\omega)By + i\omega By + \upsilon(1 + b^*)(1 + i\omega)By \quad (6.5)$$

where y is real output. This equation shows that the value of output $Py = Y$ is the sum of the wage bill, intermediate import costs, mark-up income, interest on working capital and value-added taxes.

The corresponding decomposition of the demand side of the economy is known from Chapter 2. It is simply the national account identity 2.5, which can be restated as follows:

$$Py = P[C_p + C_g + \theta I + (X - Z)] \qquad (6.6)$$

using a slightly modified notation where C_p and C_g are real private and public consumption, I real investment, and $X - Z$ should be interpreted as exports net of competitive imports. The term θ

measures the share of gross investment that is produced nationally with the balance being imported.

The next step in the structuralist approach in Taylor's macro model is to specify behavioural rules for the right-hand side of equation 6.6 (that is, C_p, I and $X - Z$ with C_g being a policy variable), and derive reduced forms for internal as well as external balances, which are also referred to as the savings and trade gaps, respectively. This will be left out here,[29] but savings rates are differentiated by social class to allow the investigation of longer-term growth effects of alternative distributional outcomes connected with the 'forced savings' mechanism.[30] The strong rigidity built into the definition of prime cost through the fixed input–output coefficient for imported intermediates (a) appears again in the foreign-trade specification. This is another common element of structuralist macro models. Finally, investment is assumed to be financed by borrowing from the banking system or the public, so investment responds to the profit rate, which is used as an index of expected future gains,[31] and negatively to the real interest rate $(i - \Delta P)$. Consumption (or savings) and investment decisions are therefore carried out independently of each other in a characteristic structuralist/Keynesian manner.

The above summary implies that four adjusting variables may be relevant in the short run: inflation (ΔP), capacity utilization (u), the trade surplus $(X - Z)$ and the interest rate (i). The cost-and-activity based derivation of the inflation rate together with the specifications of u and $X - Z$ were already referred to, and to make the system complete, an independent equation for the determination of the interest rate i can be added by assuming that loan markets clear.[32] The total model can subsequently be reduced to a 4×4 system in the four unknown variables and used for analytical purposes to understand the workings of the model and assess the impact of shocks and policy actions. A wide range of short- and long-run conclusions can be deduced from Taylor's framework. They will not all be listed here, but deriving the detailed effects of monetary tightness and of a nominal devaluation leads to classical short-run structuralist results:

(a) Monetary restraint is contractionary (due to its negative effect on investment) and possibly inflationary (through the price rule mechanism), but the trade gap is improved. A nominal devaluation may produce similar results.

(b) Devaluation is capable of producing an expansionary effect on y, but only when exports rise briskly and exceed intermediate imports. In practice, the export response will, however, take time, which raises dynamic problems.

(c) Nominal devaluations cannot avoid contributing to increasing costs and nominal wage pressures. This leads to inflation.

(d) Financial liberalization (and interest rate increases) lead to questionable results in a similar manner. Taylor (1989a:42) notes that such policies have in any case been overtaken by events, since the problem today is not excessively low interest rates but excessively high ones, especially in countries such as in sub-Saharan Africa, which are heavily affected by the international financial system.

Capacity utilization is the key closure mechanism behind the classic structuralist short-run adjustments, and output adjustment does indeed appear reasonable when typical stabilization measures such as those just referred to are applied in a harsh manner. On the other hand, neo-structuralists readily recognize that other sectors and policy measures should be considered, and alternative adjustment mechanisms may in some circumstances be of overriding importance.

Price-quantity interactions between different sectors with respectively fix- and flex-price behaviour are often crucial, so disaggregations based on common sense as well as institutional awareness are required. Yet, the analyst and policy-maker should, in any case, be aware of what the chosen closure rule is and how it can change over time. This specification affects not only the size, but also the direction of the results the model produces in the short run, and in the long run results which are unexpected from an orthodox perspective may appear.[33]

For example, orthodox arguments assume that higher profits or real wage cuts will stimulate production in an 'exhilarationist' manner.[34] But it can also be hypothesized that higher profits or real wage cuts lead to depression, and that wage increases (and the extra demand to which this redistribution gives rise) may stimulate an otherwise 'stagnationist' system. Progressive redistribution through lenient wage increases can, of course, drive demand and inflation too far, and if capacity limits are reached, a 'forced savings' mode of adjustment sets in, making redistributive initiatives self-defeating.

Country circumstances differ and generalized statements about the impact of economic shocks and, for the reasons just outlined, policy measures should be treated critically. With this in mind, it is none the less clear that neo-structuralists are more inclined to suggest less austere adjustment packages with relatively more monetary and fiscal ease than the IMF and World Bank approaches tend to imply, in particular if the initial activity level is low so that output adjustment appears more feasible. It is also held that selective policy interventions directed by the state in a conscious manner makes sense. For example, careful allocation of foreign exchange may be justified when this constraint is seriously binding. In addition, the use of export subsidies and import quotas is often proposed as an alternative to avoid the potentially unfavourable economy-wide effects of changes in the nominal exchange rate.

Similarly, proposals for outright financial liberalization are treated with suspicion. Attention is drawn to the stagflationary consequences of such moves, and it is maintained that the inflationary consequences of raising state-controlled prices for intermediate goods and food as well as other consumer goods should be carefully considered. Exchange and price controls should not be ruled out *a priori* due to their linkages with demand and income distribution. Furthermore, if the economy adjusts in a stagnationist fashion, stabilization is not necessarily incompatible with carefully controlled income redistribution in favour of the poor.

Analysing a foreign-exchange-constrained economy such as those of sub-Saharan Africa within the model formulated by Taylor (1989a) can be done by assuming that the trade gap is exogenously determined as in the World Bank RMSM. This amounts to adding a restriction to the model which must be solved by adding another degree of freedom. The simplest way of doing this is to solve the model with the capacity utilization level u and inflation as a function of $X - Z$, implying that the trade gap is suppressed. This brings into focus the key role additional foreign resources can play, since additional resource transfers to SSA will allow u (and employment) to increase.

Taylor (1989a:35) notes in this regard that the outcome of specific models should not, however, be taken too literally. A binding trade constraint can be met by many devices, including reductions in the import coefficient a in equation 6.1, reduction of inventories, policy changes such as the imposition of quotas as well as reduced public spending.[35] Assuming that at least some of these devices work and that the trade gap is reduced significantly, the economy will also have to generate additional savings to avoid a fall in u (that is, the rate of capacity utilization).

If capacity utilization is simply eliminated as an adjusting variable in the model, this illustrates a situation where only inflation can bring about internal balance through 'forced savings'. This is not, however, an automatic and smooth process as suggested by the stability of the money-demand function in the IMF financial programming model. On the contrary, demand is affected in various complicated ways by changes in the inflation rate, and competing social claims are involved. Distributional consequences will also have differing longer-term consequences, depending on whether the economy is stagnationist or not. It is relevant to note that some of the empirical studies listed in Taylor (1987, 1988) point in the former direction. There is also mounting evidence that growth prospects have become increasingly impaired by fiscal constraints. This means that crowding in effects of public sector activity are not captured. Further observations in this regard are included in Chapter 7 together with references to the growing literature on three-gap models.

RADICAL PERSPECTIVES

The various approaches to stabilization and adjustment reviewed so far have their roots in the leading (mainstream) schools or paradigms of development economics, which have over the past forty years competed for attention and become in various ways intermixed in practical policy-making and analysis. Thus, there is reason to review as well the more radical contributions to development theory, although they were not formulated to deal with short- to medium-term stabilization and structural adjustment issues. These approaches grew out of Marxian and structuralist development thinking after the Second World War, and are often classified under the headings of Marxism, neo-Marxism and dependency theory.[36]

These different versions of radical development theory overlap in a number of important respects. They are also rife with intricate internal disputes, and the conclusions as to whether and how to alter the present state of affairs in poor countries is by no means uniform. None the less, they share an appealing holistic (or global economy) approach to the analysis of the economic, social and political problems of Third World countries.

Classical dialectical Marxism is a very original analytical method, which Marx primarily used to analyse the dynamic nature of the capitalist mode of production.[37] He did not pay much attention to the situation of Africa, Asia and Latin America. Production in these regions was regarded as feudal or backward, so social formations were perceived as stagnant. The expansion of capitalism into poor countries would in all probability have a progressive impact on pre-capitalist poor countries. That is, orthodox Marxists recognize the potential for capitalist development in what is referred to as the periphery. However, focus in their work has almost exclusively been on trying to discern the inner momentum or laws of motion of history. No framework for the determination of alternative adjustment strategies and policies is offered.

The thinking of Marx has been very influential in development studies and his insistence that struggle and conflict, rather than peaceful growth, is the engine of progress remains prevalent in many of the contributions to development economics.[38] The 'optimism' of Marx has not, however, been shared by many of his followers. Already the later work of Lenin on imperialism,[39] in which he puts emphasis on the existence of an international class struggle and on monopoly capitalism as opposed to competitive capitalism, signalled a much more pessimistic attitude toward the possibility for capitalist development in poor countries.

The ideas of a centre and a periphery as well as that of uneven development at a global scale and conflicts between rich and poor countries gained support. In the first major post-war study of neo-Marxist orientation concerning poor countries Baran (1957) put forward a theory of economic growth *and* stagnation. For Baran, as well as other North American Marxists (including, for example, Sweezy 1970, and Sweezy and Bettelheim 1972), capitalist development in the Third World is impossible due to the effects of colonial domination.

Baran argued that the continuing extraction of surplus from poor to rich countries (that is, the exploitative nature of the world capitalist system) is a main cause of underdevelopment. The perspectives for the establishment of a national capitalist class are non-existent. For development to occur, radical political changes (that is, a socialist revolution) must take place. Also the neo-Marxists have therefore been rather mute in the ongoing adjustment debate.

The original structuralist group at ECLA held hopeful views on the possibilities for economic development in the periphery, to be promoted through economic policies geared at, for example, import-substituting industrialization. However, as growth started faltering in the early 1960s and political unrest spread, doubts became widespread, and the need for reformulating earlier analyses and policy conclusions was gradually recognized. Affected *inter alia* by these experiences the contours of the dependency school, which became very influential in the 1960s and 1970s, started to take form.

The more radical dependency theorists basically reached the same policy conclusions as the early neo-Marxists. They largely focused on the world economic system as a whole and on the impact of imperialism rather than on internal causes of development failure. Frank (1969) formulated the 'development of underdevelopment' thesis, and argued that while the relations between the centre and periphery of the world economy may appear to change, they have not really done so for the countries in the periphery. The poor countries are exploited through a network of monopolistic trade relations. They are, furthermore, forced to specialize in exports of primary products, for which there is little domestic demand, whereas rich countries in the centre can specialize in production of manufactures for which demand is likely to remain high. Thus, surplus continues to be extracted, and increasing polarization is taking place in the world economy. The metropolitan centres (and their local allies, a so-called *comprador* bourgeosie) override, in other words, the interests of the periphery.

Amin (1976a and 1976b), who derived his analysis of underdevelopment in the periphery from detailed knowledge of the patterns of economic change in Africa, put somewhat more emphasis on the great variety of types of underdevelopment that occur. That is, underdevelopment is reflected in an outflow of surplus as well as in a stunted process of industrial growth.[40] Amin asserts that it is not so much the absence, but the externally-dominated nature of capitalist development which constitutes the problem.

This dominance is so widespread and distorting that it is, according to Amin, still possible to refer to a general theory of underdevelopment, underlying the various specific types. Adjustment problems reflect in this interpretation foreign exploitation and the world-wide process of capital accumulation, imposed upon the formation and behaviour of nation states. Independent national policy choices cannot be taken in poor countries as long as they are integrated in the world economy. The policy conclusion remains that delinking from the world economy is a pre-condition to development. This blocks the formulation of more pragmatic policy advice.

One can identify at least two more sub-groups of the dependency approach that emerged in the gloomy period following the economic set-backs in Latin America in the early 1960s. Cardoso and Faletto (1979), who published their original contribution in 1967, are exponents of a view emphasizing the dialectics of class conflict along classical Marxist lines of thinking. There is no denial that the dynamics of the world economic system are largely determined by the centre, as held by the neo-Marxists. Yet, the stagnationist and mechanical views of the neo-Marxists and the more radical dependency theorists are squarely refuted. The underlying assumption of this branch of dependency work is that social structures may change, and more attention is therefore given to choices and alternatives. Emphasis is on the desirable rather than on the inevitable, and the overall policy conclusion is that a measure of success in terms of development can be achieved through an evolutionary reformist process.

In other words, revolution is not inevitable as in the interpretation of the neo-Marxists, but the degree to which independence of the centre can be achieved will depend upon both the level of economic development and the constellation of political forces in individual countries of the periphery. No general theory of dependency can be formulated. This points to the conclusion that the analysis of the concrete forms of imperialism and dependency situations should be at the centre of attention. Thus, potentially, this approach should be able to contribute to the adjustment debate.

Sunkel (1969) and Furtado (1976 and 1985) are in accord with the focus on the structures of domination and exploitation in the world economic system, and agree that these processes should be seen as dynamic and flexible. They also queried some of the earlier policy recommendations of ECLA. Yet, they remain at the same time closer to the original structuralist approach. Their main contribution is, therefore, that they helped in bringing out clearly the distinction between growth and development, and they pointed to the consequences of cultural dependency and the importance of transnational corporations. For example, consumption patterns of the elites are influenced from abroad in important ways that increase the dependence upon imported technology, which is effectively controlled by multinational corporations. At the same time, the size of local markets remains limited, and this, together with the stagnation of agriculture, accentuates the effect of import-substituting policies with growing external imbalance as the consequence.

Social revolution is not advocated since this option is perceived as a false alternative. Only limited attempts are made, however, to formulate policy solutions. It is argued in rather vague terms that economic policy should be reoriented toward national economic development, and that policies to promote agricultural productivity, including agrarian reform, are desirable and so on. Progressive elements among the national elites are looked to for appropriate action inspired by national collective interests. Yet, the focus is exclusively on the problems of the periphery; it is not altogether clear what the overall strategy to diminish dependency is.

In line with the above variety of different radical approaches, a number of different interpretations of the IMF and the World Bank naturally exist. However, it would be fair to state that the Bretton Woods institutions are in general conceived by dependency theorists as important means, which the centre uses to control peripheral nations. It is accepted that the scarcity of foreign exchange contributes to continuing economic crisis. Yet it is held that the provision of more alien capital will intensify, rather than decrease, external dependence as countries are further tied into the world economic system.

Attention is, in the same vein, drawn to the effective control which Western powers hold over the IMF and the World Bank. The enforcement of orthodox macroeconomic policies, including fiscal stringency, is identified with the interests of external actors and local elites rather than with poorer segments of the population. Consequently, the role of the IMF and the World Bank, as well as the policies they pursue, are viewed as a vehicle for facilitating the penetration of foreign capital into poor countries and opening them up to external domination and increasing the power and income of the local elite through distorted patterns of development.

Attention is called to the asymmetrical and unequal nature of the pressures that are put on debtor countries through conditionalities, instead of a more balanced approach to debtor as well as creditor countries. Furthermore, in analyses of particular stabilization and adjustment programmes, it is often the constraints which the IMF and the World Bank place on the longer-term development process of the country and the political costs involved in following the orthodox policy package that are in focus. Alas, policy alternatives are yet to emerge.

The views of the dependency theorists can be subjected to scrutiny from a number of perspectives. One can, first of all, object to the validity of the concept of dependency, since it is hard to draw a line between dependent countries and those which are not dependent. Therefore, as a minimum, different degrees of dependency would have to be identified. This is yet to happen in a convincing manner. Moreover, the generality and inevitability of radical theories is questionable. It is not so much that poor countries have been hurt by imperialism, that can be debated. This has been the case. None the less, the universality of the 'delinking' argument can be objected to, since it tends to oversimplify the underlying reasons for underdevelopment, and it provides little guidance on realistic stabilization and adjustment measures.

AFRICAN ALTERNATIVE FRAMEWORK

The last alternative framework to be reviewed is the African alternative
framework to structural adjustment programmes for socio-economic
recovery and transformation (AAF–SAP), put forward by the UN
Economic Commission for Africa (see ECA 1989). The publication
of this document was anxiously awaited in view of the need for a
well-articulated African response to IMF/World Bank blueprints for
stabilization and structural adjustment. African countries should obviously play a key role in the formulation of the economic strategies
and policies they are expected to implement. Since the debate over
the 'Berg Report' in the early 1980s, little had in fact come out of the
ECA in terms of consolidated analyses of the economic problems of
sub-Saharan Africa and the needed responses. In other words, was
the ECA finally getting on the 'counter-offensive' in a coherent and
innovative manner, demonstrating how Africans can indeed take
charge of the elements necessary for recovery and development, so
the adjustment debate could become more constructive?[41]

The point of departure of the ECA approach is that adjustment
must be seen as part of a continuous self-sustaining process of
structural transformation, aiming at making African countries self-
reliant. The principles and policies of orthodox adjustment programmes
have, it is argued, not been adapted to the actual situation in most
African countries, characterized by weak production structures, imperfect markets and a low capacity to react to price signals, and so on.
The fundamental problems are, according to the ECA, structural in
nature, and cannot be dealt with through rigid orthodox actions
designed within a short time-frame. Even if successful on their own
terms, such programmes do not address the underlying structural
questions. Attention is also drawn to the human dimensions of
adjustment, and it is concluded that conventional programmes of the
Bretton Woods institutions are not only inadequate, but have in fact
made matters worse, rather than better.[42]

Developments in the 1980s are painted in bleak colours by the
ECA, and it is held that not only economic progress is at risk. Also
the social fabric of African societies and national political sovereignty
is endangered due to the austere IMF/World Bank approach, the
preoccupation with short-term crisis management and the increasing
role of foreign experts in national economic decision-making. The
need for adjustment, however, is not in question.

The concrete critique, put forward by the ECA as regards the overall approach and the more specific policies of on-going stabilization and structural programmes, is in accordance with structuralist lines of thinking. Therefore, no further comments are required in this regard, except that the ECA lumps the IMF and the World Bank together in a striking manner. The ECA shows no sensitivity to the intricate contrasts between the respective analytical frameworks of the two Bretton Woods institutions. These differences are important as discussed in Chapters 3 and 4, and the failure to recognize this is a major shortcoming of the ECA document.

The alternative approach proposed by the ECA is not a universal model or blueprint for adjustment with transformation. On the contrary, the approach is intended as a broad and flexible framework which governments can use in designing their individual programmes, with particular attention being paid to enhancing local capacities. The framework is, it is said, based on three sets of macro-entities (or modules), intended to capture the relationships between the operative forces that jointly determine production, income distribution and the satisfaction of needs. Yet these broad interlocking areas of concern are described in such a simplistic, and vague manner, that this part of the ECA framework cannot attract much attention.[43]

The policy instruments and measures proposed to promote adjustment with transformation can be divided into four groups, whose content can be briefly summarized:[44]

(a) **Strengthening and diversifying the production capacity**: this group of measures *inter alia* includes land reforms to ensure better access to land for productive use, devotion of at least 20–25 per cent of total investment and an increased share of foreign exchange to the agriculture sector, the use of selective nominal interest rates and multiple exchange rates in a rationalized manner and creation of special funds to provide loans at subsidized interest rates to certain groups of economic operators.

(b) **Improving the level of income and the pattern of its distribution**: under this heading, action to expand the tax base and reduce government expenditure on defence as much as possible is urged, together with the use of limited, realistic and decreasing deficit financing for productive and infrastructural investments. Also guaranteed minimum prices for certain strategic food crops is recommended.

(c) **Pattern of expenditure for the satisfaction of needs**: expenditure-switching (that is, without necessarily increasing total government spending) is suggested in this group to increase outlays on social sectors; and selective policies such as subsidies, pricing policies, and so on, are mentioned as options, to increase the supply of essential commodities. Similarly, selective trade policy is recommended to change existing consumption patterns and also differential export incentives are recommended to boost intra-African trade.

(d) **Institutional support for adjustment with transformation:** this involves the creation of supervised food production and credit systems, the strengthening of agricultural research, the creation of extension services and other rural institutions to support the development of cottage industries, legislation that specifies a clear framework of ownership of the different social groups, and greater mass participation in decision-making.

There is actually very little difference, if any, between the ECA and the views put forward in the long-term perspective study of the World Bank (1989b) as regards the need for a review of public expenditures,[45] including the desirability of allocating more investment resources to the agriculture sector. Similarly, the ECA and the World Bank share the opinion that while internal reforms are important, they will at least in the short-term have to be supplemented by significant external financial flows, disbursed in a flexible manner.

Significant differences remain, however, between the ECA on the one side and the World Bank and the IMF on the other, without ignoring the subtle nuances in the positions of the Bretton Woods sisters. The policy recommendations of ECA are, in the first place, based on a very different assessment of the optimal balance between the interventions of the state and the use of market forces. Furthermore, the ECA does not shy away from the use of selective policy measures as the IMF/World Bank certainly do. These are fundamental aspects which have a crucial bearing on economic policy design. Thus, the adjustment debate is far from settled. It is by no means easy to say who should carry the main burden of proof. Yet the more complex the proposals for reform, the greater the demand for scarce management skills. The larger the scope for 'rent-seeking' behaviour, the greater the potential misallocation of resources.

Even if it is taken for granted that orthodox measures have not worked, the same can be said about previous policies. They are no longer effective in the changed economic environment of sub-Saharan Africa. The continent is in many ways more dependent economically as well as politically on external actors and developments than ever before. Domestic policies have at least something to do with this. The ECA approach assumes a fairly competent state, but it has yet to present a fully convincing reasoning that African states do indeed have the political will, as well as the management ability, to implement effectively the policy measures recommended.

Relating to this, the ECA is remarkably blunt about the need for increased democratization and greater mass participation in decision-making. It is acknowledged that basic rights and individual freedom are often lacking in sub-Saharan Africa. The ECA is also aware that the pervasive lack of democracy makes mobilization of domestic support, indispensable for reforms to succeed, exceedingly difficult.

FINAL REMARKS

The alternative approaches and perspectives reviewed illuminate, each in their way, some of the shortcomings of the standard IMF and World Bank models and approaches to stabilization and structural adjustment. The UNICEF concern about the human dimensions of adjustment is a most pertinent reminder that development should be people-centred, and that social issues cannot be brushed aside without undesirable consequences. The UNICEF call has met with considerable success, judged by the very different oratory presently used in policy statements by the IMF and World Bank. All parties involved now seem to accept the need for targeting the poor and vulnerable, and recent policy framework papers (PFPs) make explicit reference to poverty-related issues.

Practical follow-up at field level in actual programme design and implementation remains more doubtful, and differences persist on how distributional issues are to be perceived. Rather than integrating distributional concerns into the analysis, the IMF/World Bank have concentrated on adding compensatory measures, focused on the poor, to existing programmes, in a manner which leaves their basic design unaltered. Therefore, trade-offs between a typical component, such as the promotion of liberalized prices and other free-market policies on the one side, and distributional concerns on the other, are yet to be explored more fully and recognized as important by the Bretton Woods agencies.[46]

The policy elements of the UNICEF approach are in line with the recommendations emanating from a number of country studies carried out by structuralist researchers and similar conclusions can be found in the AAF–SAP Framework of the ECA.[47] This reflects the evolutionary (and at times rather hazy) relationship between the basic needs and the structuralist paradigms of development. Structuralist perceptions have been highly, perhaps even increasingly, influential as the breeding ground for critiques of the IMF and World Bank adjustment models. However, few would by now subscribe to 'original structuralism', which has very limited common ground with the basic human needs approach.[48]

Besides, differences between the UNICEF approach and at least some structuralists seem to remain despite some complementary aspects. The UNICEF framework retains an 'essentially palliative' flavour. Contrary to this, structuralists argue that the position of vulnerable groups reflects the operation of deep-seated socio-economic propagation mechanisms and distributional conflicts.[49] Moreover, it is not altogether clear that the UNICEF policy package will in general have more than partial success in modifying these basic structural characteristics.

The analytical structuralist framework makes it possible to pose, in a consistent manner, a range of important questions, not considered in IMF/World Bank models. The recommended policy package does have characteristics which differ in several fundamental respects from the orthodox approach. The latter kind of programmes have been widely tested over the past decade; and while their degree of success or failure in the sub-Saharan African context is still a much-debated issue, it is clear that stabilization and adjustment packages with a greater leaning towards structuralist views have begun to be formulated.

The neo-structuralist model should, however, be used with great care in the sub-Saharan African environment. The model must, first of all, be further disaggregated, and must take account of the fact that social classes do, as a minimum, include agriculturalists, non-agricultural capitalists and wage labour. In addition, practically all of the African countries are small primary product exporters, critically short of foreign exchange. Yet the maintenance and expansion of domestic economic activity in manufacturing industry, as well as other sectors, requires crucial imported inputs. In addition, while African countries are subject to significant external shocks, they are also subject to macroeconomic mismanagement by governments.

Since financial markets are small and compressed, fiscal and monetary policy are intimately linked to each other, not to say they are two sides of the same coin. Hence, closure through typical Keynesian

147

changes in capacity utilization becomes less likely. If completely absent, this implies, strictly speaking, that only two macro adjustment mechanisms present themselves. The first involves government management of demand, and the other 'forced' savings through inflation. The latter occurs when government cannot, for whichever reason, control domestic absorption.

Under extreme circumstances, fix-price rules will be transformed into flex-price behaviour, a characteristic which is, in structuralist models, normally reserved for the food sector. Key prices may be set by government, but even if they are out of line with economic realities, this is largely irrelevant, since economic transactions drift outside the control of the state into flourishing unofficial parallel markets. Monetary and fiscal restraint cannot in such cases be brushed aside as irrelevant. On the contrary, orthodox policy approaches may appear almost ideal for inflation stabilization. Yet eliminating the inertial component of inflation cancels neither conflicting economic claims (by different social sectors) nor structural bottle-necks, and binding constraints can often be met in several ways. Thus, structuralist theory continues to provide useful insights which might otherwise be overlooked. The most recent contribution in this regard is the focus on a possible third gap (that is, that of the fiscal constraint), which should be added to the traditional savings and foreign-exchange gaps of the two-gap formulation. In fact, the three-gap model is an alternative to the RMSM and IMF financial programming, which is simpler and much more practical than the proposed synthesis reviewed in Chapter 5.

The various sub-groups within the dependency school, and the differences in views *vis-à-vis* the Marxists and neo-Marxists, gradually led to deep splits among more radical approaches to development. In the 1980s they also became somewhat subdued as compared to the 1960s and 1970s. The difficulty of translating the dependency perspective into a consolidated set of policy conclusions is obvious and, of course, understandable given the theoretical focus and historical time perspective. However, suggesting total delinking along neo-Marxist lines of thinking is less than helpful in face of existing adjustment problems and the growing structural interdependence of the world economy.

In summary, little realistic advice has appeared on stabilization and structural adjustment problems from these approaches, although they certainly point to a number of wider historical and structural issues of a longer-term nature, which are important and keep lurking in the background.[50]

The ECA (1989) contribution is somehow disappointing. The report itself contains good summary statements of structuralist positions on adjustment. Also the preoccupation of the ECA with strengthening and diversifying the productive capacity of African countries, and the concern with income distribution and poverty come out clearly. The same accounts for the need to reorder spending priorities. Yet nothing new in terms of analytical insights emerge. The reason why the ECA approach retains relevance is its insistence on putting development issues at the centre stage, and the clear recognition of the importance of political factors. These not only shape the environment in which stabilization and adjustment policies are implemented, but also influence the decision on which kind of adjustment is opted for.

7

CONCLUSIONS

This volume has reviewed the macroeconomic situation of sub-Saharan Africa and examined various frameworks within which stabilization and structural adjustment issues are analysed. It was shown that the crisis is serious, and that the need for adjustment cannot be a cause for controversy. On the other hand, the agenda is by no means completed.

At the root of the various theoretical approaches suggested lie truly different interpretations of the development process. Even if a measure of agreement seems to be emerging on the nature of the problems and the kinds of policy interventions that should be applied, considerable disagreement about the timing and dosage of policy measures remains. Data limitations continue to make it impossible to deal with many aspects of the adjustment process in an appropriate manner. Lastly, it is one thing to agree about what needs to be done, another to visualize how this can be put into practice.

The IMF and the World Bank became major actors on the African scene during the past decade. Thus, the analytical approaches and policies they advocate have had significant importance in determining the course of events. The Bretton Woods institutions have, since their establishment, promoted the use of market forces. Yet, the coming to power of conservative governments in the major Western countries in the early 1980s strongly reinforced the emphasis on the efficacy of competitive forces as an engine of development. The views of the IMF and the World Bank on the adjustment crisis in sub-Saharan Africa came, as a consequence, to acquire a very concentrated ideological flavour. The economic policy prescriptions, which became the order of the day, were certainly, in the case of the World Bank, a long way from the positions taken during the 1960s and 1970s.

Revised macroeconomic policies, involving significant changes in the structure of production, trade, prices and resource allocation, as well as in macro-aggregates, were intricately intertwined with an increased scope of the market and a reduced role of government in packages of stabilization and structural adjustment. Typical policy conditionalities included massive devaluations, strict monetary control, considerable cuts in public sector deficits, sweeping liberalization (in internal and external trade as well as in money and capital markets), stringent wage controls, and so on. Moreover, these major policy changes were prescribed to take place in an abrupt manner in the course of a very short time-span.

In the 'new' thinking of the IMF and the World Bank little, if any, room seemed to be left for a positive role of government interventions, including the indispensable structuring of markets and provision of essential public goods. The distributional concerns of the 1970s had somehow disappeared. There was, at least initially, little recognition of the fact that African governments have, *de facto*, claimed increasing responsibility for the management and direction of their economies, and that the sheer size of the public sector makes planning indispensable. Finally, the real potential of the private sector, and the possibility that substituting public with private monopoly may have uncertain effects – that is, that deregulation may cause perverse results – were not properly assessed before wide-ranging, generalized conclusions were drawn.

None the less, concern with the crisis in Africa did not erupt after 1980, but before. The conception of the theoretical core of, respectively, the IMF and World Bank analytical macro-frameworks predate the events just referred to by several decades. The IMF financial programming model for a small open economy with a fixed nominal exchange rate was developed on the basis of the Polak model, formulated in the late 1950s. The main conclusion of this approach is that balance-of-payments problems can be traced to too rapid a growth in the money supply, and that domestic credit is the key policy instrument for conducting monetary policy. In other words, the Polak-inspired framework provides a link between the balance of payments and inflation, on the one side, and key policy instruments on the other. Credit restraint, possibly supplemented with a devaluation, can be 'handled' within the model. Financial programming is the term used to describe the process of determining the values of the policy instruments, required to achieve desired values of the target variables.

Polak did not see his model as an alternative to other economic models. On the contrary, he tried, in the light of the IMF's mandate, to

151

put forward a simplified and operationally-useful framework to analyse the behaviour of the balance of payments from a different perspective than that of the Keynesian income-expenditure approach. He argued that a series of sub-models could be developed, subsequently, to explain the various exogenous variables, kept constant in the original version. Polak was certainly well aware that the demand for money function does not remain stable as in the extreme monetarist interpretations, and that economic adjustment is a dynamic process with many disequilibria and lags.

No empirical evidence was supplied in this volume to demonstrate how the Polak model has been applied in specific cases. None the less, a vast literature confirms the dogmatic and narrow-minded way in which the IMF has gone about doing its job in sub-Saharan Africa. The affirmations made by Guitián (in Corbo, Goldstein and Khan 1987) provide an illustrative example. It is also quite clear that too little sensitivity has existed on the part of the IMF to the fact that neo-classical full-employment, flex-price assumptions do not always hold in reality. The particular supply-constrained circumstances of sub-Saharan Africa imply that flex-price clearing may exist in some markets. Still, the IMF framework remains very far from capturing how African countries actually work, *inter alia* because it is purely monetary.

Excessive attention has been paid by the IMF to the money demand and supply processes, rather than to savings, investment and growth. These latter 'real' processes do, after all, have a decisive influence on the overall macroeconomic performance and the outcome of the necessary adjustment process. The widespread perception that too restrictive credit policy has in many cases led to more output contraction than strictly necessary cannot be discarded easily. The same accounts for the fact that inflation has often been brought under control through real output increases, rather than credit ceilings.[1]

Employment, income distribution and poverty are other issues which have, until very recently, been conspicuous in their absence from the IMF approach. Adjustment implies severe social costs in most cases and who will be hurt is an important concern, not at all present in the Polak model. These observations are disturbing. The IMF will continue to play a key role in attempts to achieve balance-of-payments viability, and this should, no doubt, remain a primary objective of the Fund. But it must be kept in mind that balance-of-payments equilibrium is not an objective in its own right. In other words, sub-models have not been developed and integrated into the financial programming framework as initially expected. Consequently, little has changed in the way the IMF uses this approach.

However, in spite of its superficial nature, the IMF framework should not be disregarded outright. Monetary variables do contain important macroeconomic information, which is often more accurate and timely than data on real variables. As the financial programming framework stands, it is a simple and relatively flexible analytical tool which could, in principle, be used in an eclectic and worthwhile manner as suggested by Polak. Unrealistic assumptions can be modified, and poor practice does not by itself invalidate the theoretical construct. On the other hand, the present volume has demonstrated that the financial programming model is by no means a sufficient and theoretically-satisfactory basis for recommending and undertaking complex and crucially important packages of adjustment policies. Further theoretical development and much greater care and modesty in actual programming work is called for.

Growth programming, based on thorough macroeconomic analyses, is equally, if not more, important to ensure that stabilization takes place and the economy develops in a satisfactory manner over time. In the sub-Saharan African context, this implies that particular attention be paid to the need for growth-oriented adjustment from the very beginning, and not as an eventual 'add on' after stabilization has taken place. This is in line with the recommendations of the Group of 24 (1987) and Bacha (1987). They argue that the financial programming exercises of the IMF should be preceded by a series of growth programming exercises. The results of such exercises, as regards financial requirements, should subsequently be included as a performance criteria in structural adjustment agreements in the form of 'reciprocal conditionality' clauses. Such symmetrical pressure on creditor countries and banks could, it is held, go at least part of the way in adhering to the principle of equal burden sharing of the costs of adjustment among creditor and debtor countries. This was, in fact, emphasized as a critical need by Keynes at the Bretton Woods Conference.

In practice, growth programming has so far mostly used the Revised Minimum Standard Model (RMSM). The RMSM grew out of the two-gap literature, which appeared during the 1960s, putting *ex ante* savings and foreign exchange gaps at the centre stage of attention. The main objective of the exercises based on this model is to provide a consistent set of projections covering key macroeconomic variables. More specifically, the two-gap approach demonstrates how much growth is feasible in light of the projected savings and capital inflows. Alternatively, it can establish the amount of additional assistance or savings required to achieve and sustain a targeted growth rate. This target can be interpreted as either the minimum admissible rate, or a somewhat more optimistic projection. Yet focus in the assessment of growth prospects of a given economy is on potential output, not on actual output due to the underlying full capacity assumption. Thus, the possibility of making use of excess capacity to raise output is not a possibility in the two-gap models and the RMSM.

Furthermore, in actual practice World Bank country economists assume that the trade (or foreign exchange gap) is binding. That is, the savings gap is eliminated through *ex post* adjustments in private consumption. In addition, there is practically no behavioural content in the RMSM model, which is essentially a balance-of-payments and capital flows model. Neither public finance nor the monetary sector are present. Lines of causality are missing, and the model cannot trace the effect of policy choices that work through price incentives. Such changes can only be handled through arbitrary, *ad hoc* changes in the parameters of the model. However, this does not imply that the RMSM model is totally irrelevant to the analysis of growth and adjustment in sub-Saharan Africa. In many cases lack of adequate data limit the potential use of more sophisticated models, and the routine analytic work implied in the use of the RMSM does provide a starting point for further work.

On the other hand, the extreme simplicity of the approach, and the absolute lack of sophisticated causal relationships and interpretations of the actual operation of the economy, must be squarely recognized. It is concluded that the two-gap framework does not provide an adequate basis for formulating and examining structural adjustment programmes. Many of the key issues, including the impact of individual policies, cannot be handled within this framework, and distributional as well as fiscal issues are absent. This has become critical in view of the changes in the role of the World Bank in the 1980s, and the increasing emphasis on the need to facilitate macroeconomic policy dialogue with developing countries. Thus, it has become indispensable to try to modify and develop the RMSM, adding greater behavioural content and specification. Some recent work in this direction is under way in the World Bank, based on the macroeconomic consistency framework by Easterly (1989). Extended versions of the RMSM embrace more sectors, including the financial programming aspect of the IMF and the fiscal accounts, and various structuralist price determination rules are considered. Little has, however, so far been published on these efforts.

Summing up the approaches of the Bretton Woods institutions, the following points are particularly relevant:

(a) The IMF/World Bank economy-wide modelling models are both very simple from a theoretical point of view. Their advantage is that they require very little data to be run. They are easy to use, and provide answers quickly. This is essential in operational work, where the pressure of time can be very great indeed. In addition, the IMF/World Bank models can serve a useful purpose in helping to put order to the little information available, and as such point to key gaps in the database.

(b) The IMF/World Bank macro models are entirely different. In some ways they do supplement each other, and tension between the two institutions is, at least in part, due to the difference in time perspective. It would, in principle, be better to use the two models in a complementary, rather than a mutually-exclusive manner, and work out contradictions on a case-by-case basis. This requires, however, a flexibility that does not always exist in practice. The dichotomy of the two approaches has a theoretical as well as an operational perspective.

(c) The closure mechanisms of the IMF framework and the RMSM are different in the role played by, respectively, savings and investment as the 'driving' factor. The adjustment mechanisms are similar in the sense that closure is smooth and automatic. Attention is in both cases essentially focused on the establishment of proper balance among macro-aggregates. Variations in capacity utilization and income distribution do not appear, and there is no distinction between capacity growth and actual growth.

(d) The standard IMF/World Bank macro models do not capture the nature of structural adjustment. This has made the use of partial analyses widespread in shaping the actual contours and policy content of stabilization and adjustment packages in sub-Saharan Africa. This makes it difficult to discern the differences between the IMF and the World Bank approaches in applied work. None the less, there are differences which merit careful attention.

(e) Consistency is desirable, and the IMF/World Bank approaches can contribute to the realization of this goal. On the other hand, much more needs to be known about the economic mechanisms through which policy change affects the performance of the target variables. Action in all of the areas of policy reform, proposed with such vigour by the IMF and the World Bank, involves matters of great complexity.[2] Many issues are still up in the air.[3]

Against the above background it is remarkable that the IMF and the World Bank were so self-confident in the early years of the 1980s. The conclusion that a sizeable measure of faith and ideology must have outweighed the calls for a more phased and considered approach seems inevitable. These calls appear, more recently, to have had an impact on the IMF and the World Bank. Growth-oriented adjustment has become an accepted term, and the need for a strengthened general analytical framework is appreciated.

It is by no means an easy task to operationalize the concept of growth-oriented adjustment and develop a more comprehensive analytical framework. The knowledge of the factors that affect efficiency, savings, investment and capital flows is very insufficient. Clear relationships between financial policies and economic growth are yet to be established. Furthermore, in spite of the central policy-making and analytic role the IMF and the World Bank have played over the years, the Bretton Woods institutions have only recently initiated experimental and very preliminary efforts at restating and integrating the financial programming and RMSM approaches.

The attempt made by Khan *et al.* (1986) in this regard is theoretically interesting as a first step in investigating interrelationships, areas of conflict and the possibility for developing an integrated framework. However, typical neo-classical flex-price/full capacity utilization assumptions are maintained, and the demand for money is held stable in accordance with the monetarist tradition. These assumptions about the underlying nature of the economy are troubling in the sub-Saharan African context. There, structural bottle-necks are common, a widespread absence of key markets characteristic, and those markets which do exist often operate differently from those in the standard model.

Supply-side issues are not addressed in the merged model, where the economy is always operating at full capacity. In other words, no distinction is made between growth in productive capacity, growth of output as a result of more efficient resource use, and growth reflecting changes in aggregate demand. In addition, the behavioural equations in the model are, as readily admitted by Khan and Montiel (1989:303), rudimentary. Finally, the institutional framework is extremely limited, and the model is a one-period model.

The above shortcomings imply, on the one hand, that the effect on efficiency and on savings of standard policy measures, which are present in the merged model, have been eliminated *a priori*. Aggregate output is by definition already at the production frontier. This is a questionable assumption to make. On the other hand, several of the policy measures typically included in actual adjustment programmes, are not present in the model. This makes its scope very limited. Examples of the above two different kinds of problems are, respectively, the potential impact of exchange rate and domestic credit policy on efficiency levels, and the absence of the interest rate as an instrument to affect *inter alia* domestic savings, investment and capital flows.

Crucial issues relating to employment and wage determination are also excluded from the merged model, which cannot trace the transition path of the economy from one equilibrium to another. The latter deficiency is critical in view of the policy-making environment in Africa, where concern over short- to medium-run effects may be of overriding importance. If short-run effects are unacceptable, it may become impossible to initiate and sustain an orderly and planned adjustment process over time. Lastly, the merged framework implies that a reduction in export demand promotes growth. This is unsatisfactory. The same accounts for the recommended policy response in the face of an exogenous drop in export demand. A devaluation appears as the only policy action required while, in fact, both the IMF and the World Bank work with much more complex policy packages in their stabilization and adjustment efforts.

Summing up the merged model, it can be concluded that:

(a) It is encouraging that the IMF and the World Bank have started a search for a more satisfactory analytical framework. While the attempt made by Khan *et al.* to merge the simple IMF/World Bank models provides intellectual exercise, it does, unfortunately, not meet the need for a simple but strengthened analytical framework. Key adjustment issues fade away, and supply-side as well as distributional issues are not addressed.

(b) It remains an unsettled issue whether the IMF/World Bank models can be integrated in an operationally-worthwhile manner of use in the analysis of a broader range of adjustment issues than possible within the simpler financial and RMSM programming models. Thus, disputes will continue to exist between the IMF and the World Bank in formulating specific country programmes.

(c) The fairly conventional macro model, put forward by Vines, illustrates the extreme assumptions made in the merged model very well. Much more sensible policy conclusions in the face of a negative external shock emerge in the former model.

The above conclusions about the validity of the merged model should not discourage further research towards formulating appropriate theoretical frameworks for the analysis of adjustment issues; on the contrary. However, greater receptivity on the part of the IMF and the World Bank to the shortcomings listed will be needed. This, and the distinct weaknesses of, respectively, the IMF/World Bank approaches, make it desirable to introduce improvements based on alternative approaches. Unless this is done, there is reason to fear that 'adjustment-with-growth' will turn out to be nothing but a popular 'catch-phrase',[4] which will never be translated into purposeful action and a change in IMF/World Bank practice.

No attempt was made to review the empirical evidence on the impact of stabilization and adjustment programmes in the sub-Saharan context. It remains, nevertheless, that orthodox programmes have been criticized heavily on theoretical as well as on empirical grounds. UNICEF has, with success, drawn attention to the human costs of adjustment. Similarly, the ECA has not failed to point out shortcomings in orthodox policy advice, as well as the flaws in the statistical evidence the World Bank has used in at least some of its earlier publications.

The debate over the empirical evidence has at times assumed an almost caricature nature. By now it is clear that performance has been very uneven and generally unsatisfactory. Programmes and policy measures have certainly not worked as expected.[5] Despite concerted action on the part of African countries, adjustment has, according to more recent World Bank reports, largely been a matter of running harder to stay in place. The increases in the incidence of poverty have made it apparent to even the IMF that it is essential for this issue to move again into the forefront of policy design.

The key problem behind much of the debate on the empirical evidence is that it is impossible to establish a counterfactual of what trends would have been without the structural adjustment programmes.[6] None the less, universal acceptance of the orthodox adjustment design and implementation clearly requires more positive results than have so far come forward. The frequency of failure of attempts at a solution has certainly turned something which is, from one point of view, ordinary macroeconomic management, into a major issue in development economics.[7] This is so in particular, because poverty remains, after all, the ultimate challenge of development policy.

The UNICEF policy package is an attempt to offer a more poverty-alleviation-focused approach to adjustment. Many of the UNICEF proposals have by now, at least in part, been accepted by the Bretton Woods agencies. A special social dimension of adjustment programmes has been introduced. The weakness of the UNICEF approach would seem to be its somewhat *ad hoc* character and the lack of an analytical framework, providing deeper insights into the social and political processes and root causes propagating poverty and inequality.

Analyses based on elasticity and micro-structuralist approaches have been influential in establishing that neo-classical assumptions must be handled with great care in sub-Saharan African circumstances. Similarly, the various attempts made to extend the 'pure' neo-classical computable general equilibrium (CGE) model to include structuralist features have underpinned the need for caution in generalizing about economic policy on the basis of partial equilibrium analysis.[8] It is, however, the neo-structuralist school, that is most directly challenging the IMF/World Bank models of adjustment, and macro-structuralists, such as Taylor, have made thought-provoking contributions to the analytical and policy-oriented debate on structural adjustment.[9]

The early policy advice, emanating from the ECLA-based structuralist school in the 1940s and 1950s, paid insufficient attention to the importance of short-run macroeconomic management and macroeconomic balances. This is being reverted. At the same time, neo-structuralist models maintain strong links between the 'real' and the 'monetary' side of the economy along Kaleckian and Keynesian lines of thinking. Aggregate savings and investment are specified separately, and account is taken explicitly of structural rigidities as well as changes in income distribution. This is in complete opposition to the approaches used by the IMF and the World Bank. In other words, the typical closure mechanisms of structuralist macro models are specified differently from those assumed by the Bretton Woods agencies.

The neo-structuralist approach is engaging. It recognizes that the distributional impact of decisions on economic management are linked in critical ways with political processes and as such cannot be ignored in proper policy analysis. It also allows the analyst to assess more fully the validity and consequences of different kinds of policies. Thus, alternative heterodox policy packages, taking account of output, balance of payments and inflation, as well as distributional targets, can be formulated. Finally, the macro-structuralist approach carries with it the potential of putting the existing rather dispersed critique of the orthodox stabilization and adjustment measures on a more solid analytical base.

The problems related with the structuralist approach are several:

(a) When structural rigidities exist, other equilibrating mechanisms have to be specified. This is typically done in neo-structuralist models by introducing constraints in an *ad hoc* manner, which is not related to any endogenous rational behaviour of economic agents. This is justified because of the current inadequate state of economic theory and the absence of an acceptable reconciliation of micro and macro theory. The objective of trying to capture real and stylized macro features of the issues at hand is valid, but structuralists strain received micro theory. This leaves a wide open space of doubt, relating to applicability and interpretation.

(b) Structuralist inflexibilities are often based on short-run considerations and introduced via, for example, mark-up pricing. However, the types of assumptions, adequate for a model with a short-term horizon, are different from those appropriate for long-run models. How the edges of the different perspectives overlap is an unsettled question.

(c) Empirical support for a number of the structuralist specifications, leading to adjustment problems, is uncertain.[10] Furthermore, while useful in analytical models, several of the typical assumptions made are often indefensible in applied models. The neo-structuralist school faces, in other words, the problem that many of its contributions have so far been analytic rather than applied.

(d) Households in sub-Saharan Africa earn their living from wage employment or in small production and trade units (in the 'informal' or 'traditional' sectors), and enterprises in the 'modern' sector may be either private, state or foreign-owned. All of these aspects, as well as the national economic environment and regional differences, have a bearing on how different economic agents behave, and on the particular constraints faced. It is these various distinct sets of often contradictory behaviour that interact with economic policies in the determination of the macroeconomic imbalances reviewed. Hence, structuralist models built around only two social classes will have to be further disaggregated to become more realistic.

160

(e) The various arguments for a more heterodox approach to stabilization and adjustment will, in practice, have to be balanced against the need for following an orthodox line of action, when required to convince external donors and others to maintain a sufficiently-high level of capital inflows. Influencing the views of donors is therefore an important pre-condition for success of the neo-structuralist rebuff.

In conclusion, sub-Saharan African economies are not as flexible as assumed in the neo-classical framework, and economic models must capture existing rigidities and gaps as well as the non-existence of markets to be useful in policy analysis. However, the analytical models formulated over the years by the macro structuralist school, have not been easily applicable to the generation of specific policy recommendations. It is, as Taylor (1989a:1–2) observes, high time for concrete policy models to be laid out, if structuralism is to fare better in current practice than mainstream economics has done in the past.

Motivated by the advent of the debt crisis and the severe import compression of the sub-Saharan economies during the 1980s, encouraging new work in this regard is under way. The RMSM is, as already mentioned, being extended in the World Bank; and the two-gap model is under re-examination. With regard to the latter, Bacha (1984) was the first to make two important points: (i) the two gaps are in reality just a restatement of internal and external balance relationships from open economy macroeconomics, and (ii) it is essential to try to endogenize capacity utilization in addition to potential output rather than accepting it as a technically-determined parameter. For this reason Taylor (1991:3) underlines that when a given economy is in need for adjustment one has to 'think through coherent macro adjustment mechanisms ... via which the gaps can be resolved consistently with the institutional structure at hand'.

During the past decade public investment and recurrent expenditures have been adjusted/cut back because of the burden of foreign-interest payments. At the same time, increased attention is now being paid to the crowding-in effects of public on private investment.[11] In response, structuralist economists such as Bacha (1990), Ndulu (1990) and Taylor (1991) note that a third − fiscal − gap should be added to the savings and foreign-exchange gaps in focus in the two-gap model. Their three-gap formulations, which are based on flow of funds identities and an endogenization of capacity utilization, carry a considerable potential for becoming relevant and simple/practical tools in the analysis of growth and adjustment issues in sub-Saharan Africa. They come, for sure, closer to the mark than the synthesis suggested by Khan *et al.*[12]

Foreign capital inflows can be indispensable, as they are within the orthodox and the structuralist frameworks. Such inflows can also spell continued exploitation and dependency, as proposed by more radical approaches. On the other hand, since this is not always so, mechanical and rigid interpretations of history should be avoided. The substantial growth and development in Third World countries since the Second World War remains an empirical fact. The more recent experience of the newly-industrializing countries (NICs) is another striking indication that development is possible in the periphery, with benefits extending to the relatively poor. While disagreement on the approaches of the Bretton Woods institutions may exist for perfectly valid reasons, it is much too simplistic, and not very effective, to view these agencies as Draconian instruments for continued exploitation and as a kind of scapegoat for all existing economic problems. For this, the World Bank and the IMF are much too complex and diverse establishments.

The IMF and the World Bank are, albeit slowly, able and willing to modify their positions, when particular circumstances prevail. While it is necessary to analyse stabilization and adjustment policies from a historical and structural perspective, it can hardly be undesirable to make short-run macro-management more effective in sub-Saharan Africa. The Bretton Woods institutions can play an important role in this regard and in addressing crucial development issues. Radical approaches must be modified to take account hereof. In addition, they must recognize that complete 'delinking' is very unhelpful advice, given the existing adjustment issues and the structural interdependence of the world economy.

It is difficult to test alternative macroeconomic models empirically in SSA for methodological reasons and because of the widespread lack of data. Only a few in-depth macroeconomic country studies are available. It could be hypothesized that neo-classical closure tends to be more appropriate in the long run, and that structuralist closures fit better in the short term. Conclusions in this respect must, however, remain tentative for the time being. On the other hand, it is certain that a satisfactory overall framework in which growth-oriented adjustment can be modelled, is still lacking. The right approach to adjustment depends on many things. This makes it important that policy analysts avoid parroting a single model. Instead, they should be able to examine the economy as it is, and determine which policy instruments are likely to be effective at the chosen moment.

The present volume has confirmed that IMF financial and World Bank growth-programming exercises should be improved. Relating to this, it is clear that while some countries in sub-Saharan Africa have fared better than others, many continue to perform far below expectations. There is, therefore, plenty of reason to be cautious and to develop and test alternative approaches. In this process, non-orthodox generalizations have to be ventured. Otherwise, they are unlikely to have any impact. However, in the final analysis, it is likely that a more appropriate general analytical approach must draw on elements from orthodox as well as structuralist thinking. As a minimum, the missing equations must be added to the IMF/World Bank methodologies.[13]

It may also be that adjustment with growth cannot be modelled in a generally satisfactory manner within a common analytical framework without making it very complicated. This is another good reason for adopting a flexible, eclectic approach in the use of economic models and analytical methods in the design of structural adjustment programmes. In any case, to be able to construct a good programme, one must know the specifics of the country. Tailoring is indispensable.

Changes are required in the economic policies of previous decades to manage the African adjustment process. Governments must no doubt improve routine planning activities and take concerted measures to increase economic efficiency. However, sub-Saharan Africa faces a deep-seated production crisis, very severe foreign-exchange constraints, high rates of population growth and inadequately developed organizational and managerial capabilities. Thus, for adjustment to be growth oriented, attention needs to be paid to supply-side issues and structural constraints. More external finance is also crucial. Finally, the very vulnerable nature of the African economies should be taken account of in policy analysis and projections. This is so from the perspective of the world economy as well. Permanent changes seem to be taking place, and the high growth record experienced since the Second World War should, in all likelihood, not be taken as a trend for the coming decades.

Agreement on the need to adjust does not imply agreement on the more specific packaging of policies and their sequencing. Too little continues to be known about the exact impact of individual economic policies in the sub-Saharan African context. This obviously makes the task of African policy-makers exceedingly difficult. Programmes will, as a consequence, have to rely on rather diverse judgements of the ultimate consequences of policy actions. Hence, the design of policy packages, aiming at simultaneously eliminating macroeconomic imbalances and raising the rate of growth, will remain a much-debated issue for some time to come.

Studying the interaction of instruments and indicators in a general equilibrium framework is regularly put forward among the actions recommended for the future.[14] It is also reasonable to expect that computable general equilibrium (CGE) models, which allow the analyst to examine the impact of domestic resource allocation and individual policy instruments on growth, will become gradually more important in policy analysis related to African countries. Only a few attempts have been made so far,[15] and at present the use of CGE models in, for example, World Bank applied work is extremely limited.[16] Less ambitious approaches than these highly-disaggregated, all-purpose and data-demanding models, such as the three-gap formulations, must therefore, in most cases, be adhered to for the time being.

The crisis in sub-Saharan Africa is multi-dimensional and complex. Consequently, no single study of the limited size of this book can attempt to address all pertinent issues in a satisfactory manner. The guiding principle chosen for this inquiry has been to focus on the contributions and analytical insights emerging from existing macroeconomic frameworks, and sub-Saharan Africa has been treated as a homogenous whole. This approach, although applied in a broadminded manner, certainly has its weaknesses. Adjustment programmes will, in the African condition, involve significant distributional effects. Consequently, to be successful they must be based on political coalitions in favour of initiating and sustaining reform. The issue of how such coalitions can be forged and maintained is vital. Analyses of 'who gains' and 'who loses' are important.

Failure to design compensating devices, or negotiated 'social contracts', for 'losers' may cause political difficulties and delay or abort programme implementation. In other words, African policy-makers will have to consider the trade-offs between technical efficiency and speed and political sustainability, as well as the economic costs of politically-failed or abandoned adjustment efforts. It seems pertinent to expect that outside agencies do the same, before conditionalities are defined. Yet, this has, until recently, not been the case in the politics of negotiating adjustment programmes between the Bretton

Woods agencies and African governments. This may be changing, however. While the World Bank and the IMF had considerable leverage in the early phases of the adjustment process in SSA, African countries have by now 'reverse leverage'. As the process goes on without obvious success, the cost of programme failures also has to be faced by the Bretton Woods agencies.[17]

Linked with, and to some extent overlapping, the above points is the debate about the nature and role of the African state. Economists have in most of their work used the 'rational actor' model of government behaviour; that is, a view of government as a monolithic entity trying to correct market imperfections and promote long-run development. It is, so far, an unsettled issue what the elements of a more realistic, analytic policy model should be. However, account must be taken of the existence of personal rule, and ethnic and regional background can, at least in the short run, be more important in sub-Saharan Africa than, for example, class interests based on economic classifications.

The conclusions that can be drawn from this vary. In some countries adjustment will only be successful if fundamental reforms take place in the political systems. In others, more evolutionary patterns of change are possible. The quality and capacity of political leadership and the existence of a well-defined strategic vision for the future can matter a great deal. But popular involvement in decision-making and in the implementation of adjustment programmes is more crucial than often realized. Only through mass participation will the greater confidence of the people in their society and government, as well as the needed commitment to development, come about. It is appropriate and healthy that this perspective comes out so clearly in the ECA contribution.

The above observations suggest that there is a need for reworking the role of the state in sub-Saharan Africa. This has far-reaching implications for the formulation and implementation of sound macro-economic and development policies, but this issue was only referred to in passing. The same accounts for the distinction between liberalization and reduced state intervention, almost as ends in themselves, and the need for using market forces as an integral part of a strategy for social transformation and development. Strengthening the economic role of the government may imply it focuses its attention on a somewhat more narrow range of strategic concerns.[18] The issue is what the more precise limits of the boundaries of the state should be in its various economic and political functions.

Macroeconomics matters a great deal in sub-Saharan Africa today through its impact on overall resource allocation, institutional structures, public expenditures and taxation and the formation of an environment conducive to improved microeconomic performance. Progress in understanding the field of economic management is important because of the pressing need of formulating adequate policy advice to troubled policy-makers. Macro models, such as those reviewed, can play a useful role in setting out frameworks for thinking about adjustment issues. These models are, however, nothing more than tools in the hands of the analysts. They prove nothing by themselves.

The search for a strengthened framework for analysing adjustment with growth should continue, but it is also high time, as pointed out by Taylor (1989:2), that concrete policy models are laid out in the context of particular country circumstances. The WIDER studies, summarized in Taylor (1987), include country papers on Ghana, Ivory Coast, Kenya, Sudan and Tanzania. This is one step in the right direction since concrete adjustment programmes must, in the final analysis, be country specific. Another step is to continue developing the three-gap models.

Economics will continue to play a predominant and crucial role in the formulation and analysis of alternative development policies and strategies, in problem-solving and in the assessment of trade-offs in light of underlying assumptions and value premises. Economics is, in other words, important in the wider context of improving governance in Africa and increasing the public awareness of the choices open to society. However, economics is not all that matters. Economic and non-economic factors are continuously interacting, at times reinforcing, and at times contradicting, each other. The imbalances in Africa between basic human needs and present levels of supply of food, shelter, social services, and so on, are not easily handled by national accounting equations. These imbalances have, however, crucial implications for macroeconomics, and the need for development is as pressing as ever before. Therefore, sub-Saharan Africa poses some of the most difficult and intricate challenges to development theory and practice. In other words, much remains to be done.

NOTES

PREFACE

1 I had not read Killick (1976) before taking up my field assignments, but his conclusions, including *inter alia* the view that government actions are often not an expression of the general good, and that planning efforts failed to deliver the benefits expected, correspond closely with my own more limited observations.

2 Healey (1972:794) was commenting on this issue when he suggested that: 'It is time we learned to strengthen and to make use of market forces instead of tilting ineffectively and disastrously against them'.

3 See, for example, Toye (1987).

4 A survey of the essentials can be found in Srinivasan (1985), but also Lal's (1983) provocative statement on the 'poverty of development economics' is useful.

5 Further details on this case may be found in an article of mine (Tarp 1990).

6 See Van Arkadie (1987).

7 The 1988 *World Development Report* of the World Bank contains much useful material on these issues (World Bank 1988a).

8 See Thomas and Chhibber (1989) for a straightforward summary overview of the kinds of issues which are being debated. Green (1986) is also useful.

9 Commander (1989), Helleiner (1986a), Meier and Steel (1989) and Onimode (1989) are good references here.

10 While policy implications of existing overall approaches will be outlined, I will not dwell in detail on the intricate and substantive issues related to the analysis of the performance of individual technical policy instruments.

11 Those listed in the bibliography are just a selection, but they illustrate this point.

INTRODUCTION

1 For further details on the magnitude of the economic difficulties and their causes, see Chapter 1.

2 Lending from the World Bank and the IMF to African countries for stabilization and structural adjustment purposes takes place through the use of a number of different lending instruments. It is not the intention here to go into the details, which can be found in the IMF and World Bank annual reports. Nevertheless, it can be noted that the IMF in 1986 and 1987 supplemented its more traditional facilities (such as the Stand-by, Compensatory Financing and Extended Fund Facilities) with two new special facilities – the Structural Adjustment Facility (SAF) and the Enhanced Structural Adjustment Facility (ESAF), which are part of a broader effort to cope with the problems of the poorest countries. Most World Bank lending is given in the form of discrete projects, but since 1980 loans are also given in the form of Structural Adjustment (SAL) and Sectoral Adjustment Loans (SECAL).

3 Early debates centred around the 'Berg Report' of the World Bank (1981), which identified insufficiencies in national policies as the prime cause for decline, and the OAU *Lagos Plan of Action* (1980). A very extensive literature exists. For more recent contributions critical of the World Bank and the IMF see Onimode (1989) and Campbell and Loxley (1989).

4 Actual country programmes can and do vary, but they are in fact strikingly similar. The following lists of objectives and policy instruments have been compiled based on various sources including *inter alia* Killick (1984), Mosley and Toye (1988), World Bank (1988b), World Bank and IMF annual reports, as well as personal notes from various seminars with IMF and World Bank staff.

5 Elliot Berg, whose (World Bank 1981) work served as a catalyst in changing the debate on Africa's problems, is concerned about the spreading of conditionality as a main vehicle for extending structural adjustment assistance. In commenting on Helleiner's overview of the issues, Berg states:

> But most academic critics believe IMF conditionality has been ineffective in Africa (and elsewhere) and World Bank conditionality involves imposition of policies that are technically uncertain at best and wrongheaded or ideological at worst ... Something has gone awry here. Conditional lending has become so extensive in Africa that the donor community has become excessively intrusive in African policy making.
> (Helleiner 1986b:97)

The World Institute for Development Economics Research of the United Nations University (WIDER) study by Avramovic (1989) can be consulted for a good review of World Bank/IMF and other cross-conditionalities together with suggestions for a new approach.

6 See World Bank (1990b) for a conceptual framework of analysis of social dimensions of adjustment with particular reference to Africa.

7 Hunt (1989) provides a useful overview and analysis of competing paradigms (or economic theories) of development which are of relevance here.

8 See for example Edwards (1989b) for a critique from a moderate main-stream point of view, Bacha (1987), ECA (1989), Faber and Green (1985), Green (1986), Killick (1984), Loxley (in Helleiner 1986a) and Taylor (1988) for structuralist critiques, Kaldor (1983) for a post-Keynesian comment, and Diaz-Alejandro (1981), Pastor (1987) and Payer (1974) for viewpoints from dependency/Marxist perspectives. Please (1984) is also interesting as he has consistently argued that there is much more common ground between the World Bank and ECA approaches to development issues than is commonly perceived.

9 See Development Committee (1988) for a statement on World Bank and IMF views as expressed by the staff of these organizations. This reference also contains additional useful references.

10 According to Ravenhill (1988:179) a fragile consensus exists, as six years of intense debate have produced a measure of agreement on a solution for Africa's malaise, which is captured by the latest catchphrase of the IMF and the World Bank, 'Adjustment with Growth' (see also the editorial by Allison and Green 1985). The need for greater attention to distribu-tional concerns has been effectively promoted by the United Nations International Children's Emergency Fund (UNICEF) (see Cornia, Jolly and Stewart 1987a, 1987b) and the bibliography contains some of the more interesting contributions on distributional aspects of adjustment.

11 A joint statement on Africa's long-term development, prepared following a meeting held in May 1989, among high level staff of the World Bank, IMF, OAU, African Development Bank, United Nations Development Programme (UNDP), ECA, UNICEF and the UN Office of the Director General for Development and International Cooperation is also remarkably conciliatory in tone and content. Nevertheless, basic disagreements con-tinue to exist.

1 MACROECONOMICS OF AFRICA

1 Much of SSA is prone to droughts which have frequently had a very significant impact on agricultural production due to the low level of technologies used, including the limited development of irrigation.

2 According to ECA (1989:5) the fragmentation arises principally from the generally hostile physical environment, and the typically small nation states of Africa, coupled with low incomes. Of the forty-six countries in SSA, twenty have a population of less than five million and of these nine have a population of less than one million (World Bank 1990b:254–5 and 271). The uneven spatial distribution of the population has also inhibited the development of transport networks, thereby constraining national integra-tion.

3 See three surveys – Cassen *et al.* (1986), Mosley (1987b) and Riddell (1987) – for analyses of the broader issues related to the impact of official development assistance.

4 Acharya (1981:117) furthermore makes the point that the inherited and inappropriate public pay structures and the legacy of 'consumptionist' attitudes towards public services constrained efficiency, and resulted in a

heavy pressure for rapid expansion of government public services which tended to reduce public savings.

5 See ECA (1989:6–7) for an eloquent statement in this regard.

6 See Helleiner (1986b:65).

7 This issue will not be pursued further here. It can be noted, however, that the weaknesses of official data have no doubt been made worse because of the prolonged nature of the crisis. The consequent changes in economic structures and the increase in informal as well as illegal activities are not likely to have been fully reflected in official data (see Loutfi 1989 for an elaboration of the argument). Furthermore, it is not yet possible to reconcile available data series on balance of payments, foreign trade and national accounts (World Bank 1989a:68). Therefore, the macroeconomic balances reported in this chapter cannot in all cases be made consistent. An example is the overall resource balance. IMF data on national accounts are compiled by IMF correspondents in each government, central bank, or statistical office, whereas World Bank data are based on the UN System of National Accounts (SNA). Data from the World Bank, UN/SNA and UN trade statistics are the main original source in relation to production, domestic absorption, trade, and so on, whereas IMF international and government financial data are the principal source for fiscal and monetary accounts, as well as international transactions and price developments. A World Bank/UNDP publication (World Bank 1989a) has been used as source for some of the summary fiscal and monetary indicators in Table 1.4, but they have been calculated on the basis of IMF sources. For further technical comments see the introduction and the various notes in, for example, World Bank (1989a).

8 The Basal Metabolic Rate (BMR), that is, the amount of energy required to maintain body processes at rest, corresponds to approximately 1,800 calories/person/day. This rate does not, however, include an allowance for normal movement and work. An average of 2,250 calories is therefore sometimes used as the poverty line. This figure does not take account of variations by sex, age, and so on, and it should, of course, be recalled that food is not distributed equally.

9 See World Bank (1989a:69).

10 See, for example, IMF (1990:178).

11 Developments in the terms of trade and external financial relations will be further discussed on pages 14–25, together with developments in government finances, money and banking.

12 It can also be noted, that gross national savings as a share of GDP have consistently remained well below gross domestic savings during the 1980s (see World Bank 1989a:12–13).

13 See World Bank (1989b:110).

14 Killick (1986) provides a concise overview of the changes in perceptions over the last twenty-five years. Toye (1987) is also stimulating.

15 Ravenhill goes on to observe that the 'Berg Report' has effectively taken the Lagos Plan of Action off the development agenda, and that a similar transformation is apparent in academic work, where there is now a new emphasis on the internal characteristics of African states and an interest in policy analysis, rather than in the more radical dependency and Marxist

approaches, which were dominant in the 1970s. Further observations in this regard follow in Chapter 6.

16 A long range of similar examples that document domestic policy failures in sub-Saharan Africa can be found in World Bank (1989b). This publication is the most recent contribution in the follow-up to the 'Berg Report', and it provides an extensive list of background papers and a selected bibliography (see Sender and Smith 1984 for an earlier paper containing contrasting viewpoints and useful references). Faber and Green (1985) could also be consulted.

17 See Loutfi (1989:137).

18 See, for example, World Bank (1988a:Chapter 8) for additional information on state-owned enterprises.

19 See World Bank (1989a:116).

20 See Development Committee (1988:37–8).

21 See World Bank (1989c:65).

22 See Development Committee (1989:34).

23 Accurate data on capital flight in sub-Saharan Africa are difficult to obtain. But estimates by Chang and Cumby (1990) indicate that capital flight was an influential factor in determining developments in private sector balances in SSA during the 1980s. See Cuddington (1986) for a good general review of issues related to capital flight.

24 Note however, that these conclusions as far as the overall and the private balances are concerned and which have been based on World Bank (1989a) national accounts data, are not fully consistent with balance of payments data from IMF sources. The latter data, which are summarized in Table 1.5, indicate that the overall external financial resource balance should correspond to a net inflow of real resources to sub-Saharan Africa for the whole of the 1980–7 period. This is due, however, to the importance of services. The trade balance actually became positive from 1984 and therefore reflects that more goods were exported than imported. No attempt has been made (World Bank 1989a:68) to reconcile these differences among time-series for balance of payments, foreign trade and national accounts, as they reflect differences in definitions used, timing, recording and valuation of transactions, as well as the nature of the basic data sources.

25 According to IMF (1990), official reserves were below 10 per cent of annual imports until 1984.

26 See World Bank (1989b) for further data.

27 See World Bank (1988:23).

28 This was partly due to better weather and partly the better availability of foreign currency to finance imports, which was at least in some measure linked to the fact that African countries were beginning to accept IMF/World Bank conditionalities.

29 This position is further put into perspective by the fact, identified by Wheeler (1984), that among the most important policy variables is some form of retrenchment capability. It is quite obvious that the capability of being able to economize was not given much attention during the 1960s and 1970s, neither by newly-established African states of a developmental orientation nor by foreign agencies and advisers.

30 Internal policy-related factors, which influence developments in export volume, were found by Svedberg to be relatively more significant in explaining the overall trend in export earnings than external factors (in this case, the barter terms of trade) in the 1970–85 period. In fourteen countries, volume changes accounted for more than 75 per cent of the change in real exports, whereas barter terms of trade dominated in eleven cases. In eight countries, both volume and barter terms of trade accounted for less than 75 per cent, so their influence was judged as mixed. In the 1954–69 period, barter terms of trade only dominated in one case, whereas export volume changes dominated in twenty-eight countries.

31 See Khan and Knight (1988) for a model that incorporates feedbacks between imports and exports arising from the effect of import compression on export, and of the availability of foreign exchange on imports (see also López and Thomas 1988).

32 See Ravenhill (1988:187) for this formulation. He also points out that the volume of resources made available to Africa after 1979 was far smaller than after the first oil shock. Furthermore, African governments were not alone in misjudging that the crisis was temporary. Even IMF staff have admitted that the Fund failed to anticipate the depth of the problems that emerged. Reduced efficacy of policy effort in the face of increased exogeneity of growth has also been alluded to by Ndulu (1990).

33 See Ravenhill (1988:185–6). He notes, first, that at the heart of the matter there is a question of how the burden of adjustment should be shared at international level. Second, even if equal sharing of the burden of adjustment is not aimed at, as suggested by the designers of the Bretton Woods system, there is still a need to identify those components of previous policies that must be changed and to develop appropriate national reponses.

34 This point is made by Streeten (in Commander 1989:5).

35 See Loxley (in Helleiner 1986a:121–2).

36 Streeten (1987b) refers to a mnemonic framework for agricultural policy consistency consisting of at least six 'i's (that is, incentives, inputs, innovation, information, infrastructure and institutions). If just one of these 'i's is absent, peasants' reaction to increased price incentives may – in some cases – be negative, Streeten argues. Cleaver (1985) and Fones-Sundell (1987) are also useful studies on this subject.

37 See Loxley (in Helleiner 1986a:121). Khan (1987:34) points out the need of investigating whether the Marshall–Lerner conditions hold in the case where imported inputs loom large in the production of exports and where those imported inputs are constrained by the availability of foreign exchange.

38 See Harvey (1985) for an elaborate presentation of the arguments behind these conclusions.

39 As general background see Killick (1989) who reviews the divisions in economics and gives a stylized picture of the competing macroeconomic views.

40 See Green (1985) for an elaboration of this point.

2 MACROECONOMIC CONSISTENCY AND ADJUSTMENT POLICIES

1 It is implicitly assumed in what follows that the economy in reference is a small open economy with a fixed exchange rate.

2 Government is defined here in the budgetary sense. That is, if non-budgetary public sector operations exist, they are included in the private sector account.

3 Where independent central monetary management is feasible, it is in many cases necessary to disaggregate the monetary system into the central bank and the rest of the monetary system. This disaggregation is not, however, performed in what follows.

4 The presentation of the macroeconomic balances is partly adapted from Easterly (1989). It has, however, been formalized and considerably extended in a way which is consistent with the approaches of the IMF and the World Bank. Easterly provides a pedagogical tool (based upon an input–output conceptual framework) for deriving the various individual accounting equations and illustrates them with data from Colombia and Zimbabwe. The individual accounts give a comprehensive overview of the flows in the consistency framework. The framework can be seen as a combination of the flow-of-funds (FOF) and social accounting approaches (SAM) to macroeconomic accounting. The FOF methodology emphasizes the equality of sources and uses of funds, distinguished between current and capital accounts, whereas the SAM approach presents the macroeconomic identities in a form that shows the participation of each agent in the economy. The SAM has traditionally been used for analyses of the real economy, but has recently been extended to cover real financial interactions as well.

5 To obtain the balances in real terms it would be necessary to divide through with a price index. Furthermore, if import and interest payments to the foreign sector are registered in foreign currency they have to be converted to domestic currency by use of the exchange rate since all elements of the accounts must be measured in the same currency. Such extensions are considered in Chapter 3.

6 For ease of presentation, government lending to the private sector has been netted out from borrowing by government from the private sector (NPB_g). Similarly foreign lending by the private, government and monetary sectors has been netted out from foreign assets held by these sectors (that is, net foreign assets NFA_p, NFA_g and international reserves R).

7 Lending from the domestic economy to the external sector (that is, the external sector's borrowing) has, as noted above, been netted out from foreign assets held by the private, government and monetary sectors of the domestic economy.

8 The arguments for this position have *inter alia* found their inspiration in neo-classically-oriented growth-accounting frameworks emphasizing the importance of accumulation of capital as well as in structuralist-oriented development strategies emphasizing the role of government and import-substituting development strategies.

9 Expenditure-reducing demand management policies may, however, have

some switching effects as fiscal policy instruments can have asymmetrical effects on the tradable and non-tradable sectors.

10 See Dornbusch and Fisher (1987:483).

11 See Dornbusch and Fisher (1987:738–40).

12 The early monetarist–structuralist debate of the 1950s in Latin America comes to mind (see, for example, Kirkpatrick and Nixon, in Gemmel 1987).

13 See Dornbusch and Fisher (1987:481).

14 See Khan (1987:27).

15 See, for example, Cleaver (1985) for a discussion of the importance of agricultural output prices and Edwards (1989a), Sachs (in Corbo, Goldstein and Khan 1987) and various of the articles in Chenery and Srinivasan (1989) for some of the more recent contributions in the trade and development debate of relevance to the present discussion.

16 See, for example, Helleiner (1986b:75).

17 See Streeten (1987b) for an elaboration of this point.

18 The relationship between consumption and productivity was a concern among early writers within the field of development economics (see, for example, Myrdal 1968:Chapters 12 and 30 and Appendix 2). Also the literature on the efficiency wage hypothesis (see, for example, Basu 1984:Chapter 8) is of interest here. The stimulation of effective demand for labour-intensive consumer goods through wage and incomes policy is a well-known tenet of the structuralist paradigm within development economics (see, for example, Hunt 1989).

19 See, for example, FitzGerald (1989:Appendix A).

20 See Levačić and Rebmann (1982:121–4).

21 It is reiterated, however, that expenditure-reducing demand management policies may also have switching effects as fiscal policy instruments can have asymmetrical effects on the tradable and non-tradable sectors.

22 See, for example, Cornia, Jolly and Stewart (1987a–b), Dell (1982) and Taylor (1988).

23 For a more detailed and careful review of the analytical issues involved in the debate, see Lizondo and Montiel (1989). This reference contains an excellent analytical overview of the existing literature. The two authors aptly point out that the controversy surrounding contractionary devaluation has not yet been addressed within a proper analytical framework in which the path of macroeconomic indicators in the absence of devaluation is compared with the corresponding path implied by a given nominal devaluation. Such a dynamic model is yet to be developed. Lizondo and Montiel also stress the importance of distinguishing between the effects of an anticipated (future) devaluation and those of an unanticipated current devaluation. The latter was assumed above.

24 See Dornbusch and Fisher (1987:740–3) and IMF (1987:36–42).

25 See, for example, Balassa (1989).

26 Khan (1987) and Khan and Knight (1985) provide useful overviews of these analytic points and Green (in Commander 1989) and Loxley (in Helleiner 1986a) provide illustrative examples from a sub-Saharan context.

27 The issue of quick (shock type) versus more gradual adjustment will not be pursued here, but it can be noted that the former may involve very

considerable social and economic costs, including the considerable costs connected with unsuccessful attempts at adjustment. It can, however, also be argued that sharp shocks may sometimes be needed to overcome the risk that political opposition will have time to build up during more gradual adjustment. Careful assessment of the costs and benefits of 'sharp shock' as opposed to a phased or 'incremental approach' is required and options may vary depending on particular country circumstances.

28 This does not mean, of course, that no local savings are channelled into productive investment or that all external resources are invested.

29 The issue of the role of government investments in this context will be touched upon on pages 45–50.

30 See Khan and Knight (1985). This implies that savings decisions are not only affected by the relevant prices but by a host of other factors as well, including 'market imperfections' (or market non-existence). This is of importance in relation to the 'crowding out' review on pages 45–50.

31 See, for example, Ahamed (1986:84).

32 See also equation 2.12 on page 50.

33 This does not exclude the possibility that some structural inflation may occur due to the transformation in economic structure and subsequent reallocations in factor inputs which are being pursued by government.

34 This may not always be the case, however, depending on the size of the marginal propensities to consume.

35 That is, the public deficit is matched by an increase of savings in the private sector, which attempts to restore real money balances.

36 See Lewis (1954) for an early formulation of the arguments in the context of development economics.

37 See, for example, IMF (1987) and Taylor (1988).

38 They are, as noted by Khan and Knight (1985:24–7), fairly widely accepted. By way of illustration, it can be referred that government spending is a component of domestic expenditure $(C + I)$ and as such adds to absorption. However, if government spending is limited to traded goods, there is no impact on domestic demand (that is, on Y in equation 2.7) and excess demand fuelled inflation. The only impact will be an increase in imports (Z) or a decrease in exports (X) and a consequent drain on the resource balance. However, government spending on non-traded goods adds to aggregate domestic demand and may therefore contribute to excess demand inflation to the extent that output cannot respond. Similar kinds of considerations apply for the various sources of revenue (that is, direct and indirect taxes, net transfers from abroad, and so on).

39 See Corden (1987a) for a discussion on the 'neo-recardian equivalence theorem' and developing countries.

40 This is the so-called financial crowding-out effect.

41 See Khan (1987:26).

42 See Bacha (1990), Schapiro and Taylor (1990) and several papers by Taylor.

43 It is, in this context, interesting that it is the ECA (1989) which has been particularly forceful in drawing attention to the importance of military expenses as a heavy burden on government budgets. While the IMF does not seem to have the expertise to enter into specifics on the income/expenditure side of public budgets, the World Bank has explicitly recognized

this need and public expenditure reviews are becoming a regular feature of adjustment programmes. Further comments follow in Chapter 6.

44 $INP = INP_{gf} + INP_{pf}$, $NTR = NTR_{fg} + NTR_{fp}$ and $\Delta NFA = \Delta NFA_p + \Delta NFA_g$.

45 Another way of putting this is to say that if interest payments exceed net transfers (including aid) and new net foreign borrowing (including changes in international reserves), then a real resource transfer takes place from debtor to creditor countries. The change in net foreign borrowing (ΔNFB) is identical to the change in net foreign assets (including reserves) of the domestic economy, so $\Delta NFB = - \Delta NFA$.

46 See McFadden *et al.* (1985:179–209) for an econometric exercise on the creditworthiness of developing countries in which arrears have been built into the accounts.

47 See World Bank (1989b).

48 This expression was coined by Hans Singer of the IDS in the seminar held in August 1989 and referred to in the acknowledgements.

49 Green (in Commander 1989:43) points out that faulty estimation of crop harvests may lead to allocating too little credit to crop marketing boards. If the actual crop exceeds expectations, not enough finance will be available. This leads at best to delayed payment which may be damaging for peasant's confidence and incentives. Underestimating seasonal fluctuations may lead to the same result.

50 See Khan (1987:25).

3 FINANCIAL PROGRAMMING AND STABILIZATION

1 See, for example, Edwards (1989b:4) and Taylor (1988:154).

2 See Green (1986:5) for a more complete list of issues.

3 See, for example, Green (1986:7).

4 See IMF (1987:1).

5 See Polak (1991:62–3) for a very positive assessment of the technical competence of the negotiating teams of some IMF member countries.

6 Driscoll (1989:1) correctly makes this point, but he does not mention that the original intention had been to establish an International Trade Organization (ITO) as well. The leading figure at the Bretton Woods, Keynes, considered the ITO an indispensable third pillar of the new international financial and economic system. The ITO never came into being, however, although it was fully negotiated and agreed at Havana. The 'Havana Charter' was not ratified by the US Congress. See Singer (1989:4–9) for a stimulating review of 'the high hopes of Bretton Woods and the worm in the apple'.

7 The phrase 'to the extent possible' has obviously led to exceptions. The principle of equal sharing of the burden of adjustment among surplus and deficit countries was emphasized by Keynes. However, the IMF has always had more (asymmetrical) leverage over deficit countries than over surplus countries.

8 The original expression 'a system of stable exchange rates' was changed in the second amendment of the IMF Articles of Agreement in 1976 to

'a stable system of exchange rates'. New procedures for IMF surveillance of exchange rate policies of member countries were also introduced then, in line with the changed international monetary and financial circumstances.

9 See, for example, Edwards (1989b) for a brief but instructive assessment.
10 See Khan, Montiel and Haque (1986:8).
11 See, for example, Robichek (1985:12), who makes the point that the IMF was designed to be a 'specialized doctor' and not a 'general medical practitioner'. As a consequence, the IMF lacks the technical competence necessary to deal with many supply-side issues.
12 See Mosley (1989:275) for a useful summary of the content and sequence of stabilization and adjustment programmes.
13 This point was made, for example, by R. Williamson of the Africa Department of the IMF at study seminar 125 at IDS in August 1989, referred to under the acknowledgements.
14 See IMF (1987:12).
15 The absorption approach focuses on the need for domestic absorption to be smaller than national income if there is to be a surplus on the current account. This is, as shown on pages 43–5 of Chapter 2, equivalent to stating that domestic savings are larger than domestic investment and the difference is used for acquiring foreign assets (equation 2.10). The rate of accumulation or decumulation of foreign assets is therefore of central importance in the absorption approach. This is distinct in emphasis from the Keynesian approach to the balance of payment which is concerned with the determination of domestic product and the current account in situations which are *inter alia* characterized by involuntary unemployment, excess domestic productive capacity and price rigidity. The Keynesian approach points, in other words, to the possibility of increasing production and improving the current account through a change in the relative prices between tradable and non-tradable goods provided the Marshall–Lerner condition holds (see, for example, Levačić and Rebmann 1982:121–4).
16 If it is assumed for simplicity, first, that the private sector does not hold foreign assets and does not extend loans to the public sector and, second, that there are no interest and transfer payments with the external sector, the four balances appear as follows:

– national balance: $Y = (C + I) + X - Z$
– external balance: $X - Z = \Delta NFA + \Delta R$
– monetary balance: $\Delta M = \Delta R + \Delta DC$
– fiscal balance: $S_g - I_g = \Delta NFA - \Delta DC_g$

17 It is obvious, for example, that the private sector appears somehow subdued, although not totally absent.
18 See IMF (1987:13). Polak (1991) traces the changing nature of IMF conditionality. His account is illuminative, and points out (p. 64) that 'the frequent failures of the Fund arrangements in the 1980s appear to have had a sobering influence'.
19 That is, the effect on imports of a 1 per cent increase in real income is assumed to be about the same as the effect of a 1 per cent increase in

the domestic price level – on the assumption that prices abroad remain constant. Hence, 'the fraction of an increase in income that is spent abroad may be taken to be independent on the extent to which the expansion in money income was a "real" or a "price" phenomenon' (Polak 1957:22).

20 This amounts to using the quantity theory of money equation $Mv = Py$, where M is money demand, v velocity, P the price level and y real output. This is why the Polak model has been called the 'quantity theory of money in an open economy'. It deserves mentioning, however, that Polak (1957: section 5) considered carefully the series of other factors that may influence money demand and pointed out that the money velocity v cannot be treated as a constant at all times. Polak (1957:8) finds that 'the assumption of a constant ratio of money to income may be a worthwhile first step in a monetary theory of income formation, and that it might be profitable to investigate the full implications of this assumption', that by assuming a constant velocity 'there is in this respect, a real and perhaps unexpected gain in simplicity', and that once the quantity theory of money 'has been properly tied to income analysis it appears to be not only harmless but indeed quite useful'.

21 See Dornbusch and Fisher (1987:Chapter 11) for a brief presentation of monetary policy in a framework where the money supply is a policy instrument.

22 Polak (1957:8) puts the latter point as follows: 'The introduction of the constant ratio of money to income means *eo ipso* the discarding of the propensities to save, consume, and invest'. That is, if the marginal propensity to spend is less than one, then the model as presented would break down, as there is no way of disposing of excess money supply (generated by equation 3.3) as compared with money demand (generated by equation 3.1). However, as Polak (1957: 19) points out:

this does not mean that, in a system in which a true Keynesian spending equation is assumed to be present the quantity of money could not depend on the rate of income. It only means that in such a system there must be another variable, such as the rate of interest . . . to make separate spending and money holding equations possible.

23 See Polak (1957:24). It is not quite clear why Polak tied imports to nominal income. Lance Taylor (in a personal communication) argues that it was either a stroke of genius or because people had not quite sorted out real and nominal magnitudes in the mid-1950s. Furthermore, why the money market is always assumed to clear is vague. A specific adjustment mechanism is not provided.

24 Other specifications are of course possible and will be reviewed below.

25 Exports, credit creation, imports and income are flow variables, whereas money and international reserves are stock variables. A lasting increase in exports shifts annual exports to a higher level, where it stays permanently. A lasting increase in the rate of credit expansion means that the same additional amount of credit continues to be added to the outstanding credit stock each period. A discontinous export increase means that exports increase during one period only and then drop back to their

previous level. International reserves first increase with an amount equivalent to the extra one-period exports, and are in subsequent periods affected by increases in imports. A discontinuous credit expansion means a one-period injection of extra domestic credit, which increases the outstanding credit stock once and permanently – but not continuously. In other words, the extra foreign reserves may eventually 'disappear' but the extra credit stock will 'stay'.

26 Chand (1989:477) makes the pertinent point that, if for some reason nominal income cannot be affected, the model breaks down as there is then no way for disposing of the excess money supply.

27 Polak does not derive the expression for a discontinuous expansion in domestic credit. However, given an initial increase of domestic credit ΔDC and that the share of income, which in each period 'leaks' to imports is given by m, then the aggregate increase in imports over time will be given by the multiplier expression $m\Delta DC + m\Delta DC(1 - m) + m\Delta DC(1 - m)^2 + m\Delta DC(1 - m)^3 + m\Delta DC(1 - m)^4$ and so on. This sum is for time $t \to \infty$ equal to ΔDC. Using equation 3.4 it follows that the total change in international reserves is $- \Delta DC$, and from equation 3.3 it follows that in the end there is no change in M. A discontinuous increase in exports (ΔX) will have a similar effect on money supply, imports and income (that is, an effect that causes an initial increase but eventually subsides). In this case there is no fall in international reserves, which after the initial increase return to their previous level.

28 This can be seen by deriving the multiplier (for $t \to \infty$) for changes in the independent variable (X) on the dependent variables $(Y$ and $Z)$. A lasting increase in exports (ΔX) increases income Y by the same amount ΔX in the first 'round'. Part of this extra income is spent at home, that is, $(1 - m)\Delta X$, and a part finances extra imports $m\Delta X$. In the second 'round' income therefore increases by $(1 - m)\Delta X$. A part of this extra income is spent at home, that is, $(1 - m)^2\Delta X$, and a part is used to finance imports $m(1 - m)\Delta X$. And so the process goes on. The multiplier effect on Y adds up to $1/m$ and the multiplier for Z is 1. That is, income increases (assuming that $m < 1$) by $\Delta X/m$ and imports increase by ΔX. This implies (equation 3.4) that there is no overall change in reserves. Exports increase but the induced imports 'eat up' the initial increase in reserves.

29 See IMF (1987:12) and Kirkpatrick and Nixon (in Gemmel 1987:183–5).
30 Polak (1957:2) stated explicitly that:

Keynes' General Theory provides an adequately integrated theory of income (employment) and money. But while the part of theory dealing with income has been given a form suitable for economic analysis, the monetary part has seemed to be less tractable to such treatment.

Furthermore, the

multiplier analysis was a simplification that seemed particularly appropriate to the developed countries in the depression of the 1930's when the demand for money was highly elastic. This particular simplification is much less useful . . . with economies, such as those of the less developed countries, where money is kept exclusively for transaction purposes and its demand is not very elastic; or with countries, developed or less developed, which rely to a considerable extent on monetary policy to guide their economies.

31 See IMF (1987:12).

32 The law of one price states that the price of tradables in the domestic and external foreign economies must at the most differ by tariffs and marketing costs. If the difference is any larger, profit-seeking traders will enter the market and competition will 'push' prices towards equilibrium. That is, P_d can, if all goods are assumed to be tradables, be written as the foreign price level P_f times e where e is the exchange rate expressed as the domestic currency price of one unit of foreign currency.

33 It is reiterated that money demand is assumed here to be independent of the level of interest, i. In Johnson's original model, money demand was expressed as $M_d = f(y, i)$. However, the simplification has no implications for the basic policy conclusions, which are in focus here. Johnson eventually assumes that i is constant (see Frenkel and Johnson 1976:1976). He justifies this by viewing the domestic interest rate level as determined by the interest-parity theorem combined with an expectation that the exchange rate will stay fixed. See Levačić and Rebmann (1982:174–6) for further details.

34 It is clear, however, that Polak in his review of a lasting autonomous reduction in imports (Polak 1957:24–7) implies that a change in the exchange rate will not have a lasting effect on the balance of payments. This conclusion is in accordance with the conclusion of the 'Chicago' model as will be shown in the following.

35 See Dornbusch and Fisher (1987:740–3) for a brief account of the argument.

36 Edwards (1989b), Green (1986) and Taylor (1988) are useful secondary sources. The presentation in this section matches that of Khan, Montiel and Haque (1986), which has been published in Khan, Montiel and Haque (1990). Robichek (1985) was really written around 1960 and is probably the best description of IMF practice.

37 P_d is assumed determined by domestic forces of supply and demand in a perfectly elastic and flexible manner. P_d therefore signals flex-price clearing of domestic output markets.

38 That is, $M_d v = P\overline{y}$. The constant velocity assumption is, according to IMF (1987:13–15), only a simplifying assumption and could be replaced by a more general expression that relates money demand to a limited well-defined set of economic variables such as real income, interest rates and prices. It is crucial, however, that the relationship is stable.

39 The specification of the import function follows Khan, Montiel and Haque (1986:18, and 1990:162). The positive parameters α_0, α_1 and α_2 being respectively a constant, the marginal propensity to import and the response of imports to relative price changes (that is, the volume of imports $Z_q = \alpha_0 + \alpha_1 \overline{y} - \alpha_2 (e\overline{P}_f/P_d)$). It follows that imports denoted in foreign currency is equal to $\overline{P}_f Z_q$ and in domestic currency is equal to

$eP_fZ_q = Z_q$, due to the assumption that $P = P_d = eP_f = 1$ in the present period. Imports in foreign currency will be denoted $\tilde{Z}$ below.

40 It can also be noted that the government fiscal deficit $(S_g - I_g)$ is equal to $\Delta F_g - \Delta DC_g$.

41 In what follows, Δ refers to a change from the previous period (-1) to the present. A_{-1} is attached to indicate predetermined variables from the last period.

42 Note that equations 3.14–3.16 imply that $\Delta Y = \Delta (P\bar{y}) = \Delta P\bar{y} + P_{-1}\Delta \bar{y} = \Delta Py_{-1} + \Delta y \Delta P + P_{-1}\Delta y$; $\Delta P = (1 - \theta)\Delta P_d + \theta \Delta e\bar{P}_f$ and $\Delta M_d = (1/v)\Delta Y$. Khan, Montiel and Haque (1986) assume that Δy and ΔP are small so their product (that is, the second-order term) can be disregarded and ΔY set equal to $P\Delta y_{-1} + P_{-1}\Delta \bar{y}$, rather than the full expression $\Delta P\bar{y} + P_{-1}\Delta \bar{y} (or \Delta Py_{-1} + P_{-1}\Delta y + \Delta y \Delta P)$. However, since y is an exogenous variable that is projected separately, this assumption is not necessary. It makes no difference in principle in equation 3.32 or to the process of financial programming whether y is predetermined or exogenous.

43 Recall that $X = \tilde{X}e_{-1} + \tilde{X}\Delta e$ and similarly for ΔF.

44 Note that $Z = Z_{-1} + \Delta Z$. Furthermore, ΔZ is equal to the extra import payments due to the change in imported quantity plus the valuation change in the imports of the last period (as the exchange rate may change). The imported quantity change $\Delta Z_q = \alpha_1 \Delta \bar{y} - \alpha_2 \Delta e\bar{P}_f/P_d + \alpha_2 e\bar{P}_f\Delta P_d$. This is equal to $\alpha_1 \Delta \bar{y} - \alpha_2 \Delta e\bar{P}_f + \alpha_2 \Delta P_d$ as $P_d = eP_f = 1$, which implies that $\alpha_1 \Delta \bar{y} - \alpha_2 \Delta e\bar{P}_f + \alpha_2 \Delta P_d$ is the additional import cost in domestic currency for the extra units imported. The valuation change is equal to $Z_{-1}\Delta e\bar{P}_f$ as the foreign import price is assumed not to change. It follows that $Z = Z_{-1} + \alpha_1 \Delta \bar{y} - \alpha_2 \Delta e\bar{P}_f + \alpha_2 \Delta P_d + Z_{-1}\Delta e\bar{P}_f$ that can be rearranged.

45 The rationale behind the incomes policy prescriptions is that private sector profits play a crucial role in promoting a higher level of savings and investment and should not therefore be squeezed. Furthermore, the elimination of consumer subsidies is often recommended due to their often significant contribution to fiscal deficits.

46 See Edwards (1989b:12–19), who reviews the state of economic theory and the Fund model.

47 See, for example, Green (1986), Group of 24 (1987) and Taylor (1988), as well as the extensive number of country studies in Onimode (1989) and Campbell and Loxley (1989).

4 GROWTH PROGRAMMING AND ADJUSTMENT

1 See Whalley (1984:18). This affirmation does not mean that other types of models have not been studied in the World Bank. Extensive work has, for instance, been carried out on computable general equilibrium (CGE) models. Nevertheless, the RMSM is the only widely-used operational framework.

2 The World Bank group includes the IBRD as well as the International Development Association (IDA) and the International Finance

Corporation (IFC). IDA is an affiliate of IBRD established in 1960 to provide assistance for the same purpose as the IBRD, but on softer terms primarily to the poorer developing countries. The IFC is legally and financially separate, but is associated with the IBRD and mobilizes funding for private enterprises in developing countries. The International Center for Settlement of Investment Disputes (ICSID) and the Multilateral Investment Guarantee Agency (MIGA) are also associated with the IBRD.

3 World Bank (1991c).

4 Contrary to the IMF, only developing countries (and more recently Eastern European countries) are eligible to receive World Bank loans, and the poorer developing countries in addition have the possibility of obtaining the more concessional IDA loans.

5 A large number of reviews of the evolution and present state of development economics have come out in recent years, as may be seen from the bibliography. Killick (1986) is useful as a brief introduction with particular emphasis on policy implications.

6 See Baum and Tolbert (1985) and Gittinger (1982).

7 The importance of the macroeconomic framework – comprising fiscal, monetary, exchange rate, wage and trade policies – is, for example, very much stressed in the lessons drawn up in Baum and Tolbert (1985).

8 This statement should not be interpreted to mean that the policy conclusions drawn by the World Bank are necessarily correct or the 'best' ones available. The Bretton Woods institutions serve political ends as well, which do therefore influence the development strategy and policies pursued and they also determine in a broad sense the framework for World Bank studies and analyses. Scepticism rather than admiration is therefore called for, but Toye (1989:262–3) correctly points out that to construct 'a total picture of a uniformly oppressive Bank is ... to enter a mythical realm outside history and at odds with common sense'.

9 See Toye (1989:264).

10 Whether the IMF/World Bank relationship is one of 'creative tension', as sometimes suggested at informal levels, or not, will be left as an open issue here.

11 This raises, of course, the complex issue of cross-conditionality which has been the subject of much debate (see, for example, Toye 1989:269–70, or Avramovic 1989, for brief introductions).

12 As in Chapter 3, pages 59–60, it is important to note that this set of equations is just a sub-set of the whole set of identities which make up the national accounts, and they do not amount to a model, as no behavioural relationships have been specified. Identities do not explain how *ex ante* gaps are closed.

13 The survey article by N. Stern (1989:622) contains a useful overview.

14 The assumption of a linear capital-output relationship is not strictly required. A similar formulation can be derived from more general neoclassical production functions of the Cobb-Douglas type, if there are no significant changes in the relative costs of capital and labour. It follows that k can also be interpreted as the incremental capital-output ratio (ICOR), and will be used as such later in this chapter.

15 The Harrod–Domar models have, over the years, been further developed

by many authors (see, for example, the various articles in Sen 1970). These extensions will not be pursued here, as it is the basic Harrod–Domar model one finds at the core of the RMSM approach.

16 If, for example, the growth target is 6 per cent per year and the capital-output ratio 3:1, then the economy must save 18 per cent to accomplish its growth target. If only 12 per cent savings can be mobilized, a savings gap of 6 per cent exists. The economy can, however, still realize its growth target if sufficient foreign assistance is available to fill this gap.

17 See, in particular, Chenery and Strout (1966), but Chenery and Bruno (1962) is also useful.

18 It can be recalled from pages 59–63 of Chapter 3 that $\Delta R = X - Z + \Delta F$ (where F includes changes in net foreign assets from the capital account, as well as interest payments and net transfers from the current account). That is, if X and ΔF are given, the only way Z can be expanded in an unconstrained manner is by running down international reserves, but this will eventually deplete R and therefore cease to be an option.

19 The slopes are positive as all parameters can be assumed to be greater than nil, and since k is in all likelihood greater and s smaller than one. Theoretically it cannot a priori be said which of the two lines will have the steeper slope. If, for example, $k = 3$, $s = 0.1$, $m_1 = 0.5$ and $m_2 = 0.1$, the 'savings gap' line will be steeper than the 'trade gap' line, but if, for example, the propensities to import are very large (or k very small) the opposite could actually be true. However, for all empirically realistic values of the relevant parameters (that is, k around 3.0, s around 0.15, m_1 around 0.5 and m_2 around 0.15) the 'savings gap' line will be the steeper one. If a simpler import function, $Z = my$, were specified, the slope of the 'trade gap' line would be m. In this case the 'savings gap' line would be steeper than the 'trade gap' line as k could under normal circumstances be expected to be around 3.0 and s around 0.1, while m would no doubt be smaller than 1.0.

20 This observation follows directly from equations 4.4 and 4.5 together with the above comments about the slopes of the 'trade' and 'savings gap' lines. The greater the slope, the less the impact on Δy^* of an additional unit of foreign currency borrowed abroad.

21 See Addison (1989:1).

22 The main source used is Addison (1989), but Gelb (1984) and Whalley (1984) also provide useful information on the Bank's approach to numerical programming work.

23 These include intermediate goods and non-factor services tied to real output y, capital goods tied to investment I, and food and other imports linked to personal consumption C.

24 The model is presented in terms similar to those of Chapters 2 and 3. Addison (1989), who approaches the subject from a more operational angle, introduces time explicitly in the equations. This is not necessary to grasp the theoretical content of the model. The model is presented in real terms, so prices are assumed constant. This implies that no account is taken of changes in terms of trade. This is obviously unrealistic and is in operational simulations taken care of by distinguishing gross domestic product and gross domestic income. That is, changes in the terms of trade

is treated as an income effect. An illustrative calculation in this regard for sub-Saharan Africa as a whole was carried out in connection with the compilation of Table 1.8 in Chapter 1.

25 Determining C as a residual is equivalent to suppressing the 'savings gap' since $y = C + S$, and y is targeted.

26 It was noted above that Chenery and Strout (1966:690) actually considered the possibility of making exports dependent on a policy parameter ε, although they made it a point to stress that the effects of government policy would have limited effects, so the two-gap dilemma continued to be present.

27 The specification used here follows Khan, Montiel and Haque (1986 and 1990). Their merged model will be discussed in Chapter 5.

28 The availability of data in the sub-Saharan context is seriously circumscribed by the unrecorded economy, the importance of recent structural changes due to the crisis, and the difficulties of finding appropriate exchange rates and price deflators.

29 See Todaro (1989:90).

30 Whalley (1984:5) reports that when the last count was made in 1979, over 650 such exercises had been conducted at operational level, whereas the number at research level was more limited. The total number of RMSM exercises has increased considerably during the 1980s, but an up-to-date estimate is not available.

31 See, for example, Gelb (1984).

32 See Gelb (1984:13).

33 See Khan, Montiel and Haque (1986:30), which also contains references to some of the early empirical tests as to whether the foreign exchange constraint dominates the domestic savings constraint or not. The sources they cite generally rejected this hypothesis.

34 See Bhagwati (1982), Krueger (1974) and Srinivasan (1985) for just three examples of this literature. Schapiro and Taylor (1990) provide the elements of a counter-critique in their balanced review of the role of the state and industrial strategy.

35 See Little (1982:147–9) and Lal (1983:24–9) for summary presentations of the neo-classical 'counter-attack' on the two-gap model.

36 See Michalopolous (in Corbo, Goldstein and Khan 1987:53).

37 Williamson (in Corbo, Goldstein and Khan 1987:97–104) elaborates the argument and demonstrates in a simple model (where expenditure switching is feasible) that, under plausible conditions, situations can arise in which a foreign exchange constraint imposes 'a deadweight loss on the economy rather than an intertemporal trade-off'.

38 See Taylor (1988:Chapter 4) and Ndulu (1990:15–16). The latter observes that 'invariably all the six studies underscore the dominance of the foreign exchange constraint in the growth process'. The six SSA-countries studied included Ghana, Nigeria, Uganda, Zambia, Zimbabwe and Tanzania.

39 See, for example, Todaro (1989:486–9) and Taylor (1988:163–4).

40 These points are made by Gelb (1984:12).

41 There is no guarantee, however, that the exchange rate policy is in practice a sufficiently 'strong' policy variable, so other mechanisms may have to be introduced to explain how balance between supply and demand is in

fact established in the economy. This issue of alternative ways of closing the model, which was touched upon on pages 82–90, will be pursued further in Chapter 6, where adjustment through distributional shifts will be discussed.

5 GROWTH-ORIENTED ADJUSTMENT – AN IMF/WORLD BANK SYNTHESIS?

1 See the Group of 24 (1987).

2 The increasing attention given to growth aspects of adjustment programmes comes out clearly in a recent statement by the Managing Director of the IMF, Michel Camdessus (1989:10), who declared that:

> Our prime objective is growth. In my view, there is no longer any ambiguity about this. It is toward growth that our programs and their conditionality are aimed. It is with a view toward growth that we carry out our special responsibility of helping to correct balance of payments disequilibria and, more generally, to eliminate obstructive macroeconomic imbalances.

3 The IMF/World Bank meeting whose deliberations are summarized in the volume edited by Corbo, Goldstein and Khan (1987) is just one out of a long list of seminars and meetings on this approach to adjustment, and an increasing number of academic papers have also been produced in this field in recent years, as may be seen from the bibliography.

4 See Khan and Knight (1985), as well as the assessments of World Bank numerical programming activity, by Gelb (1984) and Whalley (1984).

5 The presentation of the proposal on pages 100–8 is based on Khan, Montiel and Haque (1986 and 1990) and Khan and Montiel (1989). Other appealing attempts at suggesting improvements in the IMF financial programming approach, in a more growth-oriented direction, exist – see, for example, Bacha (1987), Chand (1989), Group of 24 (1987) and Taylor (1988). Further comments in this regard follow in Chapters 6 and 7.

6 The specification of the model presented here applies various restrictive assumptions regarding the growth process, foreign debt, interest payments and the endogeneity of exports. These assumptions are not strictly necessary as demonstrated by Khan and Montiel (1989). In this more recent paper they put forward a much more elegant version of their original, simpler model in Khan, Montiel and Haque (1986). The simpler version of the merged framework is used here to facilitate the exposition and to ensure consistency with previous chapters. However, the above assumptions, and the way in which they can be made less restrictive, are discussed in what follows.

7 If a price determination rule such as the one in equation 3.15 $(P = (1 - \theta)P_d + \theta\, e\bar{P}_f)$ is introduced at this stage, together with an assumption that the foreign price of importables P_f remains constant (that is, $\Delta P_f = 0$), it follows that ΔR may be expressed as a function of the parameter θ and the predetermined variables P_{-1} and y_{-1} together with Δy and ΔP_d as well as the exchange rate e and the change in domestic

credit ΔDC. Even if the exchange rate and domestic credit are considered policy variables under the control of the government, there are nevertheless three unknown variables, ΔR, Δy and ΔP_d. Consequently, additional constraints are required to close the system.

8 No distinction is made here between non-trade-related foreign currency inflows to the private sector and to the government (as in equations 3.23 and 3.24). This is for convenience only and does not alter the nature of the model and its conclusions.

9 Therefore α_1 and α_2 reflect the responsiveness of the import volume to changes in respectively y and relative prices P_f/P_d.

10 The aggregate price level is expressed as the price level of the previous period P_{-1} plus ΔP since the model is specified in discrete time intervals with all adjustments taking place in one period. It can also be noted that for convenience no distinction is made between private and public investment.

11 Reference is made to pages 68–73 for the derivation of this equation.

12 The domestic currency equivalent of the import price P_f may – even if P_f remains constant – change due to changes in the exchange rate. Changes in e must be taken into account when calculating the overall change in the price index ΔP.

13 Khan, Montiel and Haque (1986:37) refer to these two ways of using the model as respectively the 'positive' and the 'programming' modes. A similar distinction was made when discussing the Harrod–Domar equation on pages 82–6.

14 See Khan and Montiel (1989). This kind of illustration is in fact known from the IS-LM diagrams, used to illustrate models of income determination, also referred to in Chapter 2.

15 Khan and Montiel (1989) contain full details.

16 See Khan and Montiel (1989:302). They also consider the impact of changes in the velocity of money circulation (that is, changes in the demand for money) and changes in factor productivity which are not commented upon here.

17 This end net result relating to the balance of payments does, however, represent several conflicting effects of the devaluation in the money market. Given the initial domestic price of domestic goods, a devaluation will cause a flow excess demand for money (equation 5.1) as the aggregate price level increases due to the increase in import prices. But a flow excess in the money supply is also created (equation 5.2), since the change in relative prices encourages production of import substitutes and exports (provided the latter are set depending on the exchange rate and not exogenously). Khan and Montiel (1989:294) show that under various assumptions (including the Marshall–Lerner condition) about the size of these relative money market effects (depending on the share of importables in the aggregate price index, on the velocity of money and on the degree of substitutability between tradables and non-tradables), the effect of Δe on the balance of payments will be positive.

18 Equation 5.9 implies that a decrease in C_g increases investment and therefore growth, and this increase in output must put a downward pressure on prices to clear the flow money market.

19 A reduction in the fiscal deficit through a decrease in taxes would operate in a similar manner except that the impact on domestic savings would be $(1 - s)$ rather than unity.

20 See Khan and Montiel (1989:297).

21 An increase in the savings rate will increase investment through equation 5.9 which increases y through equation 5.8. This leads to a deterioration of the balance of payments (through equations 5.7 and 5.4) but, since domestic prices fall imports are reduced (through equation 5.7), making the final result in equation 5.4 indeterminate.

22 The increase in the flow supply of money caused by the greater availability of foreign exchange (in equation 5.2) is neutralized by the outflow of foreign reserves caused by the increased imports.

23 Khan and Montiel (1989:302) demonstrate that a capital inflow devoted to investment will only increase national income if the marginal product of capital exceeds the interest charged on the loan.

24 Reference is made to Reinhart (1989) for full details on the econometric methodology used in estimating the parameters of the merged model and its underlying assumptions. Nevertheless, attention is drawn to the fact that each behavioural equation was estimated separately using either ordinary least squares (OLS) or generalized least squares (GLS) to make more efficient use of the limited data available (including different starting points for the various time series). That is, the model was not estimated as a system, and the methodology used did not therefore involve a direct comparison of the actual and the fitted values of the endogenous variables. Instead, the estimated parameter values were used to construct reduced form multipliers for each of the endogenous variables, and the range of values these multipliers take as parameters change was taken as an indication of the 'robustness' of the policy implications of the model.

25 Investment can therefore be represented by the term $-\mu \Delta r$, since an increase in the interest rate is assumed to lower investment.

26 A change in the real exchange rate is reflected by $(\Delta e - \Delta P_d)$, that is, the difference between the changes in the nominal exchange rate and the domestic price level. The process by which such a change in the real exchange rate is supposed to affect capacity output is that a depreciation will reduce the consumption wage which affects labour supply negatively. This in turn leads for a given capital stock to an equilibrium with a lower level of output and a higher real product wage (see Vines 1990:5). It can be noted that, if the elasticity of the labour supply is zero, this effect obviously vanishes.

27 Such a negative external shock is not considered by Khan and Montiel (1989) within their integrated framework as set out above. This kind of shock does, however, have considerable importance in the sub-Saharan context as discussed in Chapter 1.

28 It may be recalled that a similar simplification was made in Chapter 4.

29 See, for example, Levačić and Rebmann (1982:Chapter 3).

30 See Vines (1990:13, 21–2) for full details on the assumptions made, but note that there is an error in the derivation of his money demand multiplier.

31 Detailed algebraic derivations of these conclusions can be found in Vines (1990:23).

32 This is done quite simply by rewriting equations 5.17, 5.18, 5.19, 5.21 and 5.22 noting that output y is at full capacity $\hat{y}$.

33 See Chapters 3 and 4 as well as pages 108–10.

34 The positive slope of this curve is based on the assumption that the capital output ratio $(1/\alpha) > s(1 - t) + t + b$. This is empirically unproblematic.

35 This assumes that $(v^{-1} + b)/[v^{-1}(1 - \theta) + a] > 0$, but this is empirically unproblematic.

36 See Vines (1990:10).

37 The depreciation in the real exchange rate required in equation 5.27 is exactly the same as that emanating from equation 5.30. Therefore for Δy not to change, government expenditure must remain constant, and similarly in equation 5.28 which shows that no change in credit policy is required.

38 See Vines (1990:23–4) for the algebraic manipulations.

39 See Taylor (1988:154) for this formulation.

40 See Ndulu (1990) for a paper on the issue of distinguishing between growth in productive capacity and actual output in the sub-Saharan context.

6 ALTERNATIVE APPROACHES

1 Reference to this debate was made in Chapter 2 and it was noted that, for example, Kirkpatrick and Nixon (in Gemmel 1987) provide a useful overview of this debate where particular attention is paid to the fundamental causes and adequate policy responses to inflation.

2 Edwards (1989b) contains a most valuable assessment of the IMF from the perspective of a mainstream economist, who is nevertheless critical of the theoretical framework of this institution. Other mainstream economists have coincided with structuralist critiques in pointing to the striking absence of distributional concerns in the IMF/World Bank models, or contributed to the debate on contractionary devaluation. The main piece signalling a modified World Bank stance in the adjustment debate is World Bank (1989b), whereas the modified IMF views come out most clearly in a number of policy statements by its managing director (see, for example, Camdessus 1989). While there is reason to think that these statements are more than plain rhetoric, they have so far led to only limited modifications in actual adjustment programmes, except for the introduction of a number of new lending facilities already referred to in Chapters 3 and 4.

3 See Chapelier and Tabatabai (1989) which includes a set of proposals for a more active role for the United Nations Development Programme (UNDP) in stabilization and structural adjustment.

4 See Cornia, Jolly and Stewart (1987:5).

5 See, for example, the ten country studies compiled in Cornia, Jolly and Stewart (1987), and various of the studies listed in the bibliography.

6 See Hunt (1989:Chapter 9).

7 See Killick (1986) for a useful review of the points made in this paragraph.

8 See, for example, IMF (1989b).

9 See Cornia, Jolly and Stewart (1987:7).

10 See the Introduction and Chapter 2.

11 Stewart (in Cornia, Jolly and Stewart 1987:156–7) asserts that, whatever the policy package, the macro policies must be married with their consequences for the distribution of resources between priorities, and meso policies must be designed so that the two together (the macro policies and the meso consequences) protect vulnerable groups during adjustment. She goes on to compare macro targets with the speed of a wheel (rotations per second), and points out that the consequences of the rotation for the rest of the system will depend on the size and number of cogs on that wheel and other wheels linked to it. Therefore, while timing the speed of rotation may be broadly defined by external finance, the meso consequences can be greatly altered by altering the dimension and associated cogs and wheels.

12 See Bhardan (in Chenery and Srinivasan 1988:40).

13 See Seers (1963).

14 This implies that the original ideas of the structuralist school emphasizing import-substitution development strategies, and so on, are not taken up. And contributions from a dependency point of view, which in some ways grew out of the structuralist school, will only be commented upon in the context of more radical approaches. The one-dimensional classification of structuralist-inspired views that is used in what follows should therefore not be taken too literally. It is nevertheless useful as a kind of 'sorting mechanism' of arguments that puts relatively more focus on issues of short- to medium-term economic management.

15 See Robinson (in Chenery and Srinivasan 1989) for an excellent survey of multi-sector models which is relevant to the discussion here. Robinson's illuminating classification of structuralist models into 'neo-classical-structuralist', 'micro-structuralist' and 'macro-structuralist' models is incorporated in what follows.

16 Among the more recent contributions from the neo-classical structuralists, the two companion volumes by Bevan, Collier and Gunning (with Bigsten and Horsnell) (1989a, 1989b) are prominent. They contain interesting analyses of the channels through which governments influence peasants in a sub-Saharan African context. Particular areas studied include the effect of trade, investment and stabilization policies, producer pricing, availability of non-agricultural consumer goods in rural areas and the provision of public services.

17 Please (1984) is a good exponent of more pragmatic World Bank views.

18 Rattsø (1988, 1989 and 1990) is a prominent Nordic development economist working along this line of thinking. His country-focused work has so far centred on India, but work on sub-Saharan Africa is in the pipeline, although not yet available in published sources. FitzGerald (1988) is leading among the Dutch development economists working from a neo-structuralist starting point.

19 See Hunt (1989:Chapter 5) for a brief but useful overview, but there is also an extensive literature in Spanish not referred to here.

20 Eshag (1983) is a useful reference following post-Keynesian lines of thinking.

21 The model could theoretically also be closed by suppressing the trade gap by assuming that net foreign capital inflows can be set at the level needed

for overall balance. This possibility has, however, been seriously constrained during the 1980s as discussed in Chapter 1, and has not therefore
been an option on which sub-Saharan Africa could rely, contrary to what
happened during the 1970s.

22 Other closure mechanisms along the above lines of thinking are, of course,
possible. One example, well known from the literature, is the introduction
of a loanable funds market where the savings-investment balance is
brought about by changes in the interest rate. See, for example, Kogiku
(1968:120–1). This closure rule is not normally given major attention in
sub-Saharan Africa due to the underdeveloped nature of the financial
markets and the long list of other factors that influence savings and
investment decisions.

23 See Robinson (in Chenery and Srinivasan 1989:925).

24 Taylor (1990) is an excellent theory book on socially-relevant policy
analysis from a structuralist perspective, which should be consulted on
the issues raised here.

25 The basic model put forward in Taylor (1989a) is identical to the one in
Taylor (1987), which provides a slightly more condensed overview of the
approach. Both references can therefore be consulted for further details.

26 That is, u is the inverse of the capital/output ratio, which in Chapters 4
and 5 was denoted k. However, this ratio is not considered a (historically
or technologically-determined) constant in the macro-structuralist approach. Potential changes in capacity utilization are, in other words, an
important closure mechanism, although it is not excluded that u may under
special circumstances be inflexible.

27 The sign of α has important implications for how the economy responds
in the long run to shocks and policy interventions. Taylor (1987:1409)
argues that an uncertain sign is the most reasonable assumption contrary
to the orthodox view of a positive sign (implied by assuming that more
profit income goes hand in hand with economic expansion).

28 See Taylor (1989a:8).

29 See Taylor (1989a:8–17) for these details, as well as Taylor's treatment of
the financial markets that determine the nominal interest rate i and public
sector flows of funds.

30 It can, for example, be assumed that wage-earners consume all their
income whereas profit earners save a share s.

31 Capacity utilization u was already defined as y/K where K is the capital
stock. Capital is formed of nationally-produced and imported components
in proportions θ and $(1 - \theta)$ so its price $P_k = \theta P + (1 - \theta) eP_i$ where P_i is
the world price of imported capital goods. Total profits are equal to
$h^*(1 + i\omega)By$, and the profit rate $\pi = h^*(1 + i\omega)By/P_kK$. The profit rate is
therefore proportional to capacity use u, which is equal to y/K.

32 See Taylor (1989a:15). It should be noted, however, that it is still unclear
how financial assets are best included in structuralist models. Further work
on making the financial sector analysis more complete and specifying the
linkages between the real and monetary sides of the economy is still
required (see also Robinson, in Chenery and Srinivasan 1989:931).

33 The various references by Taylor contain all the necessary formalized
models and policy conclusions to substantiate this observation.

NOTES

34 This can be interpreted as a situation where $\alpha > 0$ in equation 6.3.
35 The limits to which this is possible remains one of the important unknowns in the debate on stabilization and adjustment.
36 See, for example, Hunt (1989), which contains a much more careful and detailed review of the different radical contributions as well as references to the extensive literature on these issues.
37 Marx asserts that society must undergo a series of successive transformations. The analysis of capitalism occupies the centre stage in the analysis, since capitalism at the same time unleashes the productivity of labour and leads to increasing misery, creating the basis for the socialist revolution and the eventual passage to communism.
38 Marx's materialistic interpretation of history and concepts such as the forces and relations of production, social classes (capitalists and proletariat), surplus value and exploitation are immensely intriguing. And, together with the prediction of a falling rate of profit, they have appealed not only to researchers concerned with understanding the processes of social and economic transformation, but also served as a political rallying point for billions of people all over the world.
39 See Lenin (reprinted in 1970).
40 See Hunt (1989:188) for this formulation.
41 This question should, of course, be seen against the series of reports published by the World Bank on the plight of sub-Saharan Africa during the 1980s culminating in the long-term perspective study outlining a possible path from crisis to sustainable growth (World Bank 1989b), which was issued almost simultaneously with the ECA (1989) framework.
42 A rather heated debate has been going on between the ECA and the World Bank over the interpretation of the statistics on the results of structural adjustment programmes. The essence of the matter is that both institutions initially took rather extreme positions (see, for example, UNECA 1989, and World Bank and UNDP 1989). However, the positions in both of these documents are hard to defend. Performance has on the one side been very uneven and it is very difficult to sort out the significance of the real resource flows that have followed the adoption of adjustment programmes. On the other hand, the counterfactual is missing. In other words, it is not really known what would have happened if the programmes had not been adopted. These issues deserve much more study but will not be pursued further here. An excellent and comprehensive up-to-date analysis of the results of economic reform is Mosley, Harrigan and Toye (1991).
43 Module 1 should, according to ECA (1989:55–6), be used to define the production functions in which the relevant parameters operate on human, natural and financial resources to determine various outputs. Module 2 should be used to define income distribution functions in which relevant parameters operate on the generated output to determine the income of various institutions. Module 3 should be used to generate expenditure functions for the satisfaction of essential needs, given the pattern of domestic production and income distribution.
44 The description here is admittedly incomplete, but nevertheless tries to capture the essence of the ECA approach. For further details see ECA (1989:38–43).

45 The way African governments have oriented their priorities concerning public expenditures actually comes in for strong criticism by ECA. It is pointed out that public expenditure on health is less than one-third of the military budget, and policy statements by the ECA Executive Secretary make repeated reference to the squandering of human resources that is taking place, when the welfare of the majority is neglected (see Lone 1988:23).

46 In a recent World Bank (1990b) study, Addison *et al.* make a very useful attempt to clarify the distributional issues from a theoretical perspective in order to make adjustment work for the poor in sub-Saharan Africa.

47 See ECA (1989) and Taylor (1988).

48 See Hunt (1989:339).

49 See Taylor (1988:165).

50 The formulation of the UN-supported demand for a New International Economic Order (NIEO) in the early 1970s was, for example, very much influenced by more radical approaches to development issues and these demands still retain their relevance.

7 CONCLUSIONS

1 See, for example, the country studies summarized in Taylor (1988) and Green (in Commander 1989:42).

2 Fiscal and monetary restraint can often damage the perspective for long-run growth, devaluations can be destabilizing, and while there are certainly potential gains to be derived from trade, these are not necessarily achieved in the most effective manner through the non-interventionistic free-trade policy that underlies much of the IMF and World Bank advice to African countries.

3 See Khan (1987:39).

4 See Ravenhill (1988:179).

5 An excellent guide here is Mosley, Harrigan and Toye (1991).

6 Mosley, Harrigan and Toye (1991) contains a fine assessment of the effectiveness of policy-based lending and the various evaluation methodologies.

7 See Nicholas Stern (1989:640).

8 An example is that fallacy of composition may become important when many countries pursue the same outward-oriented development strategy recommended by the IMF and the World Bank.

9 For a recent contribution see Taylor (1990).

10 See Robinson (in Chenery and Srinivasan 1989:894–5) for a much more detailed review which has inspired these comments. Robinson *inter alia* notes that 'the Walrasian model is an uneasy host for incorporating macro phenomena'.

11 See, for example, World Bank (1991b), but also Van Wijnbergen's commets (in McCarthy 1990:93–4) are illuminating. He states that 'in the Bank we have been too eager in shutting down everything that looks like government'. Van Wijnbergen goes on to stress that the type of investment is at least as important as the quantity.

12 There are also papers by Gibson (1985) and Rattsø (1990) on import-compressed economies, which extend the gap analysis in a traded/non-traded direction. These are theoretically interesting contributions, but are probably too complicated for widespread use in practice.

13 See Taylor (1988:159).

14 See, for example, Yagci, Kamin and Rosenbaum (1985:40–1) and Michalopolos (in Corbo, Goldstein and Khan 1987:46–8).

15 From the reviews of Robinson (in Chenery and Srinivasan 1989) and Gelb (1984) it appears that applied CGE modelling has been undertaken in sub-Saharan Africa in the Ivory Coast, Nigeria and Cameroun.

16 See Gelb (1984) and Whalley (1984).

17 This point was made eloquently by Professor Toye, in the seminar referred to in the acknowledgements.

18 For an elaboration of this point see Killick (1989).

BIBLIOGRAPHY

Acharya, S. N. (1981) 'Perspectives and Problems of Development in Sub-Saharan Africa', *World Development*, vol. 9, pp. 109–47.

Addison, D. (1989) 'The World Bank Revised Minimum Standard Model: Concepts and Issues', Policy, Planning and Research Paper WPS 231, Washington, D. C.: World Bank.

Ahamed, L. (1986) 'Stabilization Policies in Developing Countries', *Research Observer*, vol. 1, no. 1 (January), pp. 79–110.

Alexander, S. (1952) 'Effects of a Devaluation on a Trade Balance', *IMF Staff Papers*, vol. 2, April, pp. 775–884.

Alexander, S. (1959) 'The Effects of Devaluation: A Simplified Synthesis of the Elasticities and Absorption Approaches', *American Economic Review*, vol. 49, no. 2 (March), pp. 22–42.

Allison, C. and Green, R. (eds) (1985) 'Sub-Saharan Africa: Getting the Facts Straight', *IDS Bulletin*, vol. 16, no. 3 (July).

Amin, S. (1976a) *Impérialisme et sous-développement en Afrique*, Paris: Editions Anthropos.

Amin, S. (1976b) *Unequal Development. An Essay on the Social Formations of Peripheral Capitalism*, Hassocks, England: Harvester Press.

Anderson, D. (1987) 'The Public Revenue and Economic Policy in African Countries: An Overview of Issues and Policy Options', Discussion Paper no. 19, Washington, D.C.: World Bank.

Avramovic, D. (1989) *Conditionality: Facts, Theory and Policy*, Helsinki: World Institute for Development Economics Research of the United Nations University (WIDER).

Bacha, E. L. (1984) 'Growth with Limited Supplies of Foreign Exchange: A Reappraisal of the Two-Gap Model', in M. Syrquin, L. Taylor and L. E. Westphal (eds) *Economic Structure and Performance: Essays in Honor of Hollis B. Chenery*, New York: Academic Press.

Bacha, E. L. (1987) 'IMF Conditionality: Conceptual Problems and Policy Alternatives', *World Development*, vol. 15, no. 12, pp. 1457–67.

Bacha, E. L. (1990) 'A Three-Gap Model of Foreign Transfers and the GDP Growth Rate in Developing Countries', *Journal of Development Economics*, vol. 32, pp. 279–96.

Balassa, B. (1989) 'A Conceptual Framework for Adjustment Policies', Policy,

Planning and Research Paper WPS 139, Washington, D.C.: World Bank.

Baran, P. A. (1957) *The Political Economy of Growth*, New York: Monthly Review Press.

Baran, P. A. and Sweezy, P. M. (1968) *Monopoly Capital: An Essay on the American Economic and Social Order*, New York: Monthly Review Press.

Basu, K. (1984) *The Less Developed Economy: A Critique of Contemporary Theory*, Oxford: Basil Blackwell.

Baum, W. C. and Tolbert, S. M. (1985) *Investing in Development: Lessons of World Bank Experience*, New York: Oxford University Press.

Bevan, D., Collier, P. and Gunning, J. W. (with Bigsten, A. and Horsnell, P.) (1989a) *Controlled Open Economies: A Neo-Classical Approach to Structuralism*, Oxford: Oxford University Press.

Bevan, D., Collier, P. and Gunning, J. W. (with Bigsten, A. and Horsnell, P.) (1989b) *Peasants and Governments: An Economic Analysis*, Oxford: Clarendon Press.

Bhagwati, J. N. (1982) 'Directly Unproductive Profit Seeking (DUP) Activities', *Journal of Political Economy*, vol. 90, October, pp. 988–1002.

Bourguignon, F., Branson, W. and de Melo, J. (1989) 'Adjustment and Income Distribution', Working Paper Series no. 215, Washington, D.C.: World Bank.

Buiter, W. H. (1987) 'Some Thoughts on the Role of Fiscal Policy in Stabilization and Structural Adjustment in Developing Countries', mimeographed background paper no. 24 to 1988 World Development Report, Washington, D.C.: World Bank.

Camdessus, M. (1989) 'The Role of the IMF in a Challenging World Economy', *Nationaløkonomisk Tidsskrift*, vol. 127, no. 2, pp. 236–43.

Campbell, B. K. and Loxley, J. L. (eds) (1989) *Structural Adjustment in Africa*, Basingstoke: Macmillan.

Cardoso, F. H. and Faletto, E. (1979) *Dependency and Development in Latin America*, Berkeley, California: University of California Press.

Cassen, R. H. *et al.* (1986) *Does Aid Work?* Oxford: Clarendon Press.

Chand, S. K. (1989) 'Toward a Growth-Oriented Model of Financial Programming', *World Development*, vol. 17, no. 4, pp. 473–90.

Chang, P. H. K. and Cumby, R. E. (1990) 'Capital Flight in sub-Saharan Countries', mimeograph, Stern School of Business, New York University.

Chapelier, G. and Tabatabai, H. (1989) 'Development and Adjustment: Stabilization, Structural Adjustment and UNDP Policy', Policy Discussion Paper, New York: UNDP.

Chenery, H. B. and Bruno, M. (1962) 'Development Alternatives in an Open Economy: The Case of Israel', *Economic Journal*, vol. 72, pp. 79–103.

Chenery, H. B. and Srinivasan, T. N. (eds) (1988) *Handbook of Development Economics*, vol. 1, Amsterdam: North Holland.

Chenery, H. B. and Srinivasan, T. N. (eds) (1989) *Handbook of Development Economics*, vol. 2, Amsterdam: North Holland.

Chenery, H. B. and Strout, A. M. (1966) 'Foreign Assistance and Economic Development', *American Economic Review*, vol. 56, no. 4 (September), pp. 679–733.

Cleaver, K. M. (1985) 'The Impact of Price and Exchange Rate Policies on Agriculture in Sub-Saharan Africa', Staff Working Paper no. 728, Washington D.C.: World Bank.

Commander, S. (ed.) (1989) *Structural Adjustment and Agriculture*, London: Overseas Development Institute.

Corbo, V., Goldstein, M. and Khan, M. (1987) *Growth Oriented Adjustment Programs*, Washington, D.C.: IMF and World Bank.

Corden, W. M. (1987a) 'The Relevance for Developing Countries of Recent Developments in Macroeconomic Theory', *World Bank Research Observer*, vol. 2, no. 2 (July), pp. 171–88.

Corden, W. M. (1987b) 'Protection and Liberalization: A Review of Analytical Issues', Occasional Paper 54, Washington, D.C.: IMF.

Cornia, G. A., Jolly, R. and Stewart, F. (1987) *Adjustment with a Human Face*, vol. 1, *Protecting the Vulnerable and Promoting Growth*, and vol. 2, *Ten Country Cases*, Oxford: Clarendon Press.

Courier, (1989) 'Adjustment – An African Response', no. 117 (September–October), pp. 15–19.

Cuddington, J. T. (1986) 'Capital Flight: Estimates, Issues and Explanations', *Studies in International Finance* no. 58 (December), Princeton, N.J.: Princeton University, International Finance Section.

Dell, S. (1982) 'Stabilization: The Political Economy of Overkill', in C. Wilber (ed.) *The Political Economy of Development and Underdevelopment*, New York: Random House.

Demery, L. and Addison, T. (1987a) 'Stabilization Policy and Income Distribution in Developing Countries', *World Development*, vol. 15, no. 12, pp. 1483–98

Demery, L. and Addison, T. (1987b) *The Alleviation of Poverty under Structural Adjustment*, Washington, D.C.: World Bank.

Development Committee (1988) 'Proposals for Enhancing Assistance to Low-Income Countries That Face Exceptional Difficulties', Pamphlet no. 16, Appendix A, prepared by the staff of the World Bank, Washington, D.C.: World Bank and IMF.

Development Committee (1989) 'Strengthening Efforts to Reduce Poverty', Pamphlet no. 19, Washington D.C.: World Bank and IMF.

Diaz-Alejandro, C. (1981) 'Southern Cone Stabilization Plans', in W. R. Cline and S. Weintraub (eds) *Economic Stabilization in Developing Countries*, Washington, D.C.: The Brookings Institution.

Domar, E. (1946) 'Capital Expansion, Rate of Growth and Employment', *Econometrica*, vol. 14, pp. 137–47.

Dornbusch, R. and Fisher, S. (1987) *Macroeconomics*, New York: McGraw Hill.

Dornbusch, R. and Helmers, F. L. C. H. (eds) (1988) *Open Economy: Tools for Policymakers in Developing Countries*, EDI Series in Economic Development, New York: Oxford University Press.

Driscoll, D.D. (1988) *What is the International Monetary Fund?* Washington, D.C.: IMF.

Driscoll, D. D. (1989) *The IMF and the World Bank: How Do They Differ?* Washington, D.C.: IMF.

Easterly, W. (1989) 'A Consistency Framework for Macroeconomic Analysis', Policy, Planning and Research Paper WPS 234, Washington, D.C.: World Bank.

Economic Commission for Africa (ECA) (1989) *African Alternative Framework to Structural Adjustment Programmes for Socio-Economic Recovery and Transformation*, Addis Ababa: ECA.

Economic Development Institute (EDI) (1987) Various mimeographed theme papers on structural adjustment, Washington D.C.: World Bank.

Economic Development Institute (EDI) (1988) 'Structural Adjustment in Lowinca: A Case Exercise in Economic Policy Analysis', Development Policy Case Series no. 1, Washington, D.C.: World Bank.

Edwards, S. (1985) 'The Order of Liberalization of the Balance of Payments: Should the Current Account be Opened Up First?', Staff Working Paper no. 719, Washington, D.C.: World Bank.

Edwards, S. (1989a) 'Openness, Outward Orientation, Trade Liberalization and Economic Performance in Developing Countries', Working Paper no. 2908, Cambridge, MA: National Bureau of Economic Research.

Edwards, S. (1989b) 'The International Monetary Fund and the Developing Countries: A Critical Evaluation', Working Paper no. 2909, Washington, D.C.: National Bureau of Economic Research.

Eshag, D. (1983) *Fiscal and Monetary Policies and Problems in Developing Countries*, Cambridge: Cambridge University Press.

Faber, M. and Green, R.H. (1985) 'Sub-Saharan Africa's Malaise: Some Questions and Answers', in Rose, T. (ed.) *Crisis and Recovery in Sub-Saharan Africa*, Paris: Organization for Economic Co-operation and Development Centre.

FitzGerald. E. V. K. (1988) 'The Analytics of Stabilization Policy in the Small Semi-Industrialized Economy', Development Economics Seminar Paper no. 7, The Hague: Institute for Social Studies (ISS).

FitzGerald, E. V. K. (1989) 'The Impact of Macroeconomic Policies on Small-Scale Industry: Some Analytical Considerations', Working Paper – sub-series on Money, Finance and Development no. 29, The Hague: Institute for Social Studies (ISS).

Fones-Sundell, M. (1987) 'Role of Price Policy in Stimulating Agricultural Production in Africa', Issue Paper no. 2, Uppsala: Swedish University of Agricultural Sciences.

Frank, A. G. (1969) *Capitalism and Underdevelopment in Latin America: Historical Studies of Chile and Brazil*, New York: Monthly Review.

Frenkel, J.A. and Johnson, H. G. (eds) (1976) *The Monetary Approach to the Balance of Payments*, London: George Allen & Unwin.

Furtado, C. (1976) *Economic Development of Latin America: Historical Background and Contemporary Problems*, Cambridge: Cambridge University Press.

Furtado, C. (1985) *La Nueva Dependencia: Deuda Externa y Monetarismo*, Buenos Aires: Centro Editor de América Latina.

Gelb, A. (1984) 'Report by the Committee on Economy-Wide Modelling in the Bank', mimeographed second draft, Washington D.C.

Gemmel, N. (ed.) (1987) *Surveys in Development Economics*, Oxford: Basil Blackwell.

Gibson, B. (1985) 'A Structuralist Macromodel for Post-Revolutionary Nicaragua', *Cambridge Journal of Economics*, vol. 9, pp. 347–69.

Gittinger, J. P. (1982) *Economic Analysis of Agricultural Projects*, Baltimore: The John Hopkins University Press.

Green, R. H. (1985) 'Africa in the 1980s: What are the Key Issues?' in P. Ndegwa, L. P. Mureithi and R. H. Green (eds) *Development Options for Africa in the 1980s and Beyond*, Nairobi: Oxford University Press.

Green, R. H. (1986) 'The IMF and Stabilization in Sub-Saharan Africa: A Critical Review', Discussion Paper DP 216, Sussex: Institute of Development Studies.

Green, R. H. (1988) 'The Human Dimension as the Test of and Means of Achieving Africa's Recovery and Development: Reweaving the Social Fabric and Restoring the Broken Pot', mimeographed paper presented at ECA-sponsored conference in Khartoum, Sudan, 5–8 March.

Group of 24 Deputies (1987) 'Supplement on the Group of 24 Deputies' Report', *IMF Survey*, August, pp. 1–20.

Haggard, S. and Kaufman, R. (1989) 'The Politics of Stabilization and Structural Adjustment', in Jeffrey D. Sachs (ed.) *Developing Country Debt and Economic Performance*, vol. 1, National Bureau of Economic Research Project Report, Chicago: The University of Chicago Press.

Harrod, R. F. (1939) 'An Essay in Dynamic Theory', *Economic Journal*, vol. 49, pp. 14–33.

Harvey, C. (1985) *Macroeconomics in Africa*, revised Pan-African edition, London: Macmillan.

Healey, D. T. (1972) 'Development Policy: New Thinking About an Interpretation', *Journal of Economic Literature*, vol. X, no. 3 (September), pp. 757–97.

Helleiner, G. K. (ed.) (1986a). *Africa and the International Monetary Fund*, Washington, D.C.: IMF.

Helleiner, G. K. (1986b) 'The Question of Conditionality', in C. Lancaster and J. Williamson (eds) *Africa Debt and Financing*, Institute for International Economics.

Helleiner, G. K. (1987) 'Stabilization, Adjustment and the Poor', *World Development*, vol. 15, no. 12, pp. 1499–1513.

Heller, P. S., *et al.* (1988) 'The Implications of Fund Supported Adjustment Programs for Poverty: Experiences in Selected Countries', Occasional Paper no. 58, Washington, D.C.: IMF.

Holsen, J. A. (1986) 'Notes to Accompany Illustrative Country Projection using a Sources and Uses of Funds Accounting Framework', mimeographed World Bank paper.

Hunt, D. (1989) *Economic Theories of Development: An Analysis of Competing Paradigms*, New York: Harvester Wheatsheaf.

International Monetary Fund (IMF) (various years) *Annual Report*, Washington, D.C.

International Monetary Fund (IMF) (1977) *The Monetary Approach to the Balance of Payments*, Washington, D.C.

International Monetary Fund (IMF) (1987) 'Theoretical Aspects of the Design of Fund Supported Adjustment Programs', Occasional Paper no. 55, Washington, D.C.

International Monetary Fund (IMF) (1988) *World Economic Outlook – April*, Washington, D.C.

International Monetary Fund (IMF) (1989a) *World Economic Outlook – April*, Washington, D.C.

International Monetary Fund (IMF) (1989b) *Ten Common Misconceptions About the IMF*, Washington, D.C.: IMF, External Relations Department.

International Monetary Fund (IMF) (1990) *World Economic Outlook – May*, Washington, D.C.

Johnsson, G. G. (1985) 'Formulation of Exchange Rate Policies in Adjustment Programmes', Occasional Paper no. 36, Washington, D.C.: IMF.

Kaldor, N. (1955) 'Alternative Theories of Distribution', *Review of Economic Studies*, vol 23, pp. 83–100.

Kaldor, N. (1957) 'A Model of Economic Growth', *Economic Journal*, vol. 67, no. 268 (December), pp. 591–624.

Kaldor, N. (1975) 'What is Wrong with Economic Theory', *Quarterly Journal of Economics*, vol. 89, no. 3 (August), pp. 347–57.

Kaldor, N. (1983) 'Devaluation and Adjustment in Developing Countries', *Finance and Development*, vol. 20, no. 2 (June), pp. 35–7.

Kaldor, N. (1986) *The Scourge of Monetarism*, 2nd edn, Oxford: Oxford University Press.

Kalecki, M. (1971) *Selected Essays on the Dynamics of the Capitalist Economy 1933–1970*, London: Cambridge University Press.

Kalecki, M. (1976) *Essays on Developing Economies*, Brighton: Harvester.

Keynes, J. M. (1973) *The General Theory of Employment, Interest and Money*, London: Macmillan.

Khan, M. S. (1987) 'Macroeconomic Adjustment in Developing Countries: A Policy Perspective', *World Bank Research Observer*, vol. 2, no. 1 (January), pp. 23–42.

Khan, M. S. and Knight, M. D. (1981) 'Stabilization Programs in Developing Countries: A Formal Framework', *IMF Staff Papers*, vol. 28, no. 1 (March), pp. 1–53.

Khan, M. S. and Knight, M. D. (1985) 'Fund Supported Adjustment Programs and Economic Growth', Occasional Paper no. 41, Washington, D.C.: IMF.

Khan, M. S. and Knight, M. D. (1988) 'Import Compression and Export Performance in Developing Countries', *Review of Economics and Statistics*, vol. 70, no. 2 (May), pp. 315–21.

Khan, M. S. and Montiel, P. J. (1989) 'Growth Oriented Adjustment Programs: A Conceptual Framework', *IMF Staff Papers*, vol. 36, no.2, pp. 279–306.

Khan, M. S. and Montiel, P. J. (1990) 'A Marriage Between Fund and Bank Models – Reply to Polak', *IMF Staff Papers*, vol. 37, no. 1 (March), pp. 187–91.

Khan, M. S., Montiel, P. J. and Haque, N. U. (1986) 'Adjustment with Growth: Relating the Analytical Approaches of the World Bank and the IMF', Development Policy Issues Series Discussion Paper VPERS8, Washington, D.C.: World Bank.

Khan, M. S., Montiel, P. and Haque, N. U. (1990) 'Adjustment with Growth: Relating the Analytical Approaches of the IMF and the World Bank', *Journal of Development Economics*, vol. 32, pp. 155–79.

Killick, T. (1976) 'The Possibilities of Development Planning', *Oxford Economic Papers*, vol. 28, no. 2 (July), pp. 161–84.

Killick, T. (ed.) (1984) *The Quest for Economic Stabilization: The IMF and The Third World*, London: Heinemann.

Killick, T. (1986) 'Twenty-five Years in Development: the Rise and Impending Decline of Market Solutions', *Development Policy Review*, vol. 4, no. 2 (June), pp. 99–116.

Killick, T. (1989) *A Reaction Too Far: Economic Theory and the Role of the State in Developing Countries*, London: Overseas Development Institute.

Kogiku, K. C. (1968) *An Introduction to Macroeconomic Models*, New York: McGraw-Hill.

Krueger, A. O. (1974) 'The Political Economy of the Rent-Seeking Society', *American Economic Review*, vol. 64, no. 3 (June), pp. 291–303.

Lacey, R. (1989) 'The Management of Public Expenditures: An Evolving Bank Perspective', Discussion Paper no. 56, Washington, D.C.: World Bank.

Lal, D. (1983) *The Poverty of 'Development Economics'*, Hoberbart Paperback 16, London: Institute of Economic Affairs.

Lamb, G. (1987) 'Managing Economic Policy Change: Institutional Dimensions', Discussion Paper no. 14, Washington, D.C.: World Bank.

Lawrence, P. (ed.) (1986) *World Recession and the Food Crisis in Africa*, London: James Currey.

Lele, U. (1989) 'Agricultural Growth, Domestic Policies, the External Environment, and Assistance to Africa: Lessons of a Quarter Century', Managing Agricultural Development in Africa (MADIA) Discussion Paper no. 1, Washington, D.C.: World Bank.

Lenin, V. I. (1970) *Selected Works*, Moscow: Progress Publishers.

Levačić, R. and Rebmann, A. (1982) *Macroeconomics: An Introduction to Keynesian-Neoclassical Controversies*, Basingstoke: Macmillan.

Lewis, W. A. (1954) 'Economic Development with Unlimited Supplies of Labour', *The Manchester School*, vol. 22, May, pp. 139–91.

Little, I. M. D. (1982) *Economic Development: Theory, Policy and International Relations*, New York: Basic Books.

Lizondo, J. S. and Montiel, P. J. (1989) 'Contractionary Devaluation in Developing Countries: An Analytical Overview', *IMF Staff Papers*, vol. 36, no. 4 (December), pp. 182–227.

Lone, S. (1988) 'Adjustment Programmes under Fire', *Africa Recovery*, vol. 2, no. 2 (June).

López, R. and Thomas, V. (1988) *Import-Growth Relationship and Growth: Some Considerations for Africa*, draft document prepared for Policy, Planning and Research Seminar on Import and Growth in Africa, Washington, D.C.

Loutfi, M. (1989) 'Development Issues and State Policies in Sub-Saharan Africa', *International Labour Review*, vol. 128, no. 2, pp. 137–54.

Marx, K. (1967) *Capital: A Critique of Political Economy*, New York: International Publishers.

McCarthy, F. D. (ed.) (1990) 'Problems of Developing Countries in the 1990s. World Bank Discussion Papers 97, vol. I, *General Topics*, Second Global Prospects Conference, Washington, D.C.

McFadden, D. *et al.* (1985) 'Is There Life After Debt? An Econometric Analysis of the Creditworthiness of Developing Countries', in G. W. Smith and J. T. Cuddington (eds) *International Debt and the Developing Countries*, Washington, D.C.: World Bank.

Meier, G. M. and Steel, W. F. (eds) (1989) *Industrial Development in Sub-Saharan Africa*, Economic Development Institute Series in Economic Development, New York: Oxford University Press.

Mills, C. A. (1985) 'Priorities for Industrial Policy Reform in Africa', mimeographed paper, Dakar.

Mosley, P. (1987a) 'Conditionality as Bargaining Process: Structural Adjustment Lending, 1980–86', Essays in International Finance no. 168 (October), Princeton, N. J.: Princeton University, International Finance Section.

Mosley, P. (1987b) *Overseas Aid: Its Defence and Reform*, Brighton: Wheatsheaf.

Mosley, P. (1989) 'Effective Stabilization Policy in Less Developed Countries', *Journal of International Development*, vol. 1, no. 2 (April), pp. 273–80.

Mosley, P., Harrigan, J. and Toye, J. (1991) *Aid and Power: The World Bank and Policy-based Lending*, vol. 1, *Analysis and Policy Proposals* and vol. 2, *Case Studies*, London: Routledge.

Mosley, P. and Toye, J. (1988) 'The Design of Structural Adjustment Programmes', *Development Policy Review*, vol. 6, pp. 395–413.

Mussa, M. (1987) 'Macroeconomic Policy and Trade Liberalization: Some Guidelines', *World Bank Research Observer*, vol. 2, no. 1 (January), pp. 61–77.

Myrdal, G. (1968) *Asian Drama: An Inquiry into the Poverty of Nations*, London: Penguin Books.

Ndulu, B. J. (1990) 'Growth and Adjustment in sub-Saharan Africa', a paper presented at the World Bank Africa Economic Issues Conference, Nairobi, June.

Nellis, J. R. (1986) 'Public Enterprises in sub-Saharan Africa', Discussion Paper no. 1, Washington, D.C.: World Bank.

Nelson, J. (1984) 'The Political Economy of Stabilization: Commitment, Capacity and Public Responses', *World Development*, vol. 12, no. 10 (October), pp. 983–1006.

O'Connell, S. A. (1988) 'Fiscal Policy in Low-Income Africa', Policy, Planning, and Research Working Paper 39, Washington, D.C.: World Bank.

Onimode, B. (ed.) (1989) *The IMF, the World Bank and the African Debt*, vol. 1, *The Economic Impact* and vol. 2, *The Social And Political Impact*, London: Zed Books.

Organization of African Unity (OAU) (1980) *Lagos Plan of Action for the Economic Development of Africa: 1980–2000*.

Organization for Economic Co-operation and Development (OECD) (1989) *Development Co-operation in the 1990s*, Report by the Chairman of the Development Assistance Committee, Paris.

Organization for Economic Co-operation and Development (OECD) (1990) *Financing the External Debt of Developing Countries 1990*, Paris: OECD.

Pastor, M. (1987) 'The Effects of IMF Programs in the Third World: Debate and Evidence from Latin America', *World Development*, vol. 15, no. 2, pp. 249–67.

Patinkin, Don (1982) *Anticipations of the General Theory? and Other Essays on Keynes*, Chicago: University of Chicago Press.

Payer, C. (1974) *The Debt Trap: The IMF and the Third World*, New York: Penguin Books.

Pinstrup-Andersen, P. (ed.) (1990) *Macroeconomic Policy Reforms, Poverty and Nutrition: Analytical Methodologies*, Monograph 3, Ithaca, New York: Cornell Food and Nutrition Policy Program.

Please, S. (ed.) (1984) *The Hobbled Giant: Essays on the World Bank*, Boulder, Colorado: Westview.

Polak, J.J. (1957) 'Monetary Analysis of Income Formation and Payments Problems', *IMF Staff Papers*, vol. 6, no. 1 (November), pp. 1–50.

Polak, J.J. (1990) 'A Marriage Between Fund and Bank Models? – Comment on Khan and Montiel', *IMF Staff Papers*, vol. 37, no. 1 (March), pp. 183–6.

Polak, J.J. (1991) 'The Changing Nature of IMF Conditionality', *Essays in International Finance* no. 184 (September), Princeton, N.J.: Princeton University, International Finance Section.

Ranis, G. and Fei, J. C. H. (1988) 'Development Economics: What Next?', in Gustav Ranis and T. P. Schultz (ed.) *The State of Development Economics*, Oxford: Basil Blackwell.

Rattsø, J. (1988) 'Macroeconomic Adjustment Mechanisms in India', *World Development*, vol. 16, no. 8, pp. 959–73.

Rattsø, J. (1989) 'Macrodynamic Adjustment Mechanisms in a Dual Semi-industrialized Economy', *Journal of Development Economics*, vol. 30, pp. 47–69.

Rattsø, J. (1990) 'Import Compression, Investment Determination and Macro-economic Adjustment: A Macroeconomic Model Relevant for Sub-Saharan Africa', Institute of Economics, University of Trondheim, cyclostyled.

Ravenhill, J. (ed.) (1986) *Africa in Economic Crisis*, London: Macmillan.

Ravenhill, J. (ed.) (1988) 'Adjustment With Growth: A Fragile Consensus', *The Journal of Modern African Studies*, vol. 26, no. 2, pp. 179–210.

Reinhart, C. M. (1989) 'A Model of Adjustment and Growth: An Empirical Analysis', unpublished Working Paper WP/89/32, Washington: IMF.

Riddell, R. C. (1987) *Foreign Aid Reconsidered*, Baltimore: The Johns Hopkins University Press.

Roberts, J. (1989) 'Liberalizing Foreign-Exchange Rates in Sub-Saharan Africa', *Development Policy Review*, vol. 7, pp. 115–42.

Robichek, E. W. (1985) 'Financial Programming as Practiced by the IMF', mimeographed paper, pp. 1–13.

Schapiro, H. and Taylor, L. (1990) 'The State and Industrial Strategy', *World Development*, vol. 18, no. 6, pp. 861–78.

Scott, M. and Lal, D. (eds) (1990) *Public Policy and Economic Development: Essays in Honour of Ian Little*, Oxford: Clarendon Press.

Seers, D. (1963) 'The Limitations of the Special Case', *Bulletin of the Oxford Institute of Economics and Statistics*, vol. 25, May, pp. 77–98.

Seers, D. (1969) 'The Meaning of Development', *International Development Review*, vol. 11, no. 4 (December), pp. 3–4.

Sen, A. (ed.) (1970) *Growth Economics*, Harmondsworth, England: Penguin Books.

Sender, J. and Smith, S. (1984) 'What's right with the Berg Report and what's left of its critics?', Discussion Paper DP 192, Sussex: Institute of Development Studies.

Serageldin, I. (1989) *Poverty, Adjustment and Growth in Africa*, World Bank: Washington, D.C.

Shalizi, Z. and Squire, L. (1989) 'Tax Policy in Sub-Saharan Africa: A Framework for Analysis', Policy and Research Report no. 2, Washington, D.C.: World Bank.

Shirley, M. (1989) 'Reform of State-Owned Enterprise: Lessons from World Bank Lending', Policy and Research Report no. 4, Washington, D.C.: World Bank.

Singer, H. (1989) 'Lessons of Post-War Development Experience: 1945–1988', Discussion Paper 260, Sussex: Institute of Development Studies.

Srinivasan, T.N. (1985) 'Neo-classical Political Economy, the State, and Economic Development', *Asian Development Review*, vol. 3, no. 2, pp. 38–58.

Stern, E. (1989) 'The Lessons of the Eighties for Development', *Nationaløkonomisk Tidsskrift*, vol. 127, no. 2, pp. 244–54.

Stern, N. (1989) 'The Economics of Development: A Survey', *Economic Journal*, vol. 99, September, pp. 597–685.

Streeten, P. (1987a) 'Structural Adjustment: A Survey of the Issues and Options', *World Development*, vol. 15, no. 12, pp. 1469–82.

Streeten, P. (1987b) *What Price Food?*, Basingstoke: Macmillan Press.

Sunkel, O. (1969) 'National Development Policy and External Dependence in Latin America', *Journal of Development Studies*, vol. 6, no. 1 (October), pp. 23–48.

Svedberg, P. (1991) 'The Export Performance of Sub-Saharan Africa', *Journal of Economic Development and Cultural Change*, vol. 39, no. 1 (April), pp. 549–66.

Sweezy, P. M. (1970) *The Theory of Capitalist Development: Principles of Marxian Political Economy*, New York: Modern Reader.

Sweezy, P. M. and Bettelheim, C. (1972) *On the Transition to Socialism*, New York: Monthly Review.

Tarp, F. (1990) 'Prices in Mozambican Agriculture', *Journal of International Development*, vol. 2, no. 2 (April), pp. 172–208.

Taylor, L. (1983) *Structuralist Macroeconomics: Applicable Models for the Third World*, New York: Basic Books.

Taylor, L. (1987) 'Macro Policy in the Tropics: How Sensible People Stand', *World Development*, vol. 15, no. 12, pp. 1407–35.

Taylor, L. (1988) *Varieties of Stabilization Experience: Towards Sensible Macroeconomics in the Third World*, Oxford: Clarendon Press.

Taylor, L. (1989a) *Stabilization and Growth in Developing Countries: A Structuralist Approach*, Fundamentals of Pure and Applied Economics, vol. 29, Economic Development Studies Section, New York: Harwood Academic.

Taylor, L. (1989b) 'Gap Disequilibria: Inflation, Investment, Saving and Foreign Exchange', Working Paper 76, Helsinki: World Institute for Development Economics Research (WIDER).

Taylor, L. (ed.) (1990) *Socially Relevant Policy Analysis: Structuralist Computable General Equilibrium Models for the Developing World*, Cambridge, Massachusetts: The MIT Press.

Taylor, L. (1991) 'Gap Models', Massachusetts Institute of Technology, cyclostyled, pp. 1–32.

Thomas, V. and Chhibber, A. (eds) (1989) *Adjustment Lending: How It Has Worked, How It Can be Improved*, Washington, D.C.: World Bank.

Todaro, M. P. (1989) *Economic Development in the Third World*, New York: Longman.

Toye, J. (1987) *Dilemmas of Development*, Oxford: Basil Blackwell.

Toye, J. (1989) 'Can the World Bank Resolve the Crisis of Developing Countries?', *Journal of International Development*, vol. 1, no. 2 (April), pp. 261–74.

UNECA (1989) *Statistics and Policies: ECA Preliminary Observations on the World Bank Report*, Addis Ababa: Economic Commission for Africa.

UNICEF (1989) 'The Social Consequences of Adjustment and Dependency on Primary Commodities in Sub-Saharan Africa', mimeo, New York.

Van Arkadie, B. (1987) 'A Note on New Directions in Planning', *CEPAL REVIEW*, no. 31 (April), pp. 33–41.

Van der Hoeven, R. (1988) 'External Shocks, Adjustment and Income Distribution', mimeographed paper prepared for Middlebury Centre for Economic Studies sponsored seminar, 28–30 April, New York: UNICEF.

Vines, D. (1990) 'Growth Oriented Adjustment Programs: A Reconsideration', Discussion Paper no. 406, London: Centre for Economic Policy Research.

Whalley, J. (1984) 'A Review of Numerical Modelling Activity at the World Bank', mimeographed.

Wheeler, D. (1984) 'Sources of Stagnation in sub-Saharan Africa', *World Development*, vol. 12, no. 1 (January), pp. 1–24.

World Bank (1981) *Accelerated Development in Sub-Saharan Africa: An Agenda for Action*, Washington, D.C.

World Bank (1988a) *World Development Report 1988*, Washington, D.C.

World Bank (1988b) 'Adjustment Lending: An Evaluation of Ten Years of Experience', Policy and Research Report no. 1, Washington, D.C.: World Bank, Country Economics Department.

World Bank (1988c) *Targeted Programs for the Poor during Structural Adjustment*, a summary of a Symposium on Poverty and Adjustment, 11–12 April. Washington, D.C.

World Bank (1988d) *World Debt Tables 1987–88*, Washington, D.C.

World Bank (1988e) *World Bank Annual Report 1988*, Washington, D.C.

World Bank (1989a) *African Economic and Financial Data*, Washington, D.C.

World Bank (1989b) *Sub-Saharan Africa: From Crisis to Sustainable Growth*, Washington, D.C.

World Bank (1989c) *World Development Report 1989*, Washington, D.C.

World Bank (1989d) *World Debt Tables 1989–90*, Washington, D.C.

World Bank (1990a) *World Development Report 1990*, Washington, D.C.

World Bank (1990b) *Making Adjustment Work for the Poor: A Framework for Policy Reform in Africa*, Washington, D.C.

World Bank (1990c) *World Debt Tables 1990–91*, Washington, D.C.

World Bank (1990d) *World Bank Annual Report 1990*, Washington, D.C.

World Bank (1991a) *World Tables 1991*, Washington, D.C.

World Bank (1991b) *World Development Report 1991*, Washington, D.C.

World Bank (1991c) *World Bank Annual Report 1991*, Washington, D.C.

World Bank and UNDP (1989) *Africa's Adjustment and Growth in the 1980s*, New York: World Bank.

Yagci, F., Kamin, S. and Rosenbaum, V. (1985) 'Structural Adjustment Lending: An Evaluation of Program Design', Staff Working Paper no. 735, Washington, D.C.: World Bank.

INDEX

Goldstein, M. 69, 96, 152
government: and adjustment
policies 45–50; balance, and
economic performance 16–17;
budget constraints of 30–2;
consumption, and economic
performance 12–14, 17;
spending, and growth-oriented
adjustment model 106–7, 116.
See also deficits, government
Green, R.H. 37, 128
gross domestic product (GDP): in
economy of sub-Saharan Africa
7–10; growth of, and economic
performance 11–13, 16
gross national product (GNP): in
economy of sub-Saharan Africa
7–10; growth of, and economic
performance 11–13, 16
growth models in growth
programming 82–6
growth-oriented adjustment
99–119: conceptual framework
100–4; empirical analysis 108–10;
issues and problems 110–16;
policy analysis 104–8. *See also*
adjustment policies
growth programming: accounting
framework 81–2; and adjustment
79–98; discussion of 93–8;
growth and resource gap models
82–6; in practice 90–3; Revised
Minimum Standard Model
(RMSM) 86–90; and stabilization
153
Guitián, M. 69, 96, 152

Haque, N.U. 69, 88, 100–1, 106,
116–18
Harrod, R. 82–3, 93, 102
Harrod–Domar growth model
79–81, 83, 93, 110
health, and adjustment policies 122–3
Helleiner, G.K. 2, 4, 49, 128
human capital, and adjustment
policies 122–3

imports: and economic
performance 12–13, 24; in

economy of SSA 8–9; in
growth-oriented adjustment
model 109; and growth
programming 90–2
income: in accounting framework
of growth programming 82; and
African alternative framework
144; distribution, and IMF's
approach 152; growth
programming in practice 92; and
Polak model for financial
programming 61–3
industrial sector: growth of, and
economic performance 11–12, 15
inflation: and economic
performance 12–14; and
financial programming 75; and
Polak model for financial
programming 151; in Taylor's
model of adjustment policies
133–5
institutional content in structuralist
models of adjustment process 131
institutional reform in sub-Saharan
Africa 2
institutional support, and African
alternative framework 145
interest rates: and economic
performance 23; in policy in
sub-Saharan Africa 2; and
savings and investment 44; in
Taylor's model of adjustment
policies 133, 135–6
International Bank for
Reconstruction and
Development (IBRD) 57, 80–1
International Development
Association (IDA) 80–1
International Labour Organization
(ILO) 123
International Monetary Fund (IMF)
1, 75, 77–8; and adjustment
policies 36, 38, 48, 50; in Africa
150–1; and African alternative
framework 143–6; and financial
programming 56–9, 68–9, 73,
75; growth-oriented adjustment
99–119; and growth
programming 96–8; merged

model of 157–8; models of
155–6; objectives in sub-Saharan
Africa 2–5; and radical
adjustment models 138–42; and
structuralist-inspired adjustment
models 126–38; and UNICEF
approach to adjustment policies
120–6, 146–7
investment: in accounting
framework of growth
programming 82; and adjustment
policies 42–5; and economic
performance 12–13, 17, 20; in
growth-oriented adjustment
model 103, 110; and growth
programming 91; and IMF's
approach 152, 156; and national
balance 34–5; in structuralist
views of adjustment process
130–1, 161; in Taylor's model of
adjustment policies 134–5. *See
also* foreign investment
IS–LM model, and growth-oriented
adjustment model 112–13

Johnson, H.G. 39, 64–5, 68
Jolly, R. 122

Kaldor, N. 129
Kalecki, M. 129
Keynes, J.M. 129, 153
Khan, M. 69, 88, 96, 100–2, 106,
108, 110–11, 113–18, 152,
156–7, 162
Killick, T. 128

labour: in growth-oriented
adjustment model 110–11;
market segmentation, and
national balance 37–8; in
Taylor's model of adjustment
policies 132
Lal, D. 28
Latin America 8–9;
underdevelopment in 140–1
Lenin, V.I. 139
Lewis, W.A. 82
Loxley, J. 5, 128
Lucas, R. 76

macroeconomics of sub-Saharan
Africa 7–28; consistency of
29–55; crisis, sources of 14–25;
and economic performance
11–14; economy, nature of 7–11;
issues in 25–8
manufacturing in economy of SSA
8–9
market distortions and national
balance 35–6
Marshall–Lerner conditions: and
adjustment programmes 26–7;
and Chicago model for financial
programming 67–8; and
growth-oriented adjustment model
106; and national balance 39
Marx, K. and Marxism 138–41
merged model: for growth-oriented
adjustment 100–19; and IMF
approach 156–7
models: Chicago, for financial
programming 65–7; growth and
resource gap, in growth
programming 82–6;
Harrod–Domar, of growth
79–81, 83, 93, 110; of IMF and
World Bank 155–6; IS–LM, and
growth-oriented adjustment
model 112–13; merged, for
growth-oriented adjustment
100–19; monetary, for financial
programming 64–8; Polak, for
financial programming 60–3,
152; structuralist, of adjustment
policies 127–8; Taylor's, of
adjustment policies 132–8
monetary approach for financial
programming 64–8; and balance
of payments (MABOP) 64–6, 68
monetary policy: and adjustment
policies 50–4; aggregate, and
structuralist-inspired views of
development 128; and budget
constraints 31–2; and
growth-oriented adjustment
model 104–8; and national
balance 41–2; in Taylor's model
of adjustment policies 135–6; of
UNICEF 124–6